MANITOBA STUDIES IN NATIVE HIS...

Manitoba Studies in Native History publishes new ...
historical experience of Native peoples in the west...
The series is under the editorial direction of a board r... ...ative of the scholarly
and Native communities in Manitoba.

I *The New Peoples: Being and Becoming Métis in North America*, edited by Jacqueline Peterson and Jennifer S.H. Brown

II *Indian-European Trade Relations in the Lower Saskatchewan River Region to 1840*, by Paul Thistle

III *"The Orders of the Dreamed" : George Nelson on Cree and Northern Ojibwa Religion and Myth, 1823*, by Jennifer S.H. Brown and Robert Brightman

IV *The Plains Cree: Trade, Diplomacy and War, 1790 to 1870*, by John S. Milloy

V *The Dakota of the Canadian Northwest: Lessons for Survival*, by Peter Douglas Elias

VI *Aboriginal Resource Use in Canada: Historical and Legal Aspects*, edited by Kerry Abel and Jean Friesen

VII *Severing the Ties that Bind: Government Repression of Indigenous Religious Ceremonies on the Prairies*, by Katherine Pettipas

VIII *The Ojibwa of Western Canada, 1780 to 1870*, by Laura Peers

IX *Women of the First Nations: Power, Wisdom, and Strength*, edited by Christine Miller and Patricia Chuchryk, with Marie Smallface Marule, Brenda Manyfingers, and Cheryl Deering

Christine Miller

MANITOBA STUDIES IN NATIVE HISTORY IX

Women of the First Nations: Power, Wisdom, and Strength

Edited by

Christine Miller and Patricia Chuchryk

With Marie Smallface Marule, Brenda Manyfingers, and Cheryl Deering

THE UNIVERSITY OF MANITOBA PRESS

© The University of Manitoba Press 1996
Winnipeg, Manitoba R3T 5V6

Printed in Canada

Printed on recycled, acid-free paper ∞

Design: Norman Schmidt

Cover/jacket illustration: Catherine, wife of Napoleon Lafferty, HBC river pilot and hunter, with her two children, James and Edward, 1911 or 1912. Photographer: Henry Jones. (Hudson's Bay Company Archives, Provincial Archives of Manitoba, HBC photo collection 1987/363-I-43/14 [N8347])

Canadian Cataloguing in Publication Data

Main entry under title:
Women of the First Nations

    (Manitoba Studies in Native History, ISSN 0826-9416 ; 9)
    Papers presented at the National Symposium on Aboriginal Women of Canada, University of Lethbridge, October, 1989.
    0-88755-161-0 (bound) - 0-88755-634-5 (pbk.)

1. Native women - Canada - Congresses.* I. Miller, Christine, 1932-   II. Chuchryk, Patricia Marie. III. National Symposium on Aboriginal Women of Canada (1989 : University of Lethbridge)

E78.C2W65 1996 305.48'897071 C96-920084-6

This series is published with the financial support of the people of Manitoba, the Honourable Harold Gilleshammer, Minister of Culture, Heritage and Citizenship.

Manitoba Studies in Native History Board of Directors: J. Burelle, J. Fontaine, G. Friesen, E. Harper, E. LaRocque, R. McKay, W. Moodie, G. Schultz, D. Young.

Contents

vii   Acknowledgements

ix   Invocation: The Real Power of Aboriginal Women
Jeannette Armstrong

3   Introduction
Patricia Chuchryk and Christine Miller

11   The Colonization of a Native Woman Scholar
Emma LaRocque

19   *"La vie en rose"*? Métis Women at Batoche, 1870 to 1920
Diane P. Payment

39   Subsistence, Secondary Literature, and Gender Bias: The Saulteaux
Laura Peers

51   First Nations Women of Prairie Canada in the Early Reserve Years, the 1870s to the 1920s: A Preliminary Inquiry
Sarah Carter

77   Life in Harmony with Nature
Beverly Hungry Wolf

83   An Examination of Sport for Aboriginal Females on the Six Nations
     Reserve, Ontario, from 1968 to 1980
     Vicky Paraschak

97   Aboriginal Women's Writing and the Cultural Politics
     of Representation
     Julia Emberley

113 Art or Craft: The Paradox of the Pangnirtung Weave Shop
     Kathy M'Closkey

127 Voices through Time
     Betty Bastien

131 The Changing Employment of Cree Women in Moosonee
     and Moose Factory
     Jennifer Blythe and Peggy Martin McGuire

151 The Exploitation of the Oil and Gas Frontier: Its Impact on
     Lubicon Lake Cree Women
     Rosemary Brown

167 Gender and the Paradox of Residential Education
     in Carrier Society
     Jo-Anne Fiske

183 Recommended Reading
     Christine Miller

189 Contributors

195 Index

Acknowledgements

The appearance of this volume brings to fruition a process begun in March 1988 when a group of us got together to discuss the possibility of organizing a conference that would address issues concerning Aboriginal women in Canada. One of our major objectives was to create a forum in which both Aboriginal and non-Aboriginal researchers, community activists, and "front-line" workers could share ideas, information, experiences, and strategies. Some of us involved in organizing this conference are also teachers concerned about the absence of appropriate Canadian materials to share with students in our courses. For this reason, another objective of the conference was to generate a woman-centred volume of readings about and by Aboriginal women focussed within the geo-political boundaries of Canada. We hope that this volume will make the voices of women of the First Nations accessible not only to students but also to any interested and concerned reader.

As with any project of this magnitude, we owe a debt of gratitude to a great many people. To all of those who assisted us in organizing The National Symposium on Aboriginal Women of Canada: Past, Present and Future, held at the University of Lethbridge, 18-21 October 1989, we are grateful for your continued support of the book project. To all of those warm and caring human beings who generously took on tasks we ourselves could not, and to all of those who gave their support and energy, we thank you. Among those to whom we are especially grateful are Samantha Archibald, Betty Bastien, Deborah Clement, Jo Anne Crate-Thomas, Dayna Daniels, Doreen Indra, Caroline Lastuka, Rosalind Merrick, Shawn Penny, Sara Stanley, Muriel Stanley-Venne, and Carol Tomomitsu.

To Katie Wells, Symposium Elder, and Jean (Tootoosis) Cuthand Goodwill, Symposium Patroness, we offer special thanks. As well, we would like to note our appreciation to Daphne Odjig and Alanis Obomsawin for permitting us the use of their art to promote and support the project; the National Film Board for assisting us in mounting a retrospective of Alanis's films; and Alfred Young Man, who designed our logo and understood our vision.

We also need to express our thanks to all the volunteers and participants in the Symposium. You brought us together, you enabled and empowered us to share our ideas and experiences, and you strengthened our resolve and commitment to the struggle of all women against social injustice.

Institutional support at the University of Lethbridge was overwhelming. The Departments of Anthropology, Dramatic Arts, Native American Studies, and Sociology, and the University Art Gallery were most helpful. We would also like to thank the Faculty of Management's Burns Food Endowment Fund for financing the production of our poster; Ray McHugh of Research Services for assisting with funding applications; Conference Services for help with the organization of the Symposium; and Dr. Howard Tennant, President of the University of Lethbridge, who provided us with start-up funding and for hosting the opening reception.

We gratefully acknowledge the following for their generous financial support of the Symposium: Alberta Culture and Multiculturalism; The Anglican Church Primate World Relief and Development Fund; the Canadian Secretary of State — Aboriginal Development; Petro Canada; Chinook County Tourist Association; The Muttart Foundation; and the Social Sciences and Humanities Research Council of Canada Colloquium Grant and Aid to Scholarly Conferences.

The process of translating the Symposium into this collection of papers has been a long and sometimes arduous one. We would like especially to thank Carol Tomomitsu for her assistance in the preparation of the manuscript. We thank the authors for their patience, perseverance, and commitment to this project. We know that our requests for numerous changes and revisions to their manuscripts did not always come at the best possible time, but our volume has been strengthened as a result of their efforts. We also thank the authors for donating all proceeds from this publication to the Aboriginal Women's Scholarship Fund of the University of Lethbridge, which will assist women of the First Nations working in the areas of Native studies and women's studies. And, finally, the editors would like to thank the staff of The University of Manitoba Press, and especially its managing editor, Carol Dahlstrom, for their unflagging encouragement, support, and commitment to this project.

Although this project is the collective product of a community of women, the co-editors of this volume accept responsibility for its shortcomings.

Invocation: The Real Power of Aboriginal Women

Keynote Address: The National Symposium on Aboriginal Women of Canada, University of Lethbridge, 19 October 1989

Jeannette Armstrong

We are all very much aware of the history of the colonization process, which has systematically achieved, through various well-known measures, a breakdown in the structures upon which the well-being and health of our peoples depended. Our present social conditions bear this out.

What is not as well known is that the influences of a patriarchal and imperialistic culture upon a people whose systems were fundamentally co-operative units has been not only devastating, but also dehumanizing to a degree that is unimaginable. I speak in particular of the damage to the family-clan systems as the base units of social order in Aboriginal societies of North America. I speak in specific of the severe and irreversible effects on Aboriginal women, and the resultant effect on our nations.

The role of Aboriginal women in the health of family systems from one generation to the next was one of immense power. The immensity of the responsibility of bearer of life and nourisher of all generations is just becoming clear in its relationship to all societal functioning.

In traditional Aboriginal society, it was woman who shaped the thinking of all its members in a loving, nurturing atmosphere within the base family unit. In such societies, the earliest instruments of governance and law to ensure social order came from quality mothering of children.

In our instruments of teaching, the use of non-gendered figures, such as animals, provided a focus for instructions based on human worth. Our languages contained no words for *he* or *she* because of the high elevation of human dignity and personal recognition in our culture. The concept of colonization of one group of people by another group of people lies outside the understanding of those of us whose language and philosophy strive for co-operation and harmony wherever possible with *all* things, as a *necessary* means to survival. It is impossible to dominate or coerce another when these basic principles are childhood requisites in the learning of a social order. Traditionally, it was woman who controlled and shaped that societal order to the state of harmony, which in this time of extreme disorder seems nearly impossible.

Let me tell you that upon European contact our societies required no prisons, armies, police, judges, or lawyers. Prostitution, rape, mental illness, suicide, homicide, child sexual abuse, and family violence were all unheard of. Upon contact, physical diseases were so rare among us that our bodies had no immunities to even simple endemic diseases.

It was through the attack on the power of Aboriginal woman that the disempowerment of our peoples has been achieved, in a dehumanizing process that is one of the cruellest on the face of this earth. In the attack on the core family system, in the direct attack on the role of Aboriginal woman, the disintegration of our peoples towards genocide has been achieved.

It is a fundamental human right for parents to nurture, to protect, and to love their children. It is a fundamental and basic human right that parents raise their own children. It is a fundamental right that parents determine their own children's culture and heritage, and what their own children learn.

These fundamental human rights were seized, and still are being seized, from Aboriginal people in this country. Aboriginal children were seized from their homes and forcibly placed in sterile, military-like, hostile institutions called residential schools. These places of horror were invariably run by people who, themselves, never had children, and whose only goal was to "civilize." This process took place during the child's most essential stages of development. The resultant breakdown in our communities emerged from helpless parents left with nothing to live for and children raised in racist hostility and dispassion.

The ensuing nightmare of the effect of residential schooling on our communities has been what those "Indian problem" statistics are all about. The placement of our children in residential schools has been the single most devastating factor in the breakdown of our society. It is at the core of the damage, beyond all the other mechanisms cleverly fashioned to subjugate, assimilate, and annihilate.

Throughout the dehumanizing years that followed those residential-school years, the struggle of Aboriginal woman has simply been to survive, under the onslaught of a people steeped in a tradition of hostile cultural supremacy. The struggle has been to survive, to be able to give protection, food, and love to our children. The struggle has been just to keep our children with us. And the struggle has been intense for those of us whose residential-school experience deprived us of essential parenting skills, parenting skills that could have been learned only through quality parenting of themselves. The struggle has been to keep families together and functioning without any behavioural models except the worst patriarchal, dictatorial models on which to base relationships. The struggle has been to try, when the males stopped struggling, to provide the essentials for our children in an employment atmosphere hostile to all Natives and to all women. The struggle has been intense, too, because we have found ourselves stripped of our basic rights to family and community support systems through loss of status. The struggle has been to nurture, to protect, to provide, and to heal in an environment in which we, as Aboriginal women, have been trodden to the edge of total despair — and in a country boasting its high standards.

Therefore, when I see my sisters in the prisons, on the streets, and in their walking coffins, I see where the battle has taken its greatest toll. I see the scars. I see that these women, my sisters, have fought the cruellest of battles on earth. I see them through eyes of love and compassion. Never disgust. My utter disgust is for those who feed on the wounded. Who abuse them further with their bodies, their eyes, and their unclean minds. Who dare to think that they are somehow better. I see that, when women of our nations are dying thus, it is we who are all in danger.

Through all the horror, it has been the struggle of those women who survived somehow against all odds to bring healing where they could to their families and nations. It has been through the struggle of these women that we have maintained some balance, so that our children could survive and contribute to our peoples. It has always been the women, the mothers, who have provided that chance.

We find our strength and our power in our ability to be what our grandmothers were to us: keepers of the next generation in every sense of that word — physically, intellectually, and spiritually. We strive to retain our power and interpret it into all aspects of survival on this earth in the midst of chaos.

It is the fierce love at the centre of our power that is the weapon our grandmothers gave us, to protect and to nurture against all odds. Compassion and strength are what we are, and we have translated these into every area of our existence because we have had to. And we must continue to do so. It is a matter of the right of females to be what we fundamentally are — insurers of the next generation. It is a matter of survival where genocide is an everyday reality.

It is our compassion and strength that have been at the forefront of change in our communications. It is the power to adapt to all situations that has enabled us to ensure health and therefore survival of the young. It is the spirit to infiltrate into and learn all the systems around us in a balanced way that has enabled us to engender compassion and understanding in our children. Only those who know the true nature of despair and suffering can express compassion and understanding in all we do. It is the spirit of the female, holding in balance the spirit of the male, in a powerful co-operative force, that is at the core of family and community.

It is the strength of this female force that holds all nations and families together in health. It is the bridge to the next generation. It is this female power that is the key to the survival of us all, in an environment that is becoming increasingly damaged and unfit for all life forms. It is woman who holds this power and becomes powerful only when catalyzing co-operation and harmony, and therefore health, at all levels — from the individual, outward to the family, to the community, and to the environment. Without it, all becomes chaos, despair, hostility, and death. That is immense power.

Let this be known as the truth to all, so that we might all come through to a world once more in balance and harmony. I pray for that and struggle for that, for my great-grandchildren to come.

To you Aboriginal women out there, to you survivors, I congratulate you, I encourage you, I support you, and I love you.

Women of the First Nations

Introduction

Patricia Chuchryk and Christine Miller

Voices. Many voices. Diverse voices. Women's voices. The voices of Aboriginal and non-Aboriginal women, community grassroots activists, Métis women, academic women, feminist women, and Native Elders. Voices brought together in October 1989 to celebrate together the power, wisdom, and strength of First Nations women in Canada.

In 1987, we[1] began with the germ of an idea to hold the first ever National Symposium on Aboriginal Women of Canada: Past, Present and Future, at the University of Lethbridge. Some of us were motivated by the need for a forum in which to bring together Aboriginal women community activists; others were looking more to create a forum in which grassroots activists could meet and exchange ideas with academic researchers. And for others of us, the principle concern was the need to generate research material on Aboriginal women of Canada that we could share with our students, thirsty for such documentation. We shared also a concern that many people defined Aboriginal peoples, and especially Aboriginal women, in terms of the social problems with which they/we had become afflicted and identified. We needed to communicate the idea that with oppression also comes strength and wisdom. We wanted our collective voices to become tools of empowerment.

We were ambitious in our vision, and in October 1989, for four intense and wonderful days, we were successful in bringing together over 300 women — Aboriginals, non-Aboriginals, activists, academic researchers, feminists and non-feminists alike, students and teachers, writers and speakers, Canadians and women from outside Canada.

The problems and issues that confront Aboriginal women in Canada are well known. For example, Aboriginal women on average live ten to twelve fewer years than non-Native Canadian women. The suicide rate is seven times higher, and the average age at which suicide occurs is fifteen years lower. Aboriginal women are also more likely than non-Native Canadian women to live at or below the poverty line. Current Canadian government figures indicate that, where one in ten non-Native Canadian women is the victim of domestic violence, six in ten Aboriginal women are victimized.

While the literature calls attention to the serious problems existing in many Aboriginal communities, colonialism has resulted in an attenuation of women's roles in tribal societies, endangering women both within the larger society and within their own communities. In a recent study involving four First Nation communities and two urban centres, Aboriginal men and women described family violence as being more associated with oppression than with gender specifically. Family violence is constructed as but one of many possible outcomes of a myriad of social, psychological, and behavioural responses to colonialism (Manyfingers 1994).

Until recently, much of the research upon which we have had to rely for our knowledge about Aboriginal women has reflected racist, sexist, and/or colonialist frameworks. Often, research is devoted only to describing Aboriginal societies, and in that description defining these societies and the women who live in them as somehow problematic. Unfortunately, such descriptions further minimize women's struggles by utilizing ethnocentric methods of community research and problem solving, and relying upon Western theoretical frameworks to guide interpretations.

Despite these considerable obstacles, Aboriginal women are actively participating in improving the quality of life in their/our communities. Many indigenous cultures embrace women as nurturers, care givers and leaders, and strive to strengthen women's roles within their communities. To do otherwise would be to foster a climate conducive to cultural suicide. As Paula Gunn Allen says, speaking of herself and other Aboriginal women, "We survive, and we do more than just survive. We bond, we care, we fight, we teach, we nurse, we bear, we feed, we earn, we laugh, we love, we hang in there, no matter what" (1986, 190).

In our view, research must provide us with information leading to the potential for change. Indeed, there are a number of researchers exploring these and other issues, but heretofore no forum in which the researchers, researched, and community workers could exchange information.

The purpose behind the conference on First Nations women, then, was two-fold: First, to encourage a fully developed research and data base devoted to examining various aspects of Aboriginal women's lives, to be accompanied by the publication of a book of readings for students, researchers, and other interested persons, encompassing various theoretical perspectives; Second, to bring together Native and non-Native scholars, community activists, artists and Elders, and to provide a safe environment where a free flow of communication and ideas could be realized.

Concretely, the objectives of the Symposium were: (a) to promote information sharing among Native women and their organizations (and establish an ongoing information network); (b) to exchange strategies among community workers regarding community development, self-help, and program delivery; (c) to develop communication links among community workers and academic researchers to evaluate future research needs; and (d) to publish a book of readings.

After the initial phase of setting up an organizing committee, we sent out a call for papers to all colleges and universities in Canada, as well as to all the First Nations women's organizations we knew about and could contact. The response was overwhelming. Papers, workshops, and panels were selected on the basis of three criteria: Canadian content, regional representation, and diversity of voices.

We tried to design an innovative and all-encompassing format that included experiential and problem-solving workshops, formal presentations of scholarly papers, and the integration of researchers in appropriate workshops. As well, we wanted the involvement and spiritual direction of Elders throughout the proceedings. The titles of some of the workshops and papers reflect the diverse nature of the Symposium: "Aboriginal Women and the Impact of Change in Northern Society"; "My Grandmothers Taught Me to Stand Tall"; and "Iroquois Women's Rights with Respect to Matrimonial Property on Indian Reserves." Topics included Bill C-31, matrimonial rights, cultural change and conflict, the delivery of health services, organized battered women's shelters on reserves, business learning opportunities, and post-secondary education. We also organized a number of cultural events: a retrospective of the films of Alanis Obamsawin; the production of George Ryga's play *The Ecstasy of Rita Joe*; a showing of Native women artists; and a fashion show of the designs of Gerry Manyfingers.

Fashion shows, art shows, political issues, legal issues, social issues — The National Symposium on Aboriginal Women contained a little bit of everything to offer the wide spectrum of interests represented by those Aboriginal women who attended the event. Indeed we can and should congratulate each other, ourselves and the organizers for the efforts put forward.[2]

We were pleased with what we had accomplished. Our efforts were rewarded with a range of congratulatory comments: participants described their experience as "excellent," "educative," "valuable," "memorable," "worthwhile," and "unforgettable"; "I was honoured to be a participant"; "the range and variety allowed everyone to go away with something"; "a well-organized conference — the topics were selected with care"; and "congratulations for your courage to attack some difficult issues."

But not all comments were positive. Perhaps we tried too hard to be all things to all people. At the same time as some participants found "the overall format exceptional," others felt that there was too much emphasis on the formal presentation of academic papers and not enough opportunities for discussion and information sharing. For example, one participant noted: "I had a difficult time sitting with a room full of smart women all lined up facing the front listening to someone talk at us."

While some talked glowingly of the "gentle, family atmosphere of mothers, daughters and grandmothers," others spoke less warmly about the tensions between academics and activists, and between Aboriginal and non-Aboriginal women. While some non-Aboriginal women felt some hostility and animosity directed towards them, some Aboriginal women thought they were under-represented among the presenters. Despite our efforts to the contrary, the conference was unable to confront, dispel, or transcend the tensions that have plagued the coming together of women in a variety of settings over the past two or three decades — tensions based on racial, cultural, or ethnic identity, and the tensions between academic women and activist women.

Nevertheless, we have maintained our commitment to diversity and our belief that in the diversity of women's voices we can find strength and wisdom. This collection of readings has been designed to reflect this commitment. After the conference we asked presenters to submit the texts of their papers, talks, or workshops. We were guided in our selection by a number of criteria: Canadian content; regional representation; accessible language; challenge to conventional notions of "victim-ness"; and the promotion of empowering "ways of knowing." Therefore, this collection of "texts" celebrates many different voices — the voices of Native and non-Native scholars, feminists, and activists who address issues of silence and invisibility. Furthermore, this collection challenges the implicitly theoretical assumption of other research that the experiences and roles of women are defined universally.

It challenges the assumption that, when we speak of Aboriginal women, we speak of a single voice, a single identity, a homogenous history, and a singular cultural experience. In our view, any group of readings must take into account the differences inherent in the distinct groups. There are tribal peoples, Status, non-Status and Bill C-31; Métis peoples; and the Inuit (Jackson 1994; Chiste 1994; Satzewich and Wotherspoon 1993). These categories can be further reduced by region, historicity, government policy, and ethnolinguistic groupings.

Ethnohistorical descriptions of tribal life in the past have placed the focus on men and men's roles — man-the-warrior, man-the-chief, man-the-hunter, and man-the-provider. The roles of women have either been ignored altogether or placed in a position of subservience and/or secondary importance. While there is extensive research on the effect that colonization has had on the traditional roles of First Nations women (for example, by Smandych and Lee 1995), much of this research assumes that the women's survival skills were acquired as a result of European contact. The amount of autonomy and control differs from tribe to tribe, and group to group; nevertheless, the growing consensus in the literature is that these roles and behaviours were indeed present at the time of contact. Equally true is that this behaviour and these roles have been attenuated by the imposition of EuroCanadian law, religion, and social control. The articles in this volume by Diane P. Payment,

Laura Peers, and Sarah Carter examine the importance of women's roles in tribal societies. In their work the *a priori* assumption that there was some phenomenon relating to contact that enabled women to become stronger does not withstand critical analysis. The research clearly demonstrates that women adapted already-existing skills, knowledge, and strength to the colonial experience.

Payment, for example, gives us fresh insight into the political, economic, and spiritual importance of women in the growth of Métis communities in northern Saskatchewan. Her work reveals the multiple roles of Métis women in the construction of the community at Batoche and the Riel rebellion, as well as the effect the rebellion had on their lives. This challenges the conventional view that makes note of women only in their role as "Halfbreeds," and as "desirable and prized mates" (Redbird 1980).

Peers challenges the way in which women have been marginalized by gender bias in the secondary literature on the Saulteaux, and in doing so she documents the importance of women not only in the development of the fur trade, but also in procuring the means of daily subsistence. Women's role in food production was significant not only in conjunction with the activities of men but also made the difference between mere survival and a decent standard of living. Similarly, Carter discusses the importance of women's contributions to prairie Indian groups during the early reserve days. She shows how women maintained the survival of their families and communities by drawing upon not only traditional skills but also skills learned from missionaries and Indian agents.

Jo-Anne Fiske, Rosemary Brown, Jennifer Blythe, and Peggy McGuire focus their attention on modes of adaptation. Increasingly, the detrimental effects of residential schools are being recognized by the non-Aboriginal community. In particular, recent media reports have focussed on the devastation still being felt by those who were caught in this destructive system. Fiske's work demonstrates, however, that there were some individuals who were able to turn parts of the residential schooling experience to their advantage. She reveals to us the strength and perseverance of Carrier women who were able to incorporate and use skills learned from the destructive system of missionary education to assist their communities. Combined with traditional knowledge, these skills enabled these women to maintain their own and their group's integrity. Fiske documents the way in which Carrier women were able to assume leadership roles in their communities, calling upon political skills learned in the residential schools.

Brown's work with the Lubicon in northern Alberta documents the effect that changes in the economy have had on women's productive and reproductive labour. Blythe and McGuire have similarly examined the changes in women's work among the Cree in Moosonee and Moose Factory. Both of these papers demonstrate clearly that the impact of environmental, economic, and political pressures on the lives and work of Aboriginal women in contemporary tribal colonialist economies has mitigated the abilities of Aboriginal women to pursue traditional activities. They show the extent to which colonialist economies endanger the viability of the extended family. While women remain the centre of family life, their ability to fulfill this role has been jeopardized by external forces over which they have no control.

As much a part of women's lives as production and reproduction are literature, art, sport, and leisure. This is as true of First Nations women as it is for other groups, although it is an area that has received little serious attention. If we are to rectify the errors and omissions brought on by colonialism, it is necessary to present First Nations women as multi- rather than uni-dimensional. The work of Kathy M'Closkey, Vicky Paraschak, and Julia Emberley provides just this kind of balance.

M'Closkey discusses the way in which art produced by women has been marginalized through the imposition of patriarchal conceptions of aesthetics. The interpretation of First Nation women's art through the filters of these assumptions has had a profound effect on women and on tribal societies where the production of art was a complementary effort in which both men and women collaborated in the production of ritual items and items for daily use (Schneider 1983).

Paraschak's research is especially important since it covers an area historically ignored in the literature. She examines the effect of gender bias on the construction of knowledge as she discusses the significant role played by organized sport in the lives of First Nations women. Emberley's discussion of Jeannette Armstrong's novel *Slash* undertakes to challenge the traditional patriarchal and colonialist framework used to experience and interpret the artistic, in this case literary, production of Aboriginal writers. She tries to provide an alternate framework in which colonialist, patriarchal, and racist assumptions can be "unlearned" in the process of "reading" the writing of Aboriginal women. Her work highlights issues related to the politics of representation, the politics of identity, and the politics of difference.

Some women (including some Native women) tend to endow First Nations women with an aura of mysticism. Such unrealistic attitudes can be as problematic and derogatory as views of women as "squaws" and "beasts of burden." Such myths are debunked by the voices of Aboriginal women themselves: Betty Bastien, Beverly Hungry Wolf, Jeannette Armstrong, and Emma LaRocque.

Bastien focusses on the way in which tribal identity, as self-identity, transcends political boundaries, encompassing intrinsic values and establishing one's place in the world. She points out that it is women who must foster and maintain the sense of self in their children, for only in this way will future generations have a complete understanding of their roles among their own people and in the world at large. Similarly, Hungry Wolf speaks eloquently of the power of the earth, of nature and of connection to the environment and the ways of our grandmothers. Her voice is one of strength, wisdom, and empowerment. Identity is a historical continuum that links who we are with our ancestors.

Noted author Jeannette Armstrong gave the Symposium's keynote address.

We begin this collection with the reproduction of the text of her talk. She spoke movingly of the destructive reality that shapes the lives of many Aboriginal women. She spoke passionately of the legacy and survival of Aboriginal women and of the victory over forces designed to rob women of their dignity. Her voice is a strong, powerful, and inspiring one.

As women, as activists, and as scholars, it falls to us to examine the pedagogy and praxis of research relating to First Nations women in Canada, and to develop strategies to speak to these concerns. The development of a feminist epistemology and research methods has provided a framework that allows for the discovery and rediscovery of women's voices, women's histories, and women's experience. Yet, many scholars are trained in the patriarchal and ethnocentric institutions of EuroCanadian scholarship. This requires that those of us working within the traditions of feminist discourse and epistemology examine our own biases and those of our disciplines.

LaRocque's work provides the theoretical framework for the collection. She calls our attention to the way in which colonialist scholarship has set parameters around theory and empiricism, establishing a false dichotomy between the "self" and the "word." She convincingly argues that the research efforts and writings of First Nations women about their own lives are neither fully appreciated nor fully understood as valid scholarly contributions within traditional academic frameworks and models. She challenges us to confront the assumptions that underlie our words.

It is important to note that many of the papers were delivered as oral texts. The reader also needs to be aware that some of the research contained in this volume is now over six years old. Nevertheless, we are confident that this collection makes an important and original contribution to the struggle for a distinctive and multi-dimensional Aboriginal woman's voice.

NOTES

1. Marie Smallface Marule and Christine Miller, both then faculty members in the Department of Native American Studies at the University of Lethbridge; Patricia Chuchryk and Doreen Indra of the departments of Sociology and Anthropology respectively; Cheryl Deering, Joanne Crate-Thomas, and Rosalind Merrick, students in the Native American Studies Department, Betty Bastien, an instructor with the University of Calgary Faculty of Social Work program, and Brenda Manyfingers, a professional with Alberta Social Services.
2. In the conference program we provided participants with space to write their comments about the various speakers and events of the conference. This, as well as other quoted remarks about the Symposium, comes from participants' submitted evaluations.

REFERENCES

Albers, Patricia. 1983. "Introduction: New Perspectives on Plains Indian Women." In *The Hidden Half: Studies of Plains Indian Women*, ed. Patricia Albers and Beatrice Medicine. Washington, DC: University Press of America.

Allen, Paula Gunn. 1986. *The Sacred Hoop: Recovering the Feminine in American Indian Tradition.* Boston: Beacon Press.

Chiste, Katherine Beaty. 1994. "Aboriginal Women and Self-Government: Challenging Leviathan." *American Indian Culture and Research Journal* 18, no. 3.

Green, Rayna. 1992. *Women in American Indian Society.* New York: Chelsea House Publishers.

Jackson, Margaret A. 1994. "Aboriginal Women and Self-Government." In *Aboriginal Self-Government in Canada: Current Trends and Issues*, ed. John H. Hylton. Saskatoon: Purich Publishing.

Manyfingers, Brenda. 1994. "Treaty Seven Community Study: Family Violence and Community Stress." Royal Commission on Aboriginal Peoples. Unpublished manuscript.

McIver, Sharon D. 1995. "Aboriginal Women's Rights as 'Existing Rights.'" *Canadian Women's Studies* 15, nos. 2 and 3:34-37.

Ontario Native Women's Association. 1989. *Breaking Free: A Proposal for Change to Aboriginal Family Violence.* Thunder Bay: Ontario Native Women's Association.

Redbird, Duke. 1980. *We Are Métis: A Métis View of the Development of Native Canadian People.* Willowdale, ON: Ontario Métis and Non Status Indian Association.

Ryga, George. 1976. *The Ecstasy of Rita Joe.* Vancouver: Talonbooks.

Satzewich, Vic, and Terry Wotherspoon. 1993. *First Nations: Race, Class and Gender Relations.* Scarborough, ON: Nelson Press.

Schneider, Mary Jane. 1983. "The Role of Sioux Women in the Production of Ceremonial Objects." In *The Hidden Half: Studies of Plains Indian Women*, ed. Patricia Albers and Beatrice Medicine. Washington, DC: University Press of America.

Smandych, Russell, and Gloria Lee. 1995. "Women, Colonization and Resistance: Elements of an Amerindian Autohistorical Approach to the Study of Law and Colonialism." *Native Studies Review* 10, no. 1.

The Colonization of a
Native Woman Scholar

Emma LaRocque

The history of Canada is a history of the colonization of Aboriginal peoples. Colonization is a pervasive structural and psychological relationship between the colonizer and the colonized and is ultimately reflected in the dominant institutions, policies, histories, and literatures of occupying powers. Yet, it is only recently that Canadian scholars from a variety of fields have begun to situate the Native/white relationship within this context of dominance-subjugation.[1] There is ample room in Canadian scholarship for macroscopic explorations of the dynamics of oppression. In other words, we must seek to understand what happens to a country that has existed under the forces of colonial history over such an extended period of time. We must seek to recognize the faces of both the colonizer and the colonized,[2] as they appear in society and in the academic community. We must become aware of the functions of power and racism, its effects on the Native population, and the significance of resistance.

Colonization has taken its toll on all Native peoples, but perhaps it has taken its greatest toll on women. While all Natives experience racism, Native women suffer from sexism as well. Racism and sexism[3] found in the colonial process have served to dramatically undermine the place and value of women in Aboriginal cultures, leaving us vulnerable both within and outside of our communities. Not only have Native women been subjected to violence in both white and Native societies, but we have also been subjected to patriarchal policies that have dispossessed us of our inherited rights, lands, identities, and families. Native women continue to experience discrimination through the Indian Act, inadequate representation in Native and mainstream organizations, lack of official representation in self-government discussions, under- and/or unequal employment, and ghettoization of the educated Native woman, for example.[4] The tentacles of colonization are not only extant today, but may also be multiplying and encircling Native peoples in ever-tighter grips of landlessness and marginalization, hence, of anger, anomie, and violence, in which women are the more obvious victims.

The effects of colonization, then, have been far-reaching, and numerous issues remain to be examined, not the least of which is how colonization affects men and women differently.[5] As a long-standing scholar in Native studies, I especially wish to bring to this discussion some of my reflections about what confronts those of us who are not only Native and women but are also intellectuals and researchers caught within the confines of ideologically rooted, Western-based canons, standards, and notions of objectivity and research.[6] We are in extraordinary circumstances: not only do we study and teach colonial history, but we also walk in its shadow on a daily basis ourselves. What do we do with our knowledge as well as with the practices of power in our lives, even in places of higher learning?

I find it impossible to study colonial history, literature, and popular cultural productions featuring Native peoples, particularly women, without addressing the social and ethical ramifications of such study. To study any kind of human violation is, *ipso facto*, to be engaged in ethical matters. And we must respond — as scholars, as men and women, Native and white alike. These destructive attitudes, unabashed biases, policies, and violence that we footnote cannot be mere intellectual or scholarly exercises. They do affect Native peoples, real human lives. I believe there is a direct relationship between racist/sexist stereotypes and violence against Native women and girls.[7] The dehumanizing portrayal of the "squaw" and the over-sexualization of Native females such as in Walt Disney's *Pocahontas* surely render all Native female persons vulnerable. Moreover, these stereotypes have had a profound impact on the self-images of Native men and women, respectively, and on their relationships with each other.[8]

In addition to the questions of the social purpose of our knowledge, we are confronted in scholarship with having to deal with Western-controlled education, language, cultural production, and history. For example, classically colonial archival and academic descriptions and data about Natives' tools, physical features, "rituals," or geography have been equated with objectivity,[9] while Native-based data has been subsumed under subjectivity. Native scholars, particularly those of us who are decolonized and/or feminist, have been accused of "speaking in our own voices," which is taken as "being biased" or doing something less than "substantive" or "pure" research. Not only are such accusations glaringly ironic given the degree of bias, inflammatory language, and barely concealed racism evident in much of early Canadian historical and literary writing on Native peoples,[10] but they are also adversarial. Native scholars' contribution to contemporary scholarship is significant, for, in a sense, we bring "the other half" of Canada into light. Not only do we offer new ways of seeing and saying things, but we also provide new directions and fresh methodologies to cross-cultural research; we broaden the empirical and theoretical bases of numerous disciplines, and we pose new questions to old and tired traditions. And often, we live with many anomalies. If we serve as "informants" to our non-Native colleagues, for example, about growing up within a land-based culture (e.g., on a trap line), our colleagues would include such information as part of their scholarly presentations; it would authenticate their research. Yet, if we use the very same information with a direct reference to our cultural backgrounds, it would be met, at best, with scepticism, and, at worst, with charges of parochialism because we would have spoken in "our own voices."

Clearly, the tension in the colonizer/colonized dichotomy has not escaped the academic community, and much work needs to be done to acknowledge the dialectics of colonization in Canadian scholarship. And I, as a Native woman, am compelled to pursue and express my scholarship quite differently from the way my non-Native counterparts do. I do this by maintaining orality in writing, taking an interdisciplinary approach to genre, calling for ethical re/considerations (not to be confused with "censorship") in the archiving of hate material, and openly (rather than covertly) referring to "voice" within academic studies. My use of "voice," for example, is a textual resistance technique. It should not be assumed, as it so often is, that using "voice" means "making a personal statement," which is then dichotomized from "academic studies." Native scholars and writers are demonstrating that "voice" can be, must be, used within academic studies not only as an expression of cultural integrity but also as an attempt to begin to balance the legacy of dehumanization and bias entrenched in Canadian studies about Native peoples. Colleagues, publishers, editors, and readers of academic material need especially to acquaint themselves with the political nature of the English language, Western history, and other hegemonic canons of scholarly and editorial practices and criticism before they are in a position to appreciate what should most appropriately be understood as "Native resistance scholarship."[11] There is no basis for assuming that Native intellectuals are somehow more predisposed to bias than are white intellectuals.

The growing body of international literature on "post-colonial voices" as expressed by non-Western scholars and writers should serve as an instructive reminder that Native scholars and writers in Canada are part of this non-Western international community. This is not to say that the colonial experience is "in the past" for Canadian Native peoples; rather, it is to say that we are responding within the post-colonial intellectual context. As Ashcroft, Griffiths, and Tiffin put it, we are emerging "in our present form out of the experience of colonization" and asserting ourselves "by foregrounding the tension" with the colonial power by writing or talking back to "the empire."[12] We are challenging our non-Native colleagues to throw off "the weight of antiquity" with respect to hegemonic canonical assumptions, which continue "to dominate cultural production in much of the postcolonial world."[13] We are challenging them to re-evaluate their colonial frameworks of interpretation, their conclusions and portrayals, not to mention their tendencies of excluding from their footnotes scholars who are Native.[14]

There are many and varied layers of "colonial" practices in current Canadian scholarship. Of interest is the less than judicious treatment of the Native women writers who contributed to *Writing the Circle*[15] by some critics who, among other things, exclude the theories, criticisms, creativity, and experience of these women.[16] A number of critical responses have based their theories about Native women writers on such small, repetitive, and highly selective samples[17] that it does raise troubling issues of exclusion especially to those of us (both male and female) who are at once scholars, critics, and/or creative writers. We do present complexities in that we are crossing cultures, disciplines, and genres, and we obviously do not fit into conventional categories or ideological formulas. But we have been writing and footnoting at least as early as the 1970s, and our combined backgrounds of scholarship and marginalization as well as critical and/or creative works do model what is at the very heart of post-colonial discourse. It remains that as scholars we are all challenged to cross borders and to seek greater understanding. Western-based assumptions (including feminist, deconstructionist, and/or "post-colonial" discourse) can no longer claim exclusive rights to the ways and means of academic methodology and insight.

The challenge is, finally, to ourselves as Native women caught within the burdens and contradictions of colonial history. We are being asked to confront some of our own traditions at a time when there seems to be a great need for a recall of traditions to help us retain our identities as Aboriginal people. But there is no choice — as women we must be circumspect in our recall of tradition. We must ask ourselves whether and to what extent tradition is liberating to us as women. We must ask ourselves wherein lies (lie) our source(s) of empowerment. We know enough about human history that we cannot assume that all Aboriginal traditions universally respected and honoured women. (And is "respect" and "honour" all that we can ask for?) It should not be assumed, even in those original societies that were structured along matriarchal lines, that matriarchies necessarily prevented men from oppressing women. There are indications of male violence and sexism in some Aboriginal societies prior to European contact[18] and certainly after contact. But, at the same time, culture is not immutable, and tradition cannot be expected to be always of value or relevant in our times. As Native women, we are faced with very difficult and painful choices, but, nonetheless, we are challenged to change, create, and embrace "traditions" consistent with contemporary and international human rights standards.

Sadly, there are insidious notions within our own communities that we as Native women should be "unobtrusive, soft-spoken and quiet," and that we should not assume elected leadership, which is taken to mean "acting like men." The "traditional Indian woman" is still often expected to act and dress like an ornamental Pocahontas/"Indian Princess." But who should our models be? How should we maintain the traditions we value without adhering to stereotype or compromising our full humanity? If one must look to the past for models and heroes, we might do well to take a second look at Pocahontas. The irony is that the real Pocahontas was neither unobtrusive nor quiet. Quite the contrary: she was in fact revolutionary — for the wrong cause, but revolutionary nonetheless!

If we wish to act on history rather than be acted on, we can ill afford to be silent or stay content in the shadows of our male contemporaries. Speaking directly to the exclusion of women's experience and the analysis of this exclusion, Joyce Green, a Native doctoral student in political science at the University of Alberta, writes: "So much of women's experience has been classified as nondata. So much of women's analysis as women has been ignored by the academy and by the activists. The consequence is male-gendered theoretical and epistemological development that is presented as authentic reflection of the human condition. . . . But knowledge is dynamic, and there is nothing preventing the incorporation of new female and Aboriginal ways of knowing."[19]

History demands of us to assume our dignity, our equality, and our humanity. We must not move towards the future with anything less. Nor can we pursue scholarship in any other way.

NOTES

1. There are fine works from various fields on the colonization of Canadian Native peoples. They include E. Palmer Patterson, *The Canadian Indian Since 1500* (1972); Mel Watkins, *Dene Nation, Colony Within* (1977); Thomas R. Berger, *Northern Frontier, Northern Homeland* (1977); Hugh and Karmel McCullum, *This Land Is Not for Sale* (1975); Anastasia M. Shkilnyk, *A Poison Stronger Than Love* (1985); Dara Culhane Speck, *An Error in Judgement* (1987); A.D. Fisher, "A Colonial Education System: Historical Changes and Schooling in Fort Chipewyan" (1981). Many more conventional studies have not placed the Native experience into any cohesive theoretical framework; instead, the emphasis has been on "the impact of" the white man, his tools, his religion, and his diseases, and so forth. Fur-trade volumes, in particular, are replete with "impact" notions and items.
2. I am suggesting, of course, that as Canadian peoples, both Native and non-Native, we may find ourselves, our respective experiences, mirrored in Albert Memmi's *The Colonizer and the Colonized* (1967).
3. Racism and sexism together result in powerful personal and structural expressions in any society, but they are clearly exacerbated under colonial conditions. However, it should be noted that sexism, in particular, did not derive solely from European culture or colonization. As alluded to throughout this paper, there are indications of pre-existing patriarchy and sexism within Aboriginal cultures.
4. For a more detailed discussion on patriarchy, see my article, "Racism/Sexism and Its Effects on Native Women" (1989). See also: Joyce Green, "Constitutionalising the Patriarchy: Aboriginal Women and Aboriginal Government" (1993); Gail Stacey-Moore, "In Our Own Voice: Aboriginal Women Demand Justice" (1993).
5. Further study is required on how colonization affects men and women differently. Diane Bell, a critical anthropologist, has pointed out that, while mainstream scholars have begun to "develop more and more sophisticated models of colonial relations, . . . they have, for the most part, paid scant attention to the different impact of colonial practices on men and women," which has led to creating "a niche for the consolidation of male power; . . . the most consistent outcome

appears to be that while men assume the political spokesperson role, the women run the welfare structures" (1989, 6).

6. On the issue of non-Western intellectuals confronting Western hegemonic canonical assumptions in post-colonial writing, see: Barbara Harlow, *Resistance Literature* (1987); Ashcroft, Griffiths, and Tiffin, *The Empire Writes Back* (1989); and Peter Hitchcock, *The Dialogics of the Oppressed* (1992).

7. For a more detailed discussion on violence against Native women, see my article, "Violence in Aboriginal Communities" (1993). See also the Aboriginal Justice Inquiry of Manitoba, Government of Manitoba (1991); and the report, *Breaking Free: A Proposal for Change to Aboriginal Family Violence*, Ontario Native Women's Association (1989).

8. Native men and women have experienced and reacted to colonial influences quite differently. This is particularly evident with respect to gender roles and stereotypes. For further comment on this, see my articles: "Racism/Sexism and Its Effects on Native Women" (1989); and "Violence in Aboriginal Communities" (1993).

9. There is an air of detachment to these descriptions, and it is this imperial aloofness that has been mistaken for objectivity. For a brilliant analysis of "textual strategies of domination" through European descriptions of Native ethnography that give "an appearance of impartiality," see Parker Duchemin, "'A Parcel of Whelps': Alexander Mackenzie among the Indians" (1990).

10. For a discussion on inflammatory language that should qualify as hate literature, see my article, "On the Ethics of Publishing Historical Documents" (1988).

11. For a more detailed discussion, but in the context of literary treatment of Aboriginal themes and writers, see my "Preface, or Here Are Our Voices — Who Will Hear?" in *An Anthology — Writing the Circle: Native Women of Western Canada* (1990); see also my article, "When the Other Is Me: Native Writers Confronting Canadian Literature," *Human Ecology: Issues in the North* 4, to be published by the Circumpolar Institute, University of Alberta.

12. Ashcroft, Griffiths, and Tiffin, *The Empire Writes Back* (1989, 2).

13. Ibid., 7.

14. Non-Native scholars are increasingly using Native sources that they, however, reformulate or discount as ethnographic or personal accounts; there has been a persistent tendency on the part of white intellectuals to disregard Native scholars and other intellectuals, apparently assuming that they cannot be "of the people," or cannot be "objective." Either way, Native-based scholarship is put in a no-win situation.

15. Perreault and Vance, eds., *An Anthology — Writing the Circle: Native Women of Western Canada* (1990).

16. See, for example, Hartmut Lutz, "Confronting Cultural Imperialism: First Nations People are Combating Continued Cultural Theft" (1995). Lutz's article is wide-ranging but, in the context of discussing "Stolen Stories" (141-42), he lists *Writing the Circle* as one of the works criticized (led by two Native women) for "cultural appropriation"; he then goes on to claim that "most Native writers support" the debate without making clear whether, by *debate*, he means the broad topic of cultural appropriation or the small controversy surrounding *Writing the Circle*. Lutz bases his conclusion on an extremely small representation, quite mysteriously (and uncharacteristically, as he usually treats Native literatures and writes with depth and scope) overlooking the theoretical ramifications of the fifty or so Native women writers involved in the production of *Writing the Circle*. For a similarly perplexing treatment of *Writing the Circle*, see also Julia Emberley, *Thresholds of Difference: Feminist Critique, Native Women's Writings, Postcolonial Theory* (1993).

17. Attention has been poured repeatedly and almost exclusively on three or four Native women writers in most "Native issues" publication specials or literary conferences over the last five years. See, for example, articles by Agnes Grant, Noel Elizabeth Currie, Margery Fee, and Barbara Godard in W.H. New, ed., *Native Writers and Canadian Literature* (1990). I should emphasize that my comment is not intended to focus on the Native writers upon whom attention

is lavished but on the literary and academic critics who persistently neglect to study the other several dozen or so Native writers in Canada.

18. Many early European observations as well as original Indian legends (e.g., Cree Wehsehkchcha stories I grew up with) point to pre-contact existence of male violence and sexism against women.

19. Joyce Green, "Democracy, Gender and Aboriginal Rights," unpublished manuscript, November 1993, 15.

REFERENCES

Adams, Howard. 1975. *Prison of Grass: Canada from the Native Point of View.* Toronto: New Press.

Ashcroft, Bill, Gareth Griffiths, and Helen Tiffin. 1989. *The Empire Writes Back: Theory and Practice in Post-Colonial Literature.* London and New York: Routledge.

Bell, Diane. 1989. "Considering Gender: Are Human Rights for Women Too?" Paper presented at the International Conference on Human Rights in Cross Cultural Perspectives, College of Law, University of Saskatchewan.

Berger, Thomas R. 1977. *Northern Frontier, Northern Homeland: The Report of the Mackenzie Valley Pipeline Inquiry,* Volume 1. Ottawa: Minister of Supply and Services Canada.

Brodribb, Somer. 1984. "The Traditional Roles of Native Women in Canada and the Impact of Colonization." *The Canadian Journal of Native Studies* 4, no. 1:85-103.

Brownmiller, Susan. 1975. *Against Our Will: Men, Women, and Rape.* New York: Simon and Schuster.

Campbell, Maria. 1973. *Halfbreed.* Toronto: McClelland and Stewart, Ltd.

Culhane Speck, Dara. 1987. *An Error in Judgement: The Politics of Medical Care in an Indian/White Community.* Vancouver: Talonbooks.

Duchemin, Parker. 1990. "'A Parcel of Whelps': Alexander Mackenzie among the Indians." *Canadian Literature* 124-25 (spring-summer):49-75.

Emberley, Julia. 1993. *Thresholds of Difference: Feminist Critique, Native Women's Writings, Postcolonial Theory.* Toronto: University of Toronto Press.

Fanon, Frantz. 1963. *The Wretched of the Earth.* New York: Grove Press.

Fisher, A.D. 1981. "A Colonial Education System: Historical Changes and Schooling in Fort Chipewyan." *Canadian Journal of Anthropology* 2, no. 1 (spring):37-44.

Fisher, Robin, and Kenneth Coates, eds. 1988. *Out of the Background: Readings on Canadian Native History.* Toronto: Copp Clark Pitman.

Green, Joyce. 1993. "Constitutionalising the Patriarchy: Aboriginal Women and Aboriginal Government." *Constitutional Forum* 4, no. 4:110-20.

Harlow, Barbara. 1987. *Resistance Literature.* New York: Methuen.

Hitchcock, Peter. 1992. *The Dialogics of the Oppressed.* Minneapolis: University of Minnesota Press.

LaRocque, Emma. 1975. *Defeathering the Indian.* Agincourt: The Book Society of Canada.

_____. 1988. "On the Ethics of Publishing Historical Documents." In *"The Orders of the Dreamed": George Nelson on Cree and Ojibwa Religion and Myth, 1823,* ed. Jennifer S.H. Brown and Robert Brightman. Winnipeg: University of Manitoba Press.

_____. 1989. "Racism/Sexism and Its Effects on Native Women." In *Public Concerns on Human Rights.* Winnipeg: Human Rights Commission.

_____. 1990. "Preface, or Here Are Our Voices — Who Will Hear?" Preface to *An Anthology — Writing the Circle: Native Women of Western Canada,* ed. Jeanne Perreault and Sylvia Vance. Edmonton: NeWest Publishers.

_____. 1990. "Tides, Towns and Trains." In *Living the Changes,* ed. Joan Turner. Winnipeg: University of Manitoba Press.

_____. 1993. "Violence in Aboriginal Communities." In *The Path To Healing*, prepared by the Royal Commission on Aboriginal Peoples, 72-89.

Lutz, Hartmut. 1995. "Confronting Cultural Imperialism: First Nations People are Combating Continued Cultural Theft." In *Multiculturalism in North America and Europe: Social Practices —Literary Visions,* ed. Hans Braun and Wolfgang Klooss. Trier, Germany: Wissenschaftlicher Verlag Trier.

Manitoba, Government. 1991. Aboriginal Justice Inquiry of Manitoba.

McCullum, Hugh, and Karmel McCullum. 1975. *This Land Is Not for Sale: Canada's Original Peoples and their Land — A Saga of Neglect, Exploitation, and Conflict.* Toronto: Anglican Book Centre.

Memmi, Albert. 1967. *The Colonizer and the Colonized.* Translated by Howard Greenfeld. Boston: Beacon Press.

New, W.H., ed. 1990. *Native Writers and Canadian Literature.* Vancouver: University of British Columbia Press.

Ontario Native Women's Association. 1989. *Breaking Free: A Proposal for Change to Aboriginal Family Violence.* Thunder Bay: Ontario Native Women's Association.

Patterson, E. Palmer. 1972. *The Canadian Indian Since 1500.* Don Mills, ON: Collier-Macmillan Canada, Ltd.

Perreault, Jeanne, and Sylvia Vance, eds. 1990. *An Anthology — Writing the Circle: Native Women of Western Canada.* Edmonton: NeWest Publishers.

Shkilnyk, Anastasia M. 1985. *A Poison Stronger Than Love: The Destruction of an Ojibwa Community.* New Haven: Yale University Press.

Stacey-Moore, Gail. 1993. "In Our Own Voice: Aboriginal Women Demand Justice." *Herizons* 6, no. 4:21-23.

Steiner, Stan. 1968. *The New Indians.* New York: Dell Publishing Co.

Van Kirk, Sylvia. 1980. *"Many Tender Ties": Women in Fur-Trade Society in Western Canada, 1670-1870.* Winnipeg: Watson and Dwyer Publishing Ltd.

Watkins, Mel. 1977. *Dene Nation, Colony Within.* Toronto: University of Toronto Press.

"La vie en rose"? Métis Women at Batoche, 1870 to 1920

Diane P. Payment

Although studies on Aboriginal women have increased in the last decade, especially in the United States,[1] Métis (Franco-AmerIndian) and "Halfbreed"[2] (Anglo-AmerIndian) women in Canada have been the subject of only a few specific inquiries, usually in relation to the fur trade or more contemporary issues.[3] (Not surprisingly, it is women who are thinking and writing about women.)

Two of the difficulties in researching and writing about women in the past generally have been the dearth of sources or personal testimonies by the "hidden half," and the male bias of the written record in general. The world of pre-twentieth-century, working-class EuroCanadian women is largely unrecorded. They had little leisure time, and many could not read or write, and so their "stories" were not collected. The women who did keep journals or were the subject of biographies were usually from the leisured upper class and reflected its values and behaviour. And few writers considered their own day-to-day lives worth recording.

In the case of Métis women, the issues of ethnicity, class, and literacy were even more a factor than among Aboriginals or EuroCanadians. Their cultural traditions were recorded both orally and in writing, reflecting their dual Aboriginal and EuroCanadian heritage. In the Aboriginal tradition, knowledge was acquired through experience and transmitted orally. Among EuroCanadian women, it was only those in the upper class who recorded their own lives. But since few Métis women could read and write in French or in English, personal written accounts are few and fragmentary.

As part of my research on Métis society for Batoche National Historic Site in 1976 and 1985, I interviewed eighteen women Elders. These women, born between 1886 and 1910, talked about their personal life experiences and those of their ancestors. These oral histories, a few letters and journals written by Métis women, and general accounts written by Métis of the events of 1885 formed the basis of my research.[4] Women were of course an integral part of Batoche society, but since their world was largely private and male directed, few of their experiences were documented by the writers of the time, most of whom were male. The oral histories were the key source of information on the lives of women at Batoche between 1870 and 1920 and provided valuable insight into the collective experience of Métis women. The picture that emerged from my interviews was not "*la vie en rose*," or the feminine idea of love, family, and home fostered by the Church and promoted in the Victorian literature of the period. Experiences were individual and varied, but most women "had to bear their cross,"[5] and in particular they had to endure the suffering and anxiety associated with war, poverty, and discrimination.

MÉTIS WOMEN: THEIR ANCESTRY AND "WORLD" BY THE NINETEENTH CENTURY

The Métis women at Batoche were almost exclusively of Cree or Ojibwa and French-Canadian origin. Some aspects of the Aboriginal heritage were still in evidence in the early 1900s, especially among the elder *mosums* (grandfathers) and *kokums* (grandmothers) who still spoke Cree or Saulteaux and practised Native medicine. The testimonies of the women at Batoche suggest a predominance of French-Canadian tradition in their music and lifestyle, but a syncretism of Cree and Canadien is illustrated in their language, mentality, religious beliefs, and other cultural traditions. The Cree and Ojibwa culture was more suppressed and undermined by the turn of the century. Fur traders, missionaries, and politicians had increasingly isolated the Métis from their AmerIndian counterparts. The Métis were encouraged to live in settlements, abandon their traditional beliefs in favour of Christianity, and adopt British institutions. The racism, bigotry, and sexism of the Victorian era persuaded many Métis to declare "*on n'est pas des sauvages*" or to deny their grandmothers' origins and to assert their French-Canadian "male" heritage. However, they remained "between two worlds." The people who called themselves *gens libres* (or *otipemisiwak*) were forced to resort to war to defend their freedom and homeland in 1870 and 1885. Their persistence and pride ensured that Batoche remained a Métis community. The credit for this achievement must go not only to politicians and traders such as Louis Riel, Gabriel Dumont, and Xavier Letendre, but also to the "invisible" majority — women such as Josephte (Paul) Tourond, Marguerite (Dumas) Caron, and Marie (Letendre) Champagne. Without legal rights as individuals and belittled as inferior *créatures d'Ève* by the Catholic Church, their identities and achievements survived *malgré tout*.

The Métis woman's world in the late nineteenth and early twentieth centuries was essentially domestic and family oriented. It was largely dominated by Victorian attitudes to ethnic origins and class, which placed Aboriginal women in an inferior position to EuroCanadian women. The Euro-Christian ideal of the submissive wife, which was consistent with the tradition of patriarchy, had been firmly established. It can be argued that the status and power of Native women, both AmerIndian and Métis, had been greatly eroded through contact with European missionaries and fur traders. In the early West, plains Aboriginal women, the main ancestors of Métisses, filled an essentially egalitarian role in relation to men in the pre-agricultural economy.[6] Women's role in the hunt was as significant and as necessary as men's. Along with the men, they built some of the buffalo pounds, acted as scouts, interpreters, and skinners, and hauled the hides and meat into the camp. Women played a central part in the distribution of meat and hides from which clothing was made. The social and economic status of women was one of complementarity with men. The fur trade restructured the plains economy and placed women in a subservient and inferior productive role.[7] The negative European attitudes and behaviour toward Aboriginal women, called "squaws,"[8] slowly but effectively eroded the AmerIndian woman's position.

FROM RED RIVER TO BATOCHE

By the time of the emergence of a Métis settlement at Red River, around 1805, the Ojibwa, Cree, Déné, and Métis women[9] who accompanied their voyageur husbands were entering a world where Christian marriages, social and economic dependence, and racial prejudice would soon dominate. The pressures and tensions experienced by "Halfbreed" and Métis women may have differed. According to Sylvia Van Kirk, the Anglo "mixed-bloods," unlike the Métis, lacked a distinct cultural identity based on their dual cultural heritage. She suggests that, because of their inferior status, "Halfbreed" women were more easily acculturated or integrated into the dominant British society.[10] A recent study on Red River society suggests that there were also important class differences among Métis and "Halfbreed" women.[11] The daughters of traders Andrew McDermott and Narcisse Marion, for example, married into economically and socially influential families and pursued a lifestyle that was very different from that of women whose fathers or husbands were employed as labourers by the Hudson's Bay Company, or were primarily hunters and freighters. The status and circumstances of Métis women in St. Boniface in the early 1800s is alluded to by l'abbé Provencher in his correspondence. Like his contemporaries, Provencher was convinced of the inferiority and dependence of women with respect to the male *chef de famille*. He referred to women as *le sexe*,[12] implying their tainted sexual role. But he also commented on the cruelty and moral depravity of many French-Canadian voyageurs who abused their wives. Provencher failed to convince many men to abandon the AmerIndian custom of marriage *à la façon du pays* in favour of a Christian marriage, as men liked the freedom of "turning off" (leaving) their wives. The views of Aboriginal women on this issue are not extensively recorded or not clear, but there is evidence of traditional flexibility and independence in the selection and maintenance of mates in many groups.[13] In the opinion of Provencher and most EuroCanadians, however, AmerIndian women were abused and would benefit from the protection and stability of a Christian marriage.[14]

Provencher perceived the Métis women's sphere as one of domesticity (*bas emplois*) but, curiously enough, also as agents of civilization and Christianization within the family. Métis women were described as generous, hard-working, and more easily acculturated than the men: "Pour les filles de nos habitants, il ne faut pas une éducation bien relevé. Le principal serait de leur apprendre à bien vivre et à travailler afin de faire de bonnes mères de famille, ce qui relevera le pays avec le temps, il en a grandement besoin."[15] Another missionary who worked among the Ojibwa and Métis in the 1840s said that "*les filles bois-brûlées*" had more potential than boys in professions such as teaching. "Il est inutile de songer aux garçons pour celà ils sont trop inconstants."[16]

Other accounts refer to the enterprise of women who were skilled weavers and spinners and provided all the clothing for the family. The French-Canadian clergy was disdainful of the Aboriginal customs of smoking the pipe, of squatting on the floor, of serving food with the hands, and other *coutumes sauvages* that persisted among Métis women. The increasing number of French-Canadian women in the community by the 1850s were presented to them as models in dress and behaviour. The wearing of the *châle* and *couverte* was being abandoned in favour of European dress, as confirmed in photographs of Métis women at Red River in the 1860s and early 1870s, whereas the men still wore the *ceinture fléchée* and the *souliers mous*. European ideals of femininity, passivity, and sexual restraint prevailed.

An ambivalent picture of Métis women in St. Boniface emerges by 1870, the year of the Métis resistance and the negotiation of Manitoba's entry into Confederation. Members of the predominant ethnic group and more educated than their male counterparts, these women were also generally more acculturated to the Catholic and French-Canadian tradition. *Métissage* was viewed positively as part of the dual Métis Canadien heritage in the early years of Manitoba. French-Canadian women who married Métis men adopted or befriended the children from their previous customary marriages. As in the case of Julie (Lagimodière) Riel (the mother of Louis Riel) and Henriette (Landry) Dumas, they were the custodians of both traditions. They had integrated into Métis society and were often even physically indistinguishable from their Native sisters. A Winnipeg journalist who interviewed Mme Riel before Louis' execution in 1885, not knowing that she was French Canadian, described her appearance and demeanour as AmerIndian: "She has exceedingly high cheek bones, . . . thick black hair, . . . and rather low forehead, [which] indicate the blood of the race which flows in her veins."[17]

RESETTLEMENT AT BATOCHE: FEMALE ROOTS

The Métis were dispossessed and displaced by the new Anglo-Ontarian majority in Manitoba in the 1870s. Whereas in 1870 the "Halfbreeds" and Métis numbered about 10,000 (or eighty percent of the population), by 1884 over 4,000 (or forty percent) had left for the North-West Territories.[18] Hundreds of Métis families from the parishes of St. Boniface, St. Norbert, and St. François-Xavier left for the South Saskatchewan River district between 1872 and 1882. They sought new economic opportunities, wished to maintain their ethnic identity, or, as incisively recalled by Gabriel Dumont in 1903, re-affirmed their freedom and independence: "Nous avons quitté le Manitoba, parce que nous n'étions plus libres et nous sommes venus ici, dans ce pays sauvage, pour être libres. Et voila qu'on vient encore nous embêter."[19] There, they established new communities with stores, river-lot farms, schools, churches, and new kinship networks. One of these communities, Batoche, was established by Xavier Letendre dit Batoche in 1872 and given his surname (or *sobriquet*).

Over half of the approximately 500 inhabitants of Batoche in 1883 were women. The general resettlement pattern was organized according to extended family — grandparents, parents, brothers, sisters, cousins, and cross-cousins — but close analysis reveals a particularly strong female kinship tie.[20] For example, Angélique Dumas, who was married to Louis Letendre, settled near Batoche in 1872. Her sister Marguerite, Marguerite's husband, Jean Caron, and their family followed in 1878. In 1882, the youngest sister, Christine (Mme Barthélémi Pilon), left St. Norbert (Manitoba) for Batoche, accompanied by her elderly widowed mother, Henriette Landry Dumas, and three brothers. Finally, in 1901, another sister, Geneviève (Mme Joseph Ladéroute), also resettled at Batoche. By that time the sisters and their large families all resided in close proximity to each other. Similar patterns of female-led resettlement could be observed in the Gervais, Delorme, and Parenteau families.[21]

Widowed women and grandmothers (or *kokums*), such as Marguerite Ouellette (née Gingras) and Marie Vandal (née Primeau), accompanied by their grown children, who were unwilling or unable to remain in Manitoba were also among those who made the trek to Batoche. Marguerite Lespérance, the sixty-year-old mother of Louis Schmidt, settled with her son and his family near present-day St. Louis in 1880. She had led a very difficult life. Abandoned by her husband, who had "borrowed" another woman in 1869, she had lived in abject poverty and now depended on her son and daughters for a livelihood.[22] Julia Henry Lépine, Marie Hallet Letendre, and Hélène McMillan Boyer, all in their eighties, were among the elderly widowed grandmothers who accompanied their families to Batoche.[23] Marie Hallet resided with her son Xavier Letendre and assisted her daughter-in-law with the education of the children and in the household. These three Métis women, all born around 1805, had participated in the establishment and consolidation of the Métis nation at Red River in the 1830s and '40s. Their children had taken part in the resistance led by Louis Riel in 1869-70. All of them also lived to see the second resistance (or *guerre nationale*) in 1885. They were not strangers to privations and dispossession. This generation of Métis women, who had been taught Ojibwa and Cree traditions by their Aboriginal mothers, were the "keepers" of this heritage at a time of increased pressure to emulate the way of life of their French-Canadian fathers.

Elders enjoyed much prestige in Métis society. In their speeches, Louis Riel and other Métis leaders insisted on the importance of honouring and respecting their Aboriginal maternal ancestors.[24] Riel's letters home attest to his devotion and consideration for his widowed mother. Women were very influential in Riel's life. He was inspired and guided by his grandmother, mother, aunts, sisters Sara and Henriette, his wife, Marguerite, and finally his daughter Angélique, whom he called *mon petit ange*. There is no evidence, however, that he saw women's influence extending much beyond the home and family, but his composition "La Métisse," and the song written in honour of his sister Henriette ("Quand je partis ma chère Henriette"), suggest sensitivity and recognition of women's contribution to the Métis nation. One of his last compositions, "La lettre de sang," also called "L'Adieu," was written for his mother, whom he considered also his soul-mate. In it, he relates how he took a pen knife and dipped it in his blood to write a letter. When she received the letter written in blood, she would share his grief and sorrow, "ses yeux baignant de larmes, son coeur allant mourant."[25]

WOMEN'S SPHERE AT BATOCHE

Métis women's own accounts of their lives at Batoche suggest a mentality and way of life strongly influenced by French-Canadian traditions and Catholic beliefs. It was a patriarchal society where the "men ruled and the women reigned," although women elders enjoyed prestige and honour. Similar to their French-Canadian sisters, Métis women bore many children, an average of ten to twelve in the years 1883 to 1920.[26] Their "métchif" language, a French-Cree and/or French-Ojibwa dialect, was predominantly French in content, unlike that in some other Métis communities, such as Ile à la Crosse and Turtle Mountain (North Dakota), where the French component was less discernible.[27] French-Canadian customs such as *pendre la crémaillère* (house warming), the crowning of Ste. Catherine, celebrations of *le Jour de l'An* (New Year), and *le temps des fêtes* were followed, and Métis women made *tourtière* (a savoury meat pie), *glissante* (a type of dumpling) and *boulettes* (meat balls). The most popular names — Catherine, Angélique, Virginie, and Josephte — were French. But, at Batoche, a syncretism of French-Canadian, Cree, and to a lesser extent Scottish and Ojibwa customs was in evidence at the turn of the century. Many women smoked a pipe (at least privately), grew or cultivated medicinal herbs, wore amulets, and prepared foods such as *le rababou* (a kind of stew), *pemikan* (pemmican), and *galette* (or bannock), which were AmerIndian in origin. Many families still migrated seasonally, or "camped out," during the deer- and duck-hunting season, berry-picking expeditions, and while gathering seneca root. Their clothing was inspired by both traditions, if predominantly western European by 1900.

Religion was an important part of Métis life, and women in particular were looked upon by the clergy as the main custodians and transmitters of the Catholic beliefs and traditions. Father Moulin, parish priest at Batoche between 1882 and 1914, reported that it was primarily the women and their children who attended daily Mass at 6:00 a.m., as well as Benediction Vespers and other religious celebrations other than the regular and obligatory Sunday Mass.[28] Nevertheless, women's position in the Church was one of subservience to a male clergy and church hierarchy. Only Sisters were allowed to enter the sanctuary and assist in the preparation of the altar. Lay women were relegated to domestic duties. When they visited the rectory to bring food, launder clothing, or even to chat with Mlle Onésime Dorval, the lay religious teacher at Batoche, women were required to enter through her side kitchen door.[29] Propriety, decorum, and "appearances" were to be maintained. Priests were issued the rules and regulations of the Oblate Order and of the clergy in general, as to appropriate conduct and behaviour in the presence of women.[30] Only older women, preferably widows, were to be hired as housekeepers, and, although the regulations against women may have been issued to prevent gossip, there is a distinct impression that women were generally perceived as Jezebels or Mary Magdalenes who would tempt lonely and isolated priests into sin and other "distractions."[31] Father Moulin was reportedly a solitary and "proper" individual, but it was known that some neighbouring priests reportedly made personal inquiries to women in the confessional[32] or were particularly condescending toward them. Women whose husbands were unfaithful or who were abused were told to overlook the "small misdemeanour" or to sacrifice themselves for God and family, as was one woman who was subjected to a *ménage à trois*.[33]

All in all, the relationship between women and the Church was ambivalent and contradictory. On the one hand, they were perceived as morally superior, the custodians of the faith and as more "civilized" or apt to adopt "superior" EuroCanadian values and lifestyles. But the church bell tolled only three times at a woman's funeral, rather than five as for a man's, and "*l'école des femmes*," or women's views and activities, were restricted to their sphere or the League of Ste Anne, charitable organizations, teas, bazaars, and cleaning chores in the church and rectory. There were three classes of Catholic women: Sisters, or women who entered the religious orders; "*les vieilles filles*," or the "old maids" who devoted their lives to the care of elderly parents or orphaned brothers and sisters, or the teaching of children and the nursing of the sick; and married women. An obedient wife and bearer of many children, however, was the Church's salvation, as "les familles nombreuses ont donné à l'Eglise les plus grands saints."[34]

THE "TROUBLES" OF 1885:
WOMEN'S PERSPECTIVES AND EXPERIENCES

It is important to look at Métis' own accounts and testimonies relating to the North-West resistance in 1885 to understand the views and activities of women at Batoche during that important event. Some women, such as Madeleine Wilkie (wife of Gabriel Dumont) and Marguerite Monet (wife of Louis Riel) emerge in these accounts as "helpmates," while others, such as Marguerite (Dumas) Caron and Josephte (Paul) Tourond, were critical to Métis strategy.[35] Accounts of the battles of Duck Lake, *la coulée des Tourond* (Fish Creek), and the siege of Batoche usually feature men fighting and dying in the trenches, the political leadership and tragic execution of Louis Riel, and the military savvy of Gabriel Dumont. Canadian military reports make only a few casual references to the "Halfbreed ladies" in the camp at Batoche. Captain Peters took only one photograph of women at Batoche during the battle, although press correspondents were curious about the appearance and condition of the "squaws." On the other hand, accounts of the resistance left by the Métis themselves, women's reminiscences, and references in the missionary correspondence reveal that women were active agents or played an important supply role outside the trenches, challenged Dumont and Riel's battle strategy, and were subjected to the humiliation and plunder of the victorious and vengeful North-West Field Force.[36]

The events of 1885 were traumatic for both men and women in the community. Riel and the Métis council (or *Exovidate*) met until March 1885, when "justice command[ed] to take up arms."[37] Meanwhile, the women prayed and lobbied in the hope that fighting would not break out. Mme Josephte Lépine (née Lavallée) warned her husband, Maxime, and the other leaders: "Vous entreprenez des affaires trop gros, que vous ne comprenez pas."[38] But when, according to Mme Angèle (Landry) Dumont (stepmother of Gabriel), "we heard Orangemen were coming to kill us, . . . we came to Batoche in the large camp where I stayed about one week."[39] The camp to which most of the women, children, and elders retreated was on a secluded flat surrounded by bluffs, on the east side of the river. They were joined by some Cree from the One-Arrow and Duck Lake reserves, while the Dakota (who did not get along with the Cree) located mainly on the other side of the river (west bank). The families settled in tents or makeshift dugouts covered with robes, blankets, or branches. They brought along their horses, wagons, cattle, personal possessions, and essential household articles. The atmosphere at the camps was one of solidarity and exchange. The women shared whatever food was available and cared for the children and elders. All available cattle were requisitioned and slaughtered for food. Madeleine (Wilkie) Dumont and the elderly Mme Marie (Hallet) Letendre cooked for the councillors and cared for the sick and wounded in the village.

There was division in the community on the issue of resort to arms and Riel's religious mission, although few women expressed their views openly, especially if they were contrary to those of their fathers or husbands. Métis accounts of the battle and the resistance collected by l'abbé Gabriel Cloutier in early 1886 reveal the divergent views of women regarding the fighting and the tactics followed. Marie-Anne (Caron) Parenteau came to warn Father Fourmond at the neighbouring parish of St-Laurent de Grandin that if the police (soldiers) came she would skin them like buffalo meat: "Si la police vient, je les épare, moi. Je vais les traiter comme on fait des buffalos de la prairie."[40] Once the fighting started, the women rallied to the cause. Mme Véronique Fidler (née Gervais) recalled: "They were melting the lead that came wrapped around the HBC goods in frying pans over a fire"[41] in order to make bullets. Rosalie Parenteau (married to councillor Philippe Gariépy) melted down lead kettles and the linings of tea tins. Sometimes the bullets were too big and they had to trim them with their knives.[42] The preparations of war were accompanied by anxiety, resignation, and in some cases outright criticisms and advice. During the battle at Fish Creek, Mme Marguerite Caron came to see Riel and admonished him for not sending reinforcements to the trapped Métis fighters, among whom were her husband and two sons.[43] Riel exhorted her to pray, but the resolute Mme Caron replied that it was time for action, not prayer. If the men did not go, she would!

Avez-vous eu des nouvelles? — En envoyer vous chercher? — Vous n'allez pas voir donc. . . . Que faites vous donc tous ici, une gagne de monde qui passez votre temps à regarder — Vous feriez mieux d'aller crier de l'autre bord, vous aurez de la force. . . . Argreillez vous donc pour aller les aider. Vous étiez plus pressés de défoncer les magasins et de piller que d'aller aider vos gens qui sont dans le risque, là. Si vous ne voulez pas aller, dites-le moi, moi je vais aller voir s'ils sont en vie oui ou non."[44]

She won the argument and the crucial reinforcements were dispatched.

The women were entrusted with the spiritual dimension of the struggle. They prayed for the safety of their men as well as for the success of the *"guerre nationale."* They went to Father Moulin's church at St. Antoine to hear Mass and receive Communion as well as to a little chapel of Riel's reformed church, "catholique, apostolique et vitale du Nouveau-Monde,"[45] in the village. There, they prayed to Our Lady of Lourdes, for whom the Métis had a special reverence.

There was desolation and despair after the sudden defeat and "capture" of Batoche. The women, children, and elders in the camp were forced to escape in a hurry, abandoning any personal articles and essentials. Most of the women, fearing for their lives and safety, fled the camp on foot and made their way to the Minatinas hills southeast of Batoche. They subsisted on what they could find, in many cases dog meat, plant roots, and hard *galette*, which they had stuffed into their pockets. Joséphine (Fleury) Delorme, who was among the refugees, recalled: "[I] put my baby in a washtub so I thought I would protect her life and my husband came to me — you had better run away because we're going to get killed."[46] Another woman, Christine (Dumas) Pilon, described her fear for her newborn "bibi": Along with other women, one of them the pregnant Mme Riel and her two children, she walked along the riverbank, hiding in the bluffs. Marguerite Riel was coughing blood. They placed their children under a light canvas cover in the cold damp weather. A distraught and haggard Louis Riel came to see them three times before surrendering. It was a pitiful sight.[47] After three days, the women, children, and a few elderly men walked the eighteen miles back to Batoche.

The farms were laid waste and the village was in ruins. The homes between Batoche and St-Laurent de Grandin, the neighbouring parish, were burnt by the victorious government troops, most of them *after* the battle or surrender. Although Riel had received from General Middleton a promise of security and protection for the women and children, the rank and file went on a rampage. Mme Amélie Fisher (née Poitras), whose husband, Georges, managed the Fisher Store at Batoche, reported that a soldier took her carpetbag containing $230.[48] Mme Blanche Henry (née Ross) "a été pillée sous sa vue, ouvert sa cassette, pris son butin et même son jonc de mariage."[49] When she cried out for her wedding ring, the soldiers laughed at her. The men also raided the trunks for clothing, furs, and food. Mme Pélagie Parenteau (née Dumont), Gabriel's sister, lost all her clothing: "Ils n'ont laissé qu'une chemise."[50] Mme Marie Champagne (née Letendre) protested vainly about the horses rounded up on her farm near the village but was especially indignant when sacks of wheat and flour were removed.[51] On the night following the battle, the Tenth Grenadiers and the Midlanders entrenched themselves in the village while the other troops, scouts, and teamsters soon scattered over the Métis and AmerIndian camps, ransacking and pillaging. In the words of one participant, "All sorts of things were captured. Among the most useful was the sum of $200 found by one of the troops, Indian curiosities, beadwork, Indian coats and innumerable odds and ends, . . . a quantity of tobacco and pipes and a lot of bread foraged out of the camp."[52] Although the loss of cattle, furs, pool tables, furniture, and other valuable items had an important long-term economic impact, it was the loss of food, transportation, and shelter that caused immediate distress and suffering among the families.

Because of the proximity of *la loge des femmes* (the women's camp) to the Métis entrenchment in the village, it was the women who were the first to witness the carnage of battle. Although reports of mutilation of Métis wounded or dead are not contained in government or military accounts, the Métis have maintained that this did occur. For example, Damase Carrière, whom the soldiers blamed for Captain French's death, was "finished off" as he lay dying near the scene: "Les femmes ont cherché les cadavres. En arrivant à Damase Carrière, elles le trouvent une ficelle au cou; voyaient la trace où traîné du buisson, au bord de la prairie."[53] Many of the women counselled their husbands, who had fled with them after the battle, to escape across the border rather than surrender, despite promises and assurances by General Middleton, through Father Végréville, that they would not be prosecuted.[54] But, ultimately, all the leaders who had not escaped to the United States, such as Moïse Ouellette, Alexandre Fisher, Maxime Lépine, and Philippe Gariépy, were arrested, brought to trial, and imprisoned.

Amidst the suffering and dispossession, few women blamed Riel or the men for the outcome. Mme Josephte Venne (née St-Arnaud), whose husband, Salomon, and sons did not take up arms or "join the movement," declared after the battle that in 1869-70 they had remained "loyal," as they had in the last conflict, but she wasn't so sure they were better off. As Métis, they were always the losers.[55] In the words of a neighbour, Mme Christine Pilon (née Dumas), "Il nous restait que le courage de Canadien et de Métis pour vivre."[56] The women blamed the government for the war and destruction and honoured their martyred leader, Riel. "Ce n'est pas Louis Riel mais le gouvernement lâche qui est venu en guerre chez les pauvres gens."[57] This conviction was strengthened over the years. Justine (Caron) St-Germain and Marie (Caron) Parenteau, whom I interviewed in 1978, both had fathers and husbands who had fought in the resistance. Both had pictures of Riel in their living rooms. When I asked her about Riel, Mme St-Germain looked up at the picture with great deference and said, "C'était un saint et ils l'ont pendu comme un chien."[58] It is possible that time erased many wounds, softened the bad memories, but similar feelings were expressed to members of the Union Nationale Métisse when they came from Manitoba to Batoche in the early 1900s and in 1935.[59]

The death and destruction of war were felt for months, even years, to come. Most of the Métis victims were middle-aged men, and they left widows with large families, as in the case of Catherine Godon, widow of André Letendre, who had twelve children at home. Judith Parenteau, widow of Isidore Dumont, Gabriel's eldest brother, was forced to accept government food relief, as was Catherine Delorme, the elderly widow of Donald Ross. Marguerite (Monet) Riel and her two children, Jean and Angélique, were cared for by Riel's aunt Julie McGillis until the end of June, when his brother Joseph came to get them and they all returned to the family home in St. Vital, Manitoba. Henriette Riel reported that her sister-in-law was very sick and heavy-hearted.[60] The young children, fortunately, remained unaware of much of the sorrow and suffering and found solace in their toys and the *gâteries* of *Mémère* Riel. Twenty-five-year-old Marguerite Riel suffered a miscarriage in October 1885, shortly before Louis' execution. She died of tuberculosis and a broken heart in May 1886. Mme Josephte Tourond, a widow with nine children, had to cope with both personal and property losses. Her house was ransacked, cattle stolen or slaughtered, and her fields lay in waste after the battle of *la coulée* (Fish Creek), which was fought on her farmstead. But, more seriously, she lost two sons on the last day of the battle at Batoche, and another died soon after that, of consumption. Two young daughters subsequently also succumbed to the disease.

Much emphasis is placed in official accounts on the fact that there was no rape and wanton killing of women and children during the war. But one Métis journal indicates that there was at least one victim; a little Métis-Dakota (Sioux) girl was killed in the crossfire and hastily buried by the soldiers.[61] An investigation of parish burials between March and December 1885 reveals that, although twelve men died directly or indirectly from wounds suffered at the battle of Batoche, nine women died of causes related to or at least aggravated by the sufferings and deprivations of war.[62] They died of consumption (tuberculosis), *la grippe* (influenza), and *fausse-couche* (miscarriage). Women accounted for the proportionately high death rate in 1886 as well.

THE RECONSTRUCTION OF THE COMMUNITY

The women of Batoche were resourceful, shrewd, and persistent, especially when dealing with the government or "*les Anglais*," whom they feared and resented. In the hope of getting some compensation after the battle of 1885, especially for their personal property, they made declarations in their "maiden," or birth, names to the Rebellion Losses Commission in 1886.[63] It was customary for a woman to receive a *dot* (dowry) when she married. This was in the form of cattle, household furniture — especially a bedstead (or *lit garni*) — or a marriage trousseau.[64] Since the women were usually in charge of the hen house and the *laiterie* (or milkhouse), they argued with the commissioners that a portion of the household goods, cattle, and farm products was theirs, for which they should receive compensation. They had not taken up arms and therefore could not be held accountable. It was a worthy and in most cases valid argument, but one that the commission lawyers did not accept, especially given that at this time a woman's property was considered her husband's. The only women who received compensation were widows of men who had died before the outbreak. Mme Josephte Tourond, widowed since 1883, presented a claim for $8,451. But since her sons had taken up arms, she was allowed only $2,805 in compensation.[65] Influence and patronage affected the approval of claims, and merchant families such as the Letendres, Vennes, Boyers, and Fishers, who had not actively or openly participated in the uprising, received compensation.[66] Virtually all of the claims from the farming, freighting, or "labouring" classes were disallowed, irrespective of their degree of participation in the events of 1885. The claims of the wives, widows, or mothers were likewise rejected on the basis of denunciations by others and the fact that "the husbands had been party to the loss."[67]

Widowhood, separation from husbands who were imprisoned, emigration, and exile were the fate of many women in the years following 1885. Madeleine Wilkie, for example, died shortly after joining her husband, Gabriel Dumont, in Montana in 1886. The younger widows were forced either to depend on their families for shelter and sustenance or to remarry. Josephte Gervais, widow of Calixte Tourond, subsequently taught at Vandal School near Fish Creek, but most women who were alone or self-supporting found work as domestics. A few older widows who had sons and daughters to assist them took over the "men's work" on the farms, in many cases quite successfully. Mme Tourond, with her sons and extended family, continued to manage the ranch and raise cattle at *la coulée* and at Batoche until about ten years before her death in 1928. Mme Marguerite Caron and Mme Marie Champagne are other examples of veterans of 1885 and "family matriarchs" who, after the deaths of their husbands (between 1905 and 1912), took up second home-steads[68] and made a living *malgré tout*.

The community of Batoche was re-established by the late 1880s, prospered again briefly in the 1890s, and subsequently maintained a certain *modus vivendi* well into the twentieth century. The resistance brought increased prejudice and isolation for the Métis, but they persisted in their demands for resurveys of their lands, political representation in the territorial and federal governments, and fa-vourable economic policies. Most of the original families remained in the district, and many refugees returned. But the Delorme, Desmarais, and Gervais families relocated to the Pincher Creek area in the 1880s, and the Goulet, Bélanger, and Arcand families were living in the Battleford area by the late 1890s. Other families lived periodically or permanently in "frontier" communities such as Jackfish Lake and Aldina, where work was more readily available. Ranching and freighting op-portunities were limited at Batoche, and the grain crops were generally plagued by frost, drought, and insects. Other employment opportunities for men, such as fur trapping, hauling cordwood, and horse breaking, were largely seasonal. As a re-sult, many married women worked as cooks and cleaners in the private homes of EuroCanadians or a few better-off Métis.

The women who stayed on the farm usually were responsible for milking the cows, maintaining the vegetable garden, and administering the family budget, as many could read and write and had more education than their husbands.[69] Milking was the farm task that was the most successful, or offered the most personal satis-faction and occasionally even "pin money." Mme Ti-Jean Caron (Véronique Parenteau) was proud of her *laiterie*, where she made sweet butter and cream and the occasional Sunday treat of homemade ice cream.[70] The butchering of pigs and beef cattle and the seasonal hunts entailed a lot of work for the women. Household tasks included baking, canning, knitting, crocheting, and the sewing of clothing for all the family. Mme Alexandrine Nicolas (née Fleury) recalled how her mother, who sewed elegant velvet and brocade outfits for the rich English and French women of Duck Lake, would use the scraps or their cast-offs to make clothing for her own family. The seasonal gathering of wild fruit, such as *pimbinas*, saskatoons, and wild pears, supplemented the basic diet of meat, root vegetables, and *galette*, and ensured occasional "fancy" desserts. Mme Adélaïde Ranger (née Pilon) related how her mother taught her and her sister Octavie their first lessons in catechism and writing: "We had to write our French very correctly. Mother had gone to the Grey Nuns school in St. Boniface in the 1870s where she had also learned to weave and embroider."[71] She also mentioned that her mother was proud of the fact that her two daughters did not have to work *pour les autres*, and remained at home until their marriages.

Most young girls, especially when orphaned or in a home where ruled an "evil" or uncaring stepmother, had to go out and find work to escape domestic drudgery. Cousins Justine St-Germain (née Caron) and Marie Parenteau (née Caron) talked about their stepmothers (their fathers' third wives) and the unhappiness of life at home where "*le diable était dans la cabane*" and "my sisters and I had to take care of the new babies and do all the dirty housework."[72] Some children in her situation went to live with their grandmothers, usually a better arrangement, while others left home or married "as soon as they could," as in the case of seventeen-year-old Justine Branconnier, who in 1913 married a man twenty years older, whom she didn't really love. "It was Freddy that I loved but he had gone to war."[73] Georgine d'Amours, whose mother had died when Georgine was an infant, was cherished by her guardian, the teacher, Mlle Dorval. But she married forty-eight-year-old, twice-widowed Auguste Lenglet at the age of twenty-four in 1900, for financial security and social position rather than love.[74] Her stepchildren disliked her, and her elderly husband was demanding, but she found her happiness with her two daughters and in various cultural and social activities that her privileged life accorded her. An intelligent and enterprising woman, she became postmistress at Duck Lake in the 1920s, taking over from her husband, who had previously held the position of postmaster.

There is little evidence in Métis women's accounts from Batoche in the late 1800s of lifelong harmonious marriages. Most were unhappy, at least from the wife's point of view. Mme Christine Dumas Pilon (wife of Barthélémi) spoke of her *cher mari*, but one of her daughters stated matter-of-factly that Barthélémi was *un ivrogne*. Another woman candidly admitted that her Louis was *un coureur de jupons* and lazy as well, but she had had fourteen children, her fate had been decided, or she was *née pour un p'tit pain*.[75] A French-Canadian–Métis folk song, "L'Adieu de la mariée,"[76] which was popular at the turn of the century, sums up the lot of many married women. The following are a few extracts:

Ce n'est point pour un an (It is not just for a year)
Qu'il soit z-bien-ou-z-mal (Whether it is good or bad)
Il faut y rester (One must stick with it)

Il faut donc tout y passer (Each one according to her lot)
Adieu! je m'en vais en ménage (Farewell, I am getting married)
Ce n'est pas pour un an (And it's not just for a year)
C'est pour l'restant de ma vie (It's for my whole life long)
Aller dans la misère (I'm looking forward to hardship)

Most of the women interviewed claimed that men had "outlets," or opportunities to leave the home. They went away to do seasonal work such as wintering cattle north of Batoche, to work as cowboys at Medicine Hat and Lethbridge, or to work as hunting and fishing guides up north. Quite a few Batoche young men went off to the Klondike gold rush between 1897 and 1900, some abandoning their wives and children altogether. At home, the men usually had Sundays off from the farm, when they played cards or pool and had a drink of *piquette* or *ti-gin*. "But us women, we were usually stuck at home. There were the cows to milk, Sunday dinners to cook and the children to take care of."[77] Social outlets for women included visiting, going to church, weddings, funerals, and special feasts such as on *la fête des Métifs* (the national feast day, 24 July), and during the period between Christmas and New Year's Day, when there was a succession of dances and banquets. The women of Batoche played a prominent role in preparing for *la fête des Métifs*. They cooked the food, made articles for the handicraft booths, and participated in games, which included women's sack races and toffee making.[78] They played the fiddle, sang, and danced jigs, polkas, and *châtises* together or along with the men. Mme Alice Paulhus reported that her mother, Elise Boyer (née Tourond), played the harmonium at many family and wedding parties in the early 1900s.[79] When the Union Nationale Métisse de St-Joseph du Manitoba celebrated its fiftieth anniversary at Batoche in 1935, it was Emma Boyer (née Ferguson) who sewed the national flag and the religious banners that were hung in the church.

Life at Batoche was not *la vie en rose*, as promised to all Francophone women who followed the call of service to God and nation. The poignant song written by Edith Piaf[80] in the 1940s, "La vie en rose," perfectly identifies the complaint of the women of Batoche in the late 1800s and early 1900s. The lives of Marie, Josephte, Mélanie, Catherine, and their "sisters" at Batoche were lives filled with hard work and constant struggle against poverty, sexual discrimination, and racial prejudice. Although proud of their dual French-Canadian and AmerIndian heritage, it was a liability in the dominant Anglo-Canadian society of the early 1900s. But their determination and resiliency ensured their survival. In the words of one woman who was interviewed in 1978:[81]

La vie, c'tait dur dans ces temps là (Life, it was hard in those days)
On avait pas de grosses pensions (We didn't have the big pensions)
Le mari, les enfants c'tait pas que l'affaire (A husband, the children, what a lot)
Puis l'prêtre qui nous disait d'endurer (And the priest who'd tell us to bear it)
Mais j'avais mon secret. (But I had my secrets.)

NOTES

1. The literature on AmerIndian women has proliferated in the last decade. See, for example, Patricia Albers and Beatrice Medicine, eds., *The Hidden Half: Studies of Plains Indian Women* (Lanham: University Press of America, 1983); Mona Etienne and Eleanor Leacock, eds., *Women and Colonization: Anthropological Perspectives* (New York: Praeger, 1980); Gretchen M. Bataille and Kathleen M. Sands, *American Women Telling Their Lives* (Lincoln: University of Nebraska Press, 1984); and, more recently, H.C. Wolfart and Freda Ahenakew, *Kôhkominawak Otâcimowiniwâwa / Our Grandmothers' Lives: As Told in Their Own Words* (Saskatoon: Fifth House Publishing, 1992). Some of the women interviewed identified themselves as Métis.

2. The term *Halfbreed* is used by the author in an ethnic context to identify women of AmerIndian and English, Scottish, or European origin other than French Canadian and who do not consider themselves Métis. Over the years, EuroCanadians have given the term a pejorative and derogatory meaning, but many people of "Native-English" origin encountered in the Prince Albert area, north of Batoche, identified themselves as such in comparison to the Métis and did not wish to be called "Mixed-Bloods," English-Métis, or other esoteric terms.

3. See, in particular, Sylvia Van Kirk, *"Many Tender Ties": Women in Fur-Trade Society in Western Canada, 1670-1870* (Winnipeg: Watson and Dwyer, 1980); Jennifer S.H. Brown, *Strangers in Blood: Fur-Trade Company Families in Indian Country* (Vancouver: University of British Columbia Press, 1980); Jacqueline Peterson, "Ethnogenesis: The Settlement and Growth of a 'New People' in the Great Lakes Region, 1702-1815," *American Indian Culture and Research Journal* (fall 1982); and, Dolores T. Poelzer and Irene A. Poelzer, *In Our Own Words: Northern Saskatchewan Métis Women Speak Out* (Saskatoon: Lindenblatt and Hamonic, 1986). Maria Campbell has written about her life as a Métis woman in *Half-Breed* (Toronto: McClelland and Stewart, 1973); and Emma LaRocque, a Cree-Métis, has also provided important insights from personal experiences in *Defeathering the Indian* (Agincourt: The Book Society of Canada, 1975). A film series produced by Norma Bailey entitled *Daughters of the Country* (National Film Board of Canada) portrays the Aboriginal and Métis women's "world" and history. Since the drafting of this article, Nathalie Kermoal has investigated the role of Métis women in the resistance of 1870 and rebellion (Kermoal's term) of 1885 in "Les rôles et les suffrances des femmes méttisses lors de la Résistance de 1870 et de la Rébellion de 1885," *Prairie Forum* 19, 2 (fall 1994):153-68. It is interesting to note that the voice of Métis women is absent in a recent publication on Saskatchewan women. See David de Brou and Aileen Moffatt, eds., *"Other" Voices: Historical Essays on Saskatchewan Women* (University of Regina: Canadian Plains Research Center, 1995).

4. Diane P. Payment, *"The Free People — Otipemisiwak": Batoche, 1870-1930* (Ottawa: Environment Canada — Parks, Studies in Architecture, Archaeology and History, 1990), Appendix B: Biographies of persons interviewed, 1976-1983, and Bibliography, 321-28. (Original edition in French under the title *"Les gens libres — otipemisiwak."*) In the spring of 1886, Rev. Gabriel Cloutier was commissioned by Bishop Taché to gather Métis accounts of the events of 1885. He visited the Batoche district and spoke to many Métis witnesses, mainly men, but a few women. He recorded their accounts in a two-volume handwritten journal (NAC, RG 15 Gabriel Cloutier, Journal, 1886 [AASB]). It is one of the few Métis testimonies of the resistance.

5. Interview with Mme Béatrice Boucher (née Lépine), 1977.

6. Etienne and Leacock, eds., Introduction to *Women and Colonization*.

7. Katherine M. Weist, "Beasts of Burden and Menial Slaves: Nineteenth Century Observations of North American Plains Indian Women," in *The Hidden Half: Stories of Plains Indian Women*, ed. Patricia Albers and Beatrice Medicine, chapter 2, 41-45; Priscilla K. Buffalohead, "Farmers, Warriors, Traders: A Fresh Look at Ojibway Women," *Minnesota History* 48, no. 6 (summer 1983):236-44.

8. The term *squaw* is a derivative or alteration of the Cree word *iskwew,* which means woman. The English term was widely used in a derogatory sense towards Aboriginal women by the mid-nineteenth century.

9. On the various Aboriginal origins of the Métis, see articles by Olive P. Dickason, Jacqueline Peterson, Irene M. Spry, and Jennifer S.H. Brown, in Jennifer S.H. Brown and Jacqueline Peterson, eds., *The New Peoples,* (Winnipeg: The University of Manitoba Press, 1985).

10. Sylvia Van Kirk, "'What if Mama is an Indian?': The Cultural Ambivalence of the Alexander Ross Family," in *The New Peoples: Being and Becoming Métis in North America,* ed. Peterson and Brown.

11. Brian Gallagher, "A Re-Examination of Race, Class and Society in Red River," *Native Studies Review* 4, nos. 1 and 2 (1988):25-65.

12. The term *le sexe* is used generally by missionaries and priests in the eighteenth and nineteenth centuries. See, for example, l'abbé N. Provencher's letters between 1820 and 1850 (Archives de l'Archevêché de St-Boniface [AASB], copies from the diocese of Québec and La Propagation de la Foi). It was a rather derogatory term that implied women's weakness, inferiority, and sexual role. Its use reflected the inferior status of women and male attitudes of the time.

13. Weist, "Beasts of Burden and Menial Slaves," 43-45.

14. AASB, Fonds Provencher, N. Provencher to Bishop Plessis of Québec, 14 February 1819.

15. Ibid., Provencher to Bishop Signay, 8 August 1841. "For the daughters of our settlers, there is no need for a very high level of education. The main thing would be to teach them to live and to work well so that they may become good mothers, this will raise the living standards of the country in time, it has great need of it."

16. Ibid., G. Belcourt to E. Cazeau, 1 January 1842. "It is useless to think of the boys, they are too fickle."

17. *Winnipeg Sun,* 11 June 1885, quoted in Diane Payment, "Riel Family: Home and Lifestyle in St. Vital, 1860-1910," Parks Canada, Manuscript Report No. 379, 1980, 71-72.

18. P.R. Mailhot and D.N. Sprague, "Persistent Settlers: The Dispersal and Resettlement of the Red River Métis, 1870-85," *Canadian Ethnic Studies* 17, no. 2 (1985):12 (table 3). On the topic in general, see D.N. Sprague, *Canada and the Métis, 1869-1885* (Waterloo: Wilfrid Laurier University Press, 1988).

19. Provincial Archives of Manitoba (PAM), MG 10, f1. "Récit de Gabriel Dumont" (n.d., ca. 1900), 1-2, cited in Payment, Foreword to *"The Free People — Otipemisiwak."* "We left Manitoba because we were not free, and we came here to what was still a wild country in order to be free. And still they will not leave us alone."

20. See Payment, "Society and Way of Life," chapter 1 in *"The Free People — Otipemisiwak."*

21. Ibid.

22. AASB, Taché Papers, Letters from Date: Wednesday, 13 September 1995 14:01:13 -0600 (MDT) Louis Schmidt, 1880-1893; PAM, MG 9 A31, "Mémoires de Louis Schmidt."

23. Diocesan Archives of Prince Albert, Parish Register of St-Antoine de Padoue, Batoche, 1881-1925. Compilation of genealogical data by author.

24. Account by Charles Nolin, published in *Le Manitoba,* 18 August 1887. Louis Riel often stated this theme in his speeches.

25. Copy, courtesy of George Burtonshaw, Calgary. It was sung and recorded by Gaspard Jeannotte of Lebret, Saskatchewan, in 1957 (Canadian Museum of Civilization, Ottawa, Richard Johnston Collection).

26. Payment, *"The Free People — Otipemisiwa,"* chapter 1, 15. Compiled from analysis of Parish Register, St-Antoine de Padoue, Batoche, 1881-1925.

27. On this subject, see Robert Papen, "Un parler français méconnu de l'Ouest canadien: le métis," *Actes du Troisième Colloque des Educateurs Franco-Manitobains* 3 (1984):121-36; and, John C. Crawford, ed., *The Michif Dictionary: Turtle Mountain Chippewa Cree* (Winnipeg: Pemmican Publications, 1983).

28. Deschâtelets Archives, Archives Générales (Rome), Letters of Father J. Moulin, 1882-1900.
29. Interview with Justine St-Germain (née Caron), Batoche, 1981.
30. Albert Pascal OMI, *Règlements, Usages et Discipline du Diocèse de Prince Albert*, 1916, chapter 35, "Prudences et convenances," 157.
31. Oblats de Marie-Immaculée, *Règles et Constitutions* (Rome: Maison Générale, 1890; 1910).
32. This was the implied reason for Father Valentin Végréville's early departure from Batoche in 1882, although a disagreement with Father André, district superior, was also a factor. Two women interviewed at Batoche mentioned the often inquisitive inquiries of some later priests.
33. Interview by author, Duck Lake, 1982. The woman shall remain anonymous. Her husband brought a second woman into the household. The wife was forced to accept the situation as she had many children and no other place to go. She grew to pity the woman, who was rather "simple minded," and raised the two children born of the liaison.
34. *Le Manitoba*, 12 January 1897. "Large families have given the greatest Saints to the Church."
35. AASB, Cloutier Journal, vol. 1, 5,064, 5,134; *Le Manitoba*, 25 June 1885.
36. See, in particular, testimonies to the Rebellion Losses Commission, National Archives of Canada (NAC), RG 15, vols. 914-931, relating to Batoche, St-Laurent, and Duck Lake, and accounts in Gabriel Cloutier, Journal, 1886 (AASB, 2 volumes).
37. Thomas Flanagan, ed., *The Collected Writings of Louis Riel / Les écrits complets de Louis Riel, Volume 3* (Edmonton: University of Alberta Press, 1985), letter 3-033, 58.
38. AASB, Cloutier Journal, vol. 1, 5,166. "You are undertaking things that are too complicated, that you do not understand."
39. NAC, RG 15, vol. 914, no. 214.
40. AASB, Cloutier Journal, vol. 1, 5,041.
41. Glenbow Archives, Papers of Marie-Rose Smith (née Delorme), Historic time recalled . . . , by Véronique Fidler (née Gervais), who was at Batoche in 1885.
42. AASB, Cloutier Journal, vol. 2, 5,220.
43. Ibid., vol. 1, 5,064.
44. Ibid. "Do you have any news? Are you sending for any? You are not going to see, therefore? What are you all doing here, a gang of people which passes the time looking. You would be better to go and shout on the other side, you would have more power. Gather your effects to go out and help them. You were more eager to break into the stores and pillage than go and help your people who are in danger there. If you do not want to go, tell me. I will go and see if they are alive or not."
45. Gilles Martel, *Le messianisme de Louis Riel* (Waterloo: Wilfrid Laurier University Press, 1984), 177. The study is an in-depth analysis of Riel's prophetic mission.
46. Reminiscences of Oscar Hayden as told to him by his mother, Joséphine Hayden, formerly Delorme (née Fleury?), ca. 1930. Her first husband, William Delorme, fought at Batoche.
47. Diocesan Archives of Prince Albert, Account by Christine (Dumas) Pilon, wife of Barthélémi Pilon, in a letter to Bishop J.-H. Prud'homme, 1924 (translation by author). See also, AASB, Cloutier Journal, "Reddition de Riel," vol. 2, 5,577-78.
48. NAC, RG 15, vol. 928, no. 708.
49. AASB, Cloutier Journal, vol. 2, 5,138. "was robbed under her eyes, her trunk opened, her belongings taken and even her wedding ring."
50. Ibid. "They only left her an undershirt."
51. AASB, E. Champagne to Bishop Taché, 6 March 1886; Saskatchewan Archives Board, *Champagne v the Queen*, 1892, Transcript by G.H. Young.
52. Vye Bouvier, "1885: Women in the Resistance," *New Breed*, 15, no. 3 (1984):18, quoted from Penryn H. Rusden, *The Suppression of the Northwest Insurrection*. See also, Saskatchewan Archives Board, R.K. Allan, Diary Kept during the North-West Rebellion, 1885.
53. AASB, Cloutier Journal, vol. 1, 5,138. "The women looked for the bodies. When they came to Damase Carrière, they found him with a cord around the neck; could see the mark where

dragged into the bush, on the side of the prairie."

54. AASB, Cloutier Journal, Account by Father V. Fourmond, vol. 1, 5,102; Provincial Archives of Alberta, OMI Collection, Journal du Père V. Végréville, 14-17 May 1885.
55. NAC, RG 15, vol. 916, no. 99.
56. Diocesan Archives of Prince Albert, account by Christine (Dumas) Pilon, 1924. "We only had the courage of the Canadiens and Métis left to live by."
57. Ibid. "It was not Louis Riel but the cowardly government that brought war to the poor people."
58. Interview with Justine St-Germain (née Caron), whose husband had fought at Batoche, 1981. "He was a saint and they hanged him like a dog."
59. PAM, MG 10, file 1, box 2, Reports by members of the Union Nationale Métisse St-Joseph du Manitoba after visits to Batoche between 1900 and 1903 and in July 1935.
60. Archives de La Société historique de St-Boniface Fonds Riel, Henriette (Riel) Poitras to Louis Riel, 30 June 1885; 24 October 1885.
61. AASB, Cloutier Journal, vol. 2, 5,212.
62. Diocesan Archives of Prince Albert, parish registers of St-Antoine de Padoue, St-Laurent de Grandin and St-Sacrement (Duck Lake), 1885-86.
63. NAC, RG 15, List of Claimants, vol. 931, 932.
64. Interview with Adélaïde Ranger (née Pilon), Batoche, 1977; NAC, RG 15, vol. 914, no. 17, Testimony of Mme Louise Ledoux; NAC, RG 15, vol. 917, no. 122, Testimony of Jean Caron.
65. NAC, RG 15, vol. 931, no. 21.
66. Ibid., vol. 531, Class A, "Approved Claims."
67. Ibid., vol. 531, Class C, "Claims rejected because claimants were party to their own losses," Queen's University Archives, Commissioner G.H. Young Papers, Book C, Particulars re: claims.
68. Widows of men who had registered a first homestead before 1889 were allowed to enter a second as "legal representatives of their deceased husbands."
69. Interviews with Justine St-Germain (née Caron), 1981. Mlle Onésime Dorval, who taught at Batoche between 1896 and 1914, reported that girls attended school more regularly and longer than boys.
70. Interview with Marie-Louise Langlois, formerly Caron (née Ethier), 1981.
71. Interview with Adélaïde Ranger (née Pilon), 1976. She was the daughter of Christine Dumas Pilon.
72. Interview with Justine St-Germain (née Caron), 1981.
73. Interview with Justine Nogier, formerly Caron (née Branconnier), 1976.
74. Interview with Marguerite Perillat, 1983.
75. Interviewee shall remain anonymous.
76. Song published in Lucinda Clemens (Nancy Hockley), *Folk Songs of the Prairie Métis / Une Chanson de Vérité* (Indian Head, SK: The Other Opera Co., 1985), accompanying booklet.
77. Interview with Justine St-Germain (née Caron), 1981, and with Alexandrine Nicolas (née Fleury), 1982.
78. L'Union Nationale Métisse St-Joseph du Manitoba, Minutes of meetings, 1887 to 1935.
79. Interview with Alice Paulhus (née Boyer), 1976.
80. Louigy, Edith Piaf, and Mae Davies, *Edith Piaf at Carnegie Hall, January 13, 1957*, New York, Pathée Marconi Recording, 1977.
81. Interview, Batoche, 1978.

Subsistence, Secondary Literature, and Gender Bias: The Saulteaux

Laura Peers

Even after two decades of revision and challenge by feminist perspectives, it is rare to find a tribal or regional history or ethnography in which women play more than the most insignificant of roles. Secondary literature on Aboriginal peoples continues to focus extensively on men and their political, religious, and economic activities. In the pages of these works it is men who make the decisions, men whose words are quoted, and men's achievements that are noted. Women are virtually invisible, their voices and movements stilled by the infrequency with which their work is noted and by the implication, when it is noted, that it was less important to the group's survival and to the cultural complex. Furthermore, women's work is generally presented as quite separate from men's, and as being largely restricted to the "private" sphere of the home, rather than intersecting with the "public" sphere of politics, war, religion, and society at large, which is considered to be men's territory. This manner of depicting Aboriginal societies is not only common to classic works of history and anthropology, but has also persisted in large degree into the present, for the basic structures of culture and history are still assumed by researchers to be the domain of men.

Many aspects of these biases have been addressed over the past two decades. Much attention has been paid, in particular, to the identification of bias against women in primary literature such as historic documents and to analysis of the origins of these biases. Less attention has been given to the larger issue of how the inaccurate portrayal of Aboriginal women and their work has shaped attitudes about the basic nature and history of Aboriginal North American societies and how these attitudes have shaped the secondary literature on these peoples. Without an adequate acknowledgement of women's contributions to the food harvesting, or subsistence, cycle, for example, Aboriginal peoples are portrayed as being supported only by men's contributions: hunting. This is especially the case in scholarly descriptions of Aboriginal societies of the North American woodlands, parklands, and plains, in which those peoples are generally said to have been dependent on large game and therefore dependent on game populations, the whim of the herds, and the skill of their hunters. The few dietary alternatives to which such descriptions will admit were supposedly the food of desperation, inadequate forms of nourishment that merely sustained life until game could again be found. This is, however, but an extension of the formerly popular myth that Aboriginal peoples were improvident, incapable of planning for or coping with ecological fluctuations; furthermore, it is an argument whose logic functions only if women and their contributions are excluded from it. Using the Saulteaux of the Canadian plains and parklands as an example, I examine in this paper the complex of biases against women and their work in the secondary literature and the implications of these biases for our understanding of the Saulteaux as a hunter-gatherer society. I argue that, once women's contributions to subsistence and daily life are restored to Saulteaux history and ethnography, their society is clearly seen to have possessed a wider, stronger, more flexible subsistence base better able to cope with ecological fluctuations and historical change than is admitted in the traditional secondary literature.

Also known as the western Ojibwa, Bungi, and Plains Chippewa, the Saulteaux are related to the Ojibwa or Chippewa of the Great Lakes, Boundary Waters, and northern Ontario region, from whom they separated in the late eighteenth century. The Saulteaux were one of a number of peoples who chose to come west with the expanding fur trade. They adapted well, were well received by local groups in the parkland and plains, and intermarried with Cree and Métis people. By 1800, Saulteaux bands could be found in the Red River Valley from Pembina north to the Manitoba Interlake region, and along the Assiniboine and North Saskatchewan rivers as far west as the Edmonton area. They survived ecological and climatic fluctuations, the decline of the fur trade and game populations throughout the plains and parkland, and finally the intertribal conflicts over the dwindling bison herds and the despair of the early reserve era. Through it all, the Saulteaux maintained a reputation for canniness and independence — or, as EuroCanadians sometimes called it in exasperation, "sauciness."

The three basic secondary works that examine the Saulteaux from the beginning of their migration through their adaptation and emergence as a distinct people in the West are Harold Hickerson's *The Chippewa and their Neighbors* [1988 (1970)]; Hickerson's earlier article, "The Genesis of a Trading Post Band" (1956); and James Howard's monograph, *The Plains-Ojibwa or Bungi* (1965, reprinted 1977).[1] These are all pioneering works that made great contributions to scholarly knowledge and are still extremely valuable; indeed, they remain standard reference materials. However, all of them show a bias in the presentation of the importance of women's contributions to Saulteaux subsistence, which is representative of the manner in which women's work is portrayed in the secondary literature for many other tribes. Essentially, these works portray the Saulteaux as evolving from a deer-dependent society in the western Great Lakes woodlands to a bison-dependent society in the parklands and prairies. In keeping with this image, women are generally depicted as mere processors of men's catches, not contributing to the diet themselves but dependent on the skill and goodwill of men. Underlying these assertions is the assumption that the Saulteaux were solely dependent on these animals and that they were frequently hungry and impoverished when the climate or their hunting luck was poor. This argument is incomplete and inaccurate, however, since it ignores both the reality and the ramifications of women's contributions to the diet.

In discussing the Ojibwa or early Saulteaux at their very earliest stages of movement westward from the Great Lakes, while they were still east of Red River in the late eighteenth century, Hickerson stated: "Without deer, . . . subsistence would have been impossible" (1988, 111). It was his belief that Saulteaux were obliged "either to try to survive on the meager game resources afforded by the barren boreal forest region surrounding western Lake Superior, . . . or to attempt to expand into new areas" (1988, 66). Thus, Hickerson believed that Saulteaux territorial expansion westward was caused primarily by a scarcity of deer in the Great Lakes forests. In large measure, this theory rested on his insistence that Saulteaux were dependent on deer and that other resources, such as small game, fish, wild rice, or cultivated maize and potatoes, were not vital to subsistance; his text includes a number of statements discounting the importance of these resources in the context of the seasonal round as a whole. Significantly, these alternate resources were largely produced and harvested by women.

Similarly, both Hickerson and James Howard emphasized the overriding importance of big game for the initial Saulteaux occupation of the Red and Assiniboine river valleys (1780-1805), and minimized the importance of other resources. The first paragraph of Hickerson's article "The Genesis of a Trading Post Band" contains the statement: "Over a period of two decades they extended their hunting territories first westward, and then south to . . . contiguous prairies where large game, especially the buffalo, was abundant" (1956, 289). In an interesting contradiction, Hickerson (1959) claimed in another article that the establishment of permanent Saulteaux settlements in the West was slowed by the absence of wild rice and maple sugar, which they were accustomed to utilizing in areas east of Red River. Despite this, he continually discounted the importance of alternate resources elsewhere in the article. James Howard's statement regarding Saulteaux adaptation to the West is equally male-biased: "The deer, moose, and beaver, the chief source of sustenance in their old Woodland home, gave way to the bison and pronghorn antelope . . ." (1977, 3). Predictably, Howard's work on the Saulteaux after they became established in the West by the mid-nineteenth century also emphasizes the importance of bison in relation to other resources:

The fact that they had almost completely changed over from their earlier Woodland Indian subsistence pattern of moose and deer hunting, lake fishing, and wild rice gathering, to Plains Indian bison nomadism does not mean that these . . . activities were completely forgotten. The Bungi appreciated the best of two worlds, and took deer, moose, elk, and even caribou when occasion afforded. Likewise some maple sugar was still made and a few of the eastern bands continued to harvest wild rice each fall. It was the bison, however, that now reigned supreme in the Bungi way of life (1977, 23).

Howard also asserted that "small animals . . . were utilized by the Bungi when larger game could not be secured," that "maize agriculture was not a very important part of aboriginal Plains-Ojibwa culture," and that fish were "obviously not so important to the Plains-Ojibway as the bison and other larger animals" (1977, 30, 33, 31). Like Hickerson, Howard contradicted himself regarding the importance of these alternate resources, first saying that fish were caught "when other game failed," but then claiming in the next sentence that "fish were caught and utilized whenever the opportunity afforded" (1977, 31).

Individually and as a group, these works present a vivid image of the Saulteaux as being dominated by men and men's economic activities. Foods other than big game, including foods harvested by women, are presented as being supplemental and incidental to the diet. The reader is given little information about Saulteaux diet at times other than the main hunting seasons. Furthermore, periods of scarcity of large game are presented as crises provoking large-scale group migrations or the necessity of relying on "low status" foods — which, by implication, are anything other than large game animals. Not only are women and the foods they harvest portrayed as having little value or prestige, then, but the entire culture, according to this image, lacks a truly integrated food harvesting cycle or the capability to deal with fluctuations in game populations, other climatic factors, or, by implication, with the changing fortunes and pressures of history.

SOURCES OF GENDER BIAS

The sources of gender bias in writings about Aboriginal peoples have been discussed most thoroughly by Alice Kehoe in her article "The Shackles of Tradition" and in companion articles appearing in the same volume (Albers and Medicine 1983). Eleanor Leacock's collection of essays, *Myths of Male Dominance* (1981), Frances Dahlberg's *Woman the Gatherer* (1981), Sylvia Van Kirk's *"Many Tender Ties"* (1980), and subsequent articles by Van Kirk (1986) and Priscilla Buffalohead (1983) also tackle the issues of gender bias, the analysis of sexism in primary and secondary literature, and the roles of women in Aboriginal societies. Anthropological theory about gender issues in hunter-gatherer societies is reviewed most recently in two articles in the 1988 *Annual Review of Anthropology*: Myers,

"Critical Trends in the Study of Hunter-Gatherers" (1988), and Mukhopadhyay and Higgins, "Anthropological Studies of Women's Status Revisited" (1988). While these sources analyze many practical and intellectual origins of gender bias in some depth, I will briefly consider but one: the transference of bias from the sources used by Hickerson and Howard to their writings on the Saulteaux.

Like other anthropologists who study Aboriginal people, Howard obtained most of his information from Saulteaux men. In Aboriginal communities, where men generally act as the nexus between the community and the outside world, it is difficult for a white male to interview Aboriginal women. Even had he been able to do so, the division of labour and knowledge by gender within Aboriginal cultures limited the amount of information that Howard's few female consultants would have given him — especially since interviews conducted by anthropologists with Aboriginal women are often held in the presence of their male relatives. Since many of the Saulteaux men Howard worked with were born in the late nineteenth century, when competency in adulthood was still defined to some extent in terms of a man's hunting ability, the men Howard interviewed would naturally have emphasized this part of their lives. Working primarily with men, and without a strong female voice to give a corresponding female perspective, Howard was prone to absorbing the male version of events and culture: a perfectly correct, but incomplete, perspective. Furthermore, it may be argued that Howard was particularly interested in the Saulteaux as an example of cultural change from a woodland-oriented to a plains-oriented society, and therefore emphasized the stereotypical plains traits he saw amongst them — including the importance of bison.

As an ethnohistorian, Hickerson's sources were historical documents, written by fur traders for business purposes and for the purposes of recording their own actions rather than the actions of the Aboriginal people they dealt with. These documents can be extremely useful, but only if one understands and deals with their cultural and economic biases. Unfortunately, Hickerson did not deal adequately with these problems in the formulation of his theories concerning the emergence of the Saulteaux. Hickerson based his ideas about the overwhelming importance of deer and other large game to the Ojibwa and early Saulteaux "on the frequency of mention in the [primary] literature" (1988, 108). It is clear, however, that the sources Hickerson used were all produced by individuals who had reasons for emphasizing big game. European and EuroCanadian cultures valued large game as a high-status food, associated with feasts, plenty, and affluence; largely because of this, fur traders preferred to eat large game. European traders often hired Aboriginal men to hunt for them, and the number of deer or moose traded from Aboriginal people is frequently mentioned in fur-trade journals. Such records say more about the traders' diet than about the diet of their Aboriginal hunters, even though we may assume that these men reserved some animals for their own use. Finally, fur traders had even more reason to be concerned about the supply of large game, for unless Aboriginal people had a ready supply of fresh game to augment stored foods they did not devote time to hunting furs.

There are many reasons, then, that bison, deer, and other large game should be frequently mentioned in historic documents and by Aboriginal interviewees, but this does not mean that large game was always crucial to Saulteaux survival. Game was important, particularly during fall and winter when other resources were in short supply, but other foods were more important during other seasons. Alternate resources such as wild rice and fish were also crucial staples throughout the nineteenth century and should not be discredited. By using their sources uncritically, Hickerson and Howard have given us not only an incomplete understanding of women's roles in Saulteaux subsistence, but also an incomplete understanding of the total annual food-gathering cycle and its integration and flexibility.

RE-EVALUATION OF SAULTEAUX SUBSISTENCE PATTERNS

The widespread re-examination of the importance of women's contributions to food gathering in Aboriginal societies was sparked, ironically, by the 1968 "Man the Hunter" conference and its published proceedings (Lee and DeVore 1968). Much emphasis was placed in that publication on Lee's studies of the !Kung San, a foraging group among whom plant foods harvested by women made up the bulk of a very nutritious diet. Lee initially used his findings to dispel the myth that hunting-and-gathering peoples led lives which were "nasty, brutish, and short," arguing against the biases of observers accustomed to the stability of an agricultural existence that hunter-gatherers could make a satisfying and healthy existence with, in fact, less work than the average farmer (1968, 43). Lee's data, based as it was on a society in which women provided the most important foods and in which plant foods supplied most of the protein, carbohydrates, and vitamins, opened the door to a re-examination of the literature on subsistence and gender in hunting-and-gathering societies. In the two decades since "Man the Hunter," scholars have become far more aware of the importance of foods other than game in the diet of hunter-gatherers, of the generally greater availability and reliability of these foods, of the role played by these foods in allowing an integrated and flexible annual food-gathering round, and of the role of women in harvesting and preparing many of these foods. Studies embracing this new perspective have ranged from quantitative nutritional analyses and the development of optimal foraging theory to studies of women's contribution to subsistence in Aboriginal societies worldwide; of women's control over production, distribution, and exchange of goods; of women's economic roles vis-à-vis their social and political status; and of historical changes in women's work and roles (Mukhopadhyay and Higgins 1988; Myers 1988).

In applying this new perspective and wealth of comparative material to the Saulteaux, an image of pre-reserve Saulteaux society has emerged that is at variance with the old stereotype of this people as being solely dependent on large game. We are now realizing that the Saulteaux had a much broader, more flexible subsistence base better able to cope with ecological fluctuations, and that the role of women in providing food and in making decisions about subsistence and group movements was far greater than previously thought.[2] In fact, what might be called "alternate" or "women's" foods were, for much of the year, the constant in the Saulteaux diet; large game was added to this base when it was available. These "women's" foods included vegetable foods, maple sugar, small game, and, to a certain extent, fish.

Both wild and cultivated vegetable foods were more important to the Saulteaux diet than either Hickerson or Howard admitted. Although he noted that the Saulteaux "placed great reliance on wild rice," Hickerson (1988, 106-07) claimed that the rice crop was successful only about one year in three and that the amount of rice stored for winter consumption each year was fairly small. In fact, the crop generally failed only one year in three, and harvests reached forty to fifty bushels per family each year in the lakes east of the Red River by 1802. Rice was an important stored food and trade product for Saulteaux along the Red and Assiniboine rivers and in the Interlake as well; families throughout the region returned to their rice caches each spring. Furthermore, Saulteaux women were adept at sowing and managing rice fields, and they deliberately extended the range of this crop throughout their territories as climate allowed (Moodie 1991).

For Saulteaux who spent more time on the plains, prairie turnips, or *tipsina* roots (*psoralea esculenta*), were the staple cereal. These roots are comprised of approximately seventy percent carbohydrates and five percent sugar, making them a good substitute for wild rice (Harrington 1972). Most histories and ethnographies of plains tribes contain vague statements that women made large harvests of these roots and other plants each year (e.g., Howard 1977, 32: "Wild vegetal foods were extensively utilized by the Bungi"); but they also contain statements denigrating the importance of turnips — implying that they were eaten only as a last resort, if there was no meat available. In fact, they were part of the most common meal eaten on the plains, a stew of meat and roots, and provided carbohydrates necessary to digest meat and cope with cold temperatures, something particularly important in winter and early spring when animals killed had little fat to supply carbohydrates. As well, they were readily available through summer and fall, could be preserved in several ways, and provided an abundant staple.

In the Red and Assiniboine river valleys and the Manitoba Interlake, cultivated corn and potatoes were also staple resources that supplemented or replaced wild rice during bad years or in areas where rice would not grow. One description of a gardening centre on an island in Lake Manitoba in 1819 stated: "The soil here is excellent and each family has a portion of it under cultivation, which the women and old men remain, and take care of it during the summer. . . . In the fall of the

year when they are going to abandon the place, they secure that part of the produce, under ground till spring" (HBCA B.122/e/1, fo.9). Interestingly, Tim
Holzkamm notes for the area just east of Red River at this time that when both rice
and garden crops were poor, fur returns fell drastically, suggesting that in some
areas the availability of stored cereal products may have been of more value in
supporting the fur trade than large game (1985, 149).

From Red River to the upper Saskatchewan River, Saulteaux women harvested
sap and sugar from maples, box elder, and other species each spring. This is another underestimated "crop," partly because of the assumption that it was always
used the way it is now: as a candy and condiment. There is evidence, though, that
sugar was actually regarded as food at a time of year that could otherwise be fairly
lean. Closer to the Great Lakes, a harvest of 1,600 pounds of sugar was reported by
Henry the Elder in the early 1760s; during the harvest, the eight people in the camp
ate 300 pounds of sugar (Quimby 1962, 228). Similarly, Hudson's Bay Company
district reports for the Fort Dauphin area around 1820 state: "Some families will
have upwards of 1000 roggans to collect the water in"; part of this harvest was
traded and part was placed in caches (HBCA B.51/e/1, fo.10; HBCA B.122/e/1,
fo.9). Sugar-making also reveals interesting aspects of Saulteaux sex relations.
Trader Peter Fidler and white captive John Tanner both noted that groups of women
maintained traditional rights to harvest from particular sugar groves, suggesting
that women's foods and labour played a significant role in the movement and transition of Saulteaux to the West (HBCA B.51/e/1, fo.10; James 1956, 125).

Small game, too, was more common in Saulteaux cooking pots than the secondary literature admits, and some of it, particularly rabbit and partridge, was
usually snared by women. Despite fluctuations in the rabbit population cycle, small
game was generally more reliable than larger mammals. When trader George Nelson and his men were facing starvation north of Lake Superior in the winter of
1815, Nelson's Saulteaux wife and another Aboriginal woman saved the lot of
them by snaring fifty-eight rabbits and thirty-four partridges in just over a week;
this kind of trapping or snaring was an everyday part of Ojibwa women's lives
farther west as well. Despite its abundance and reliability, though, small game was
often considered "second best" by Aboriginal people, as was the case with
Saulteaux in the Fort Pelly region in the 1850s who complained of starvation because they were unable to kill moose, although they reported that there were plenty
of rabbits that year (Van Kirk 1980, 59; Long 1987).

This same bias against food other than big game was picked up on and repeated by historians and ethnographers, and it is also seen in statements in the
secondary literature about fish, which Howard described as being "obviously not
so important to the Plains Ojibwa as the bison and other large animals" (1977, 31).
Such attitudes are refuted by the enormous productivity of sturgeon fisheries from
Lake Superior to the Saskatchewan River. According to a recent paper, the weight

of sturgeon brought in to Henry the Younger's trading post at Pembina in the spring of 1808 probably equalled the weight of bison brought in there during the entire year. In a related study, the "average annual production of edible sturgeon flesh by Ojibwa fishermen from the Rainy River from 1823 to 1885 [was] . . . calculated to be 275,415 pounds" (Holzkamm et al. 1988; Holzkamm 1987, 158). There has been no similar analysis for the western fisheries, or of the whitefish fishery, but there is some evidence that fishing stations such as the Lebret site in the Qu'Appelle Valley were also very productive locations for spring fishing for thousands of years (Smith 1986, 8). The bias against fish in the literature is, of course, only indirectly related to the bias against subsistence contributions by Saulteaux women, since men did most (though not all) of the fishing. It is related to this bias, though, for it maintains the spotlight on big game as the "proper" food, and downplays the importance and abundance of other resources.

CONCLUSION

Bison, deer, and other large game did play a critical part in the diet and culture of the Saulteaux. The more recent information on Saulteaux subsistence suggests, however, that they had a far more diverse and flexible subsistence base than they have generally been credited with, and an efficient and well-integrated annual cycle of subsistence activities. This has challenged the assumptions of Hickerson and other scholars that warm-weather activities such as gardening "had little influence upon the dominant winter economy [i.e., hunting]" (Holzkamm 1985, 144). Recent studies have shown that Saulteaux were very good at anticipating the effects of short-term climatic changes on resources and at switching between resources as conditions dictated: in the Boundary Waters region, for instance, when it looked in the spring as though the water levels were going to produce a poor rice harvest, larger gardens were planted to compensate (Holzkamm 1985, 145). Importantly, these "alternate" resources, discounted in the secondary literature, which allowed the Saulteaux to be so flexible and to survive in the face of ecological fluctuations and disasters, were largely harvested by women.

As well as incorporating biases from its sources, secondary literature on the Saulteaux has been shaped by the biases of its authors' basic academic frameworks, which incorporated two related and ethnocentric assumptions. The first of these assumptions was that men's activities and economic contributions were more important than those of women, and that women's contributions to subsistence (or politics, or religion, or any other aspect of Aboriginal culture) were insignificant. By leaving out women's contributions to subsistence and the many alternatives to game that these offered, the secondary literature depicts Saulteaux as having an unintegrated and inadequate subsistence round, and as therefore being dependent on large game, unable to cope with environmental fluctuations and the decline of game populations, and subject to hunger as a result. Little wonder, then, that their culture is portrayed as having been destroyed by an even greater historical change than the decline of game: contact with EuroCanadians. This is the second, related assumption in much of the secondary literature on Aboriginal peoples until the past decade: the belief that "true" Aboriginal culture was essentially extinct, destroyed by the historic encounter between Aboriginal and European peoples, and that Aboriginal people were passive victims of history. "Pawns in the [fur] trade," Hickerson called them, "exploited, despoiled, and finally extinguished" (1988, 119). James Howard, collecting "memory culture" from Elders in the 1950s, projected much the same impression in his writing. This older depiction of the Saulteaux (and many other Aboriginal peoples) as being unable to cope either with environmental difficulties or with the upheaval introduced by white contact and the fur trade is now giving way to a new image of Saulteaux as skillful manipulators of the environment and of historical events, who employed carefully laid strategies to cope with whatever difficulties and changes they encountered, and who possessed a vital cultural tradition that adapted and persisted throughout the nineteenth century. The development of this new image of Aboriginal cultures and the increasing appreciation of their vitality and viability has been based in large part on a growing understanding of the importance of foods harvested by women and of women's contribution to an integrated, flexible seasonal round.

The Saulteaux did face periodic scarcities, lean seasons, crop failures, difficult years, and times of starvation. And, while they were greatly affected, and to some extent their culture and lives were damaged by the sweeping changes of the nineteenth century, they were not passive victims of history. They were highly skilled at adapting and surviving, at anticipating and planning, at compensating and at coping. This is a side of Aboriginal society rarely shown in the secondary literature, partly because women's contributions to subsistence are seldom shown in an adequate way. By restoring women to written descriptions of their histories and cultures, we may also learn much about the strengths and resourcefulness of their peoples.

NOTES

1. Two other basic studies of the Saulteaux are not being considered here. One of these examines the position of the Saulteaux as a people "in between" two cultural areas (Skinner 1914); the other is primarily a reiteration of Hickerson's perspective with some additional data (Camp 1984).
2. For a more in-depth discussion of this topic, including Saulteaux/western Ojibwa women's roles, see Peers, *The Ojibwa of Western Canada, 1780 to 1870* (1994).

REFERENCES

Albers, Patricia, and Beatrice Medicine, eds. 1983. *The Hidden Half: Studies of Plains Indian Women*. Washington, DC: University Press of America.

Buffalohead, Priscilla K. 1983. "Farmers, Warriors, Traders: A Fresh Look at Ojibway Women." *Minnesota History* 48, no. 6:236-44.

Camp, Gregory. 1984. "The Chippewa Transition from Woodland to Prairie, 1790-1820." *North Dakota History* 51, no. 3:39-47.

Dahlberg, Frances, ed. 1981. *Woman the Gatherer*. New Haven: Yale University Press.

Harrington, H.D. 1972. *Western Edible Wild Plants*. Albuquerque: University of New Mexico Press.

Hickerson, Harold. 1956. "The Genesis of a Trading Post Band: The Pembina Chippewa." *Ethnohistory* 3, no. 4:289-345.

_____. 1988 (1970). *The Chippewa and their Neighbors: A Study in Ethnohistory*. Rev. ed. with foreword and critical review by Jennifer S.H. Brown and Laura L. Peers. Prospect Heights: Waveland Press.

Hickerson, Harold, ed. 1959. "Journal of Charles Jean Baptiste Chaboillez, 1797-1798 (concluded)." *Ethnohistory* 6:363-427.

Holzkamm, Tim. 1985. "Ojibway Horticulture in the Upper Mississippi and Boundary Waters." In *Papers of the 16th Algonquian Conference (1984: St Louis Country Heritage and Arts Center)*, ed. William Cowan. Ottawa: Carleton University.

_____. 1987. "Sturgeon Utilization by the Rainy River Ojibwa Bands." In *Papers of the 18th Algonquian Conference (1986: Winnipeg)*, ed. William Cowan. Ottawa: Carleton University.

Holzkamm, Tim, Victor Lytwyn, and Leo Waisberg. 1988. "Rainy River Sturgeon: An Ojibway Resource in the Fur Trade Economy." *The Canadian Geographer* 32, no. 3:194-205.

Howard, James. 1965. *The Plains-Ojibwa or Bungi: Hunters and Warriors of the Northern Prairies with Special Reference to the Turtle Mountain Band*. In *Reprints In Anthropology*, Volume 7. Lincoln: J. and L. Reprint Co. [Originally published in 1965, Vermillion: University of South Dakota.]

Hudson's Bay Company Archives (HBCA). 1818-19. "Manitoba District Report." B.122/e/1.

_____. 1820. "Fort Dauphin District Report." B.51/e/1.

James, Edwin, ed. 1956. *A Narrative of the Captivity and Adventures of John Tanner*. Minneapolis: Ross and Haines.

Kehoe, Alice. 1983. "The Shackles of Tradition." In *The Hidden Half: Studies of Plains Indian Women*, ed. Patricia Albers and Bea Medicine. Washington, D.C.: University Press of America.

Leacock, Eleanor Burke. 1981. *Myths of Male Dominance: Collected Articles on Women Cross-Culturally*. New York: Monthly Review Press.

Lee, Richard B. 1968. "What Hunters Do for a Living, or, How to Make Out on Scarce Resources." In *Man the Hunter*, ed. Richard B. Lee and Irven DeVore. Chicago: Aldine Publishing Company.

Lee, Richard B., and Irven DeVore, eds. 1968. *Man the Hunter*. Chicago: Aldine Publishing Company.

Long, W.H., ed. 1987. *Fort Pelly Journal of Daily Occurrences, 1863*. Regina, SK: The Regina Archaeological Society.

Moodie, Wayne. 1991. "Manomin: Historical Geographical Perspectives on the Ojibwa Production of Wild Rice." In *Aboriginal Resource Use in Canada: Historical and Legal Aspects*, ed. Kerry Abel and Jean Friesen. Winnipeg: University of Manitoba Press.

Mukhopadhyay, Carol C., and Patricia Higgins. 1988. "Anthropological Studies of Women's Status Revisited, 1977-1987." In *Annual Review of Anthropology*, Vol. 17, ed. Bernard J. Siegel. Palo Alto: Annual Reviews.

Myers, Fred R. 1988. "Critical Trends in the Study of Hunter-Gatherers." In *Annual Review of Anthropology*, Vol. 17, ed. Bernard J. Siegel. Palo Alto: Annual Reviews.

Peers, Laura. 1994. *The Ojibwa of Western Canada, 1780 to 1870*. Winnipeg: The University of Manitoba Press.

Quimby, George. 1962. "A Year with a Chippewa Family, 1763-1764." *Ethnohistory* 9, no. 3:217-39.

Skinner, Alanson. 1914. "The Cultural Position of the Plains Ojibway." *American Anthropologist* 16:314-18.

Smith, Brian. 1986. "The Importance of Assessing Aquatic Environments on the Northern Plains."
    Paper presented at 1986 Chacmool Conference.
Van Kirk, Sylvia. 1980. *"Many Tender Ties" : Women in Fur-Trade Society in Western Canada, 1670-
    1870*. Winnipeg: Watson and Dwyer Publishing Ltd.
_____. 1986. "The Role of Native Women in the Fur Trade Society of Western Canada, 1670-1830."
    In *Rethinking Canada: The Promise of Women's History*, ed. Veronica Strong-Boag and Anita
    Clair Fellman. Toronto: Copp Clark Pitman.

First Nations Women of Prairie Canada in the Early Reserve Years, the 1870s to the 1920s: A Preliminary Inquiry

Sarah Carter

Although systematic consideration of the many dimensions of the lives of First Nations women of the Canadian West in the early years of settlement on reserves has scarcely even begun, in the partial picture that has emerged, several broad and sometimes contradictory conclusions or theories have been advanced. In this paper, I outline some of the approaches that have been taken to the lives of northern plains women in prairie Canada, as well as in the western United States, in the early decades of reserve life, and suggest new directions for research by reviewing some of the sources available for such a study.

One widely shared conclusion that appears in the ethnographic and historical literature on northern plains women of both Canada and the United States is that to a certain extent they benefited from the transition to reserve life in the late nineteenth century, certainly more than their male counterparts. American anthropologist Esther S. Goldfrank's 1945 study of the Blood Indians of Alberta is representative of this point of view.[1] Goldfrank concludes that "women as a class have benefited from reserve life for the white man's law now protects their property and person."[2] Goldfrank emphasizes that the new laws favoured women in matters of inheritance, that "bulwarked by white example and force, she demands not only a stake in her father's estate but in her husband's as well." Serious assault and murder were now severely punished, and steps were being taken to ensure that deserting husbands did not abandon their responsibilities. Often, although not always, this view of women as profiting from the new regime of the reserve was firmly grounded in a perception of their former "primitive slavery," which they gladly exchanged for the new freedoms and rights offered them. Goldfrank, to a certain extent, exemplifies this point of view, quoting from European explorers who described Aboriginal women of the plains as slaves and drudges, who were bought and sold like chattels, stood in absolute awe of their husbands, and suffered many indignities.

A positive portrait of what reserve life had to offer to Aboriginal women was promoted when convenient by the Department of Indian Affairs (DIA) beginning in the later nineteenth century, and was also part of the public discourse of many missionaries, although certainly not all. A powerful conviction held by many in the colonizing society was that they were behaving altruistically toward the colonized. It was widely believed that dispossessed of nomadic habits, an Aboriginal woman would be the mistress of her home, and not a servile, degraded beast of burden continually on the move from camp to camp. She would acquire discipline, modesty, and cleanliness, virtues that non-Aboriginals believed were impossible in a nomadic society.

An influential generalization that emerged from the work of early-twentieth-century ethnologists of plains people was that the transition to reserve life had a profound negative effect upon men, because it deprived them of their former economic and political responsibilities, whereas women continued to function virtually as before. Anthropologist Clark Wissler (1870-1947) writes about the Oglala based upon his field work in Montana between 1902 and 1905:

I am sure that the Indian man was the real victim of reservation policy. When the soldiers herded a tribe onto a reservation the Indian men joined the ranks of the unemployed and went on relief. They would gladly have hunted, followed the war path and engaged in all the occupations they had been trained for, but there was no chance. So they sat around in idleness. On the other hand, the Indian woman had no time to loaf. As of old, she was the housekeeper, gathered wood, reared the children, cared for the sick and made most of the clothing. Then it was her job to gather whatever vegetable food was to be used.

Any day in camp would reveal the females toiling early and late. To see so many useless males around frequently aroused my resentment, but the women never complained about it. True, they were often vociferous in demanding the return of the old time but not with the idea that they would have less to do. So far as I could see, the morale of the women was far less shattered and it was they who saved tribal life from complete collapse.[3]

The argument that women's traditional domestic roles persisted, while the male roles of hunter, warrior, horse raider, rancher, and farmer have one by one dissipated, has been influential in subsequent analyses of the transition to reserve life. Some authors have concluded that this pattern attests to the adaptability, flexibility, and ingenuity of plains women. In *Oglala Women*, Marla Powers argues that women were better able than men to adapt to the dominant white culture, and they provided essential stability and continuity in their communities.[4] In a recent study of Blood couples in Alberta that ranges from the late nineteenth century to the contemporary period, Janet M. Billson accepts the basic premise that women adapted more readily to the new order but argues that, with the erosion of the male's ability to provide, a double burden was created for Blood women, whose added responsibilities created dissonance.[5]

More recent studies of plains women and the transition to reserve life have, like Billson's, tended to emphasize not an enhanced world of opportunity and an improved legal status, but, rather, have stressed that women's roles were altered and diminished — that efforts to impose Western patriarchal forms of family, labour, property, and production resulted in increased dependence upon men. In a study of Sioux women of Devil's Lake, North Dakota, Patricia Albers found that the women were systematically discriminated against in all federal policy initiatives beginning with the treaty negotiations.[6] Women were effectively excluded from agriculture, despite the fact that in the pre-reservation days cultivation was primarily the work of women. Men were awarded the equipment, stock, and seed. Nor did women have any say over how land was to be used, or how products were to be distributed. The few jobs made available by the government were granted exclusively to men. Albers concludes: "The new situation that Sioux women found themselves in gave them less opportunity to be autonomous and exercise influence than they had in the past."[7] She stresses that women did not become totally powerless or passive under their new circumstances; they continued to oversee food distribution, for example, and to exhibit a degree of independence in the dissolution of a marriage. Sioux women lost ground, however, in that they no longer played an active role in the affairs of their bands and villages.

In a case study of reservation policy and the economic position of Wichita women during the last half of the nineteenth century, Carolyn G. Pool concurred with many of Albers's conclusions.[8] Wichita women lost political and economic power as a result of reservation policies. The state promoted prevailing Western ideologies and assumptions about the role of women and men, of the male provider and the female dependant, which deprived women of the autonomy and influence they had in the past.

In the Canadian context, Kathleen Jamieson has documented the ways in which the Indian Act discriminated against women, leaving them with fewer fundamental rights than other Canadian women or Indian men.[9] Legislation enacted in 1869 and persisting until the revisions of 1951 reflected EuroCanadian social organization and cultural values and English common law in which the wife was virtually the property of her husband. It was assumed that women were dependent subjects who derived rights from their fathers or husbands. The most glaring example of this was the section that stipulated that an Indian woman who married a non-Indian man lost her status as a registered Indian, as did her children. On the other hand, white women who married Indian men, and their children, obtained legal status as Indians. Indian women also had to prove that they were of good "moral" character before they were entitled to receive an inheritance. Under the Indian Act, women were excluded from voting in band elections, or partaking in band business.

A more favourable view of women before the era of European contact is reflected in many of these studies. Jamieson, for example, points out the power of women in Iroquoian society, in which descent was traced through the female line, dwellings were owned by senior women, and the senior matrons elected and deposed the leaders. While, of all North American Native societies, those of the plains have widely been regarded as the most exploitive of women, even here, standard assumptions about the dominance of males have increasingly been drawn into question. Alan Klein, among others, has argued that, before European contact, women played an essential economic role, and men did not enjoy greater status or prestige, but, rather, the work of men and women was complementary.[10] Women possessed and wielded considerable power, reflected especially in the control they had over the distribution of the resources of the household. Only through involvement in the European fur trade were women placed in an inferior position to males. Women became more dependent, and their status declined with the advent of European contact — there was a more rigid separation between male and female with unequal treatment and different standards of behaviour. In plains societies of the nineteenth century, according to Klein, there was an increasing subservience of females who became part of the labour force, while men gained in prestige and in wealth as a result of their ability to channel women's labour. Women were oppressed as a source of cheap labour with the introduction of individual wealth, obliterating the equality the community had previously enjoyed. Even after the advent of the European and American fur and robe trade, however, it is thought that plains women had more important responsibilities and powers than their white counterparts. In some societies, women played a dominant role in the religious and ceremonial life. Some women excelled as warriors and achieved high status, and they also acted as peacemakers.[11]

The most comprehensive treatment of women in the early reserve years in western Canada is Pamela M. White's Ph.D. dissertation in geography, "Restructuring the Domestic Sphere — Prairie Indian Women on Reserves: Image, Ideology and State Policy, 1880-1930."[12] White argues that the officials of the DIA inherited from generations of European explorers and traders a rich legacy of negative imagery of Aboriginal women, which gave them assurance and confidence in their opinion that their lives had to be altered to free them from the centuries of oppression. A central strategy of the state was to restructure the domestic economy of women living on reserves, a measure seen as vital to the "civilization of the Indian." Efforts to restructure the reserve domestic economy included the introduction of new housekeeping and cooking skills and more "moral" living quarters. The state also intervened in areas of mothering and child care through the residential school system, which trained girls for domestic work and boys for farming and other trades. By the 1920s the state had become involved in virtually all aspects of an Aboriginal woman's life, according to White. An important central argument of the dissertation is that throughout the period between 1880 and 1930 the DIA deliberately promoted a largely negative image of Indian women. The high infant mortality rate and the tuberculosis epidemic were all attributed to the supposedly "slovenly" housekeeping habits, and poor mothering and nursing skills, of Aboriginal women. In this way, the well-entrenched negative images of Aboriginal women continued to be an important aspect of the Canadian state policy well into the twentieth century.

Our understanding of the many dimensions of the lives of women in the early reserve years in the West remains at best fragmentary. A major problem for historians is with the nature of the evidence, which rarely provides the first-hand voices of the women of this era. Evidence that tells us about the bases of settler and government actions is easier to assemble than that which provides insight into Aboriginal understandings and interests. Historians rely upon documentary evidence that was generated by predominantly male EuroCanadian government officials, missionaries, or other observers. A further problem with these record keepers is that they were concerned to a much greater degree with the activities and transactions of men; they regarded as insignificant or misunderstood the role of women in Aboriginal society.

It has proven easier, then, to define the social practices and beliefs upon which state policies toward Aboriginal women were based than to evaluate the extent to which the new laws and policies succeeded in remodelling women and families according to white middle-class ideals. As Pamela White has written, the DIA vigorously promoted the point of view that these policies, which were designed to alter and reshape women, had *not* succeeded, that the women willfully clung to the "old ways" and refused to take up cleanliness and other housewifery skills. More recently, however, it has been argued that the policies, laws, and programs that accompanied reserve life *did* affect women and alter their lives, although there is fundamental disagreement over whether these alterations had positive or negative consequences. An approach that stresses the subjugation of Aboriginal people by a dominant society with attendant emphasis only upon cultural decline and disintegration has increasingly been criticized as a blunt instrument. Such an approach ignores the motives, interests, and understandings of Aboriginal people themselves, and overlooks the degree of cultural continuity. The idea that Aboriginal cultures were disintegrating and ought to disappear proved useful and was promoted by powerful interests in the late nineteenth and twentieth centuries. In some of the most recent studies of culture contact in the American West, a new framework has been suggested in which one culture does not subjugate another, but, rather, two or more cultures interact, each mutually influencing the other.[13] While some of these arguments and approaches are reflected in Canadian histories of the fur-trade era, little effort has been made to extend the interpretation to the reserve era.

My preliminary investigation of some of the sources that might be drawn upon for a study of women in the early reserve era suggests that, in this time of unprecedented scarcity and upheaval when the disappearance of the buffalo coincided with settlement on reserves, and efforts to establish agriculture produced little in the way of an edible or marketable produce, women made a vital contribution to the cultural and physical survival of their communities, a contribution that is overlooked in histories of both Aboriginal people and women of the prairies. For a time, there remained scope to practise their traditional gathering economy and strategies. Based upon the sources I am familiar with, there appears to be substance to the generalization that women's roles continued and were essential to stability and continuity in the early reserve years. There is also evidence of a time during which the host and incoming cultures interacted, each mutually influencing, even assisting, the other. Reserve women were anxious to learn new skills that could be of use in the new order, but there were rarely adequate equipment, tools, and textiles to put new knowledge to work. Instead, it was the more traditional work of women in diversifying the economic base of the community that saw the people through these lean years. Although government officials blamed women for clinging to their "backward" methods, their strategies made sound economic sense. Other rural women, newcomers to the prairie West, profited from the remarkable store of knowledge that women had of what was consumable or medicinally useful as they learned to cope with the unstable prairie environment.

The level of cultural interaction receded, however, as settlement became more dense and the DIA made greater formal efforts to create boundaries between the newcomers and the host population. For the people of the "settlement belt" that hugged the Canadian Pacific Railway, the mid-1880s were the years when opportunities and freedom began to decline markedly. The resources available to Aboriginal women to assist in feeding their families diminished as the habitat of native plant species was restricted as the prairies became a land of cultivated fields and fences. A system of confining people to reserves was introduced, and women were further constrained in their ability to move about the land through the efforts of the North West Mounted Police (NWMP), who appeared particularly intent on limiting the mobility of women. The control of the DIA officials who were resident on the reserves was strengthened in the late 1880s. It would be a mistake, however, to assume that federal policies and agencies like the NWMP became the key determinants of the lives of Aboriginal women. Within the reserve framework they continued to develop strategies and to show their customary resourcefulness and ingenuity. Ideological pressures from the dominant society, however, combined with government policy and agencies, economic constraints, and an education that focussed on domestic skills to narrow the options open to women. For the Aboriginal people of prairie Western Canada, the late nineteenth century could be compared to the Depression of the 1930s, as the collapse of the economy combined with years of drought. Destitution, unemployment, and malnutrition resulted, with the added hardship of disease. Conditions were particularly grim by 1878 in southern Saskatchewan. Native catechist Charles Pratt reported from the

Touchwood Hills that year that there was not a morsel of food to be found and all were starving.[14] Thousands of destitute people congregated at posts such as Carlton, Pitt, Battleford, Walsh, and Macleod. The experiences of those who had already settled on their reserves by this time (in Treaties Four and Six) did not encourage others to follow their lead. A farm instructor in the Qu'Appelle Valley found that during the bitterly cold winter of 1879-80 Aboriginal people were in acute distress, suffering greatly, and showing clear signs of starvation. "The children," he wrote, "were *really* 'crying for food.'"[15]

Reserve residents received rations, but these were not distributed generously and were often suspended for days at a time. Relief was viewed by government officials as dangerous, demoralizing, and enfeebling, and recipients were discouraged from thinking that they could rely on this as a means of support. Aboriginal people were regarded as having somehow brought about this state of affairs themselves and as refusing to take steps to improve their condition. The solution was to feed reserve residents only a little, in order to teach them the virtues of hard work and thrift. The department salt pork that they were issued was described by a farm instructor in 1880 as "*musty* and *rusty* and totally unfit for use — although we are giving it out to the Indians, in the absence of anything better, but we *cannot use it ourselves.*"[16]

The mortality rate was high among prairie Aboriginal people in the late 1870s and 1880s, and the rate may have been higher among the males, although further study would be needed to confirm this. A EuroCanadian fur trader at Fort Qu'Appelle recorded that, between the years 1867 and 1874, 700 males within his circle of acquaintance lost their lives — "in battle, by murder and by sudden death," so that the number of females largely exceeded that of males.[17] But disease and malnutrition affected everyone. In the winter of 1878-79, a group of about seventy-five Aboriginal people described as starving arrived at Fort Qu'Appelle.[18] Toward spring they all contracted an unspecified fatal disease and died within three or four days. In the winter of 1883, forty-two members of Piapot's band died. The doctor who visited the reserve that spring concluded that the deaths were caused by a form of scurvy, due to the exclusive use of salt foods.[19] Epidemics that periodically flared up took a heavy toll. In the winter of 1889 there were thirty-six deaths on an Onion Lake reserve from scarlet fever, and on the File Hills Reserves in 1891 thirty children died of chicken pox.[20]

Aboriginal people were often reported to be too weak from sickness to work, and they were also severely hampered in their ability to perform labour because of a lack of proper clothing and footwear. To cover up their feet they cut up old leather lodges, but these also rapidly diminished, and three or four families were crowded together into one lodge.[21] Hunters could not stalk game in winter without adequate footwear and clothing. Distress was particularly acute for some after the North West resistance of 1885. Bands who were regarded as having acted in a "disloyal" manner had their horses, guns, and ammunition taken from them, and their annuities were withheld so that it was impossible to even acquire items such as matches. Officials on reserves frequently reported that residents were "down cast and afraid they are going to starve," and "profoundly depressed at the thought of the future."[22]

It was during these years of low resources and shattered morale that the work of women on reserves was vital, materially as well as spiritually. Aboriginal sources in particular lend credence to the point of view that women's roles continued to a great extent as before, providing security and stability. Women were perhaps even more essential to family and band survival than ever before. Cree author Joseph F. Dion writes that, when spirits were low on the Onion Lake Reserve in the 1880s, "much of the inspiration for the Crees came from the old ladies, for they set to work with a will that impressed everybody."[23] "Their cheerfulness," he writes, "could not help but be infectious, thus everyone was soon striving to do his share, and the Crees were able to look on the bright side of things."[24] Even in these days of great destitution and upheaval, the women kept alive traditions of communal activity and the sharing of resources. As Dion writes, "Everything that the elderly ladies gathered and stored away during the summer months was for the enjoyment and benefit of others."[25]

A number of Aboriginal women Elders were interviewed in the early 1970s for a film project that never materialized, yet their oral histories, housed at the Saskatchewan Archives Board in Regina, constitute an invaluable record of everyday life on prairie reserves at the turn of the century. They attest to the resourcefulness and ingenuity of women as they both drew on traditional talents and adapted to new conditions, and many of them dwell upon such activities as berry picking. The river and creek valleys provided a great variety of wild berries that were picked and processed as they came into season. Marion Dillon, of Seekaskootch Reserve at Onion Lake, remembers that berries were dried then stored in birch-bark boxes decorated with porcupine quills, and that in these containers they would keep all winter.[26] She recalls: "There were a few white settlers here and there already at the time. They would come by and buy berries from us. They had no money, but they traded us homemade butter and other things for the berries we had to trade."[27] Prairie turnip, known to the Plains Cree as the "big grass root," was still abundant on uncultivated prairie. It was harvested with slightly curved, fire-hardened digging sticks. The harvest time for the prairie turnip lasted only a few weeks in the late spring and early summer, and after that it was nearly impossible to locate the underground tuber because the flower and stalk broke off and blew away.[28] Many bushels were collected at a time and they were peeled, cut into shreds, and dried in the sun. Prairie turnip was eaten in a variety of ways — uncooked, boiled, roasted, in soups, or it was dried, crushed into a powder and stored in skin bags for the winter. The flour of this root, mixed with saskatoon berries, was a favourite dish among the Plains Cree.

Women's excursions were undertaken communally, and the food procured on these excursions was collectively distributed. Large groups of women and children headed off, walking great distances when it was considered that the season for the harvest of a certain resource was at hand. Each of these trips, according to Dion, was "a well organized affair, every detail being prearranged, hence there was never a hitch in the work once the location was reached. If the distance was too great for the old ladies they went prepared to camp out."[29] The different events of the season were anticipated with great enthusiasm because they were opportunities for visits and entertainment. "They derived a great deal of enjoyment," Dion writes, "when, in company with their sisters and friends, they raided Mother Nature of her different stores, each in its proper time. . . . The many different excursions organized by the women were as happy picnics, leaving no time for moping or self pity."[30] The products were often communally processed, and they were evenly distributed among the participants, as well as issued to the sick, the aged, and those unable to attend the outing.

Marie Osecap's description of an excursion for wild rhubarb on the Sweet Grass Reserve is typical of women's activities.

Below a bank beside . . . [Drumming Creek] grew many maple trees. With these maple trees grew many wild rhubarb. After a lunch and a good rest, we cut the rhubarb, putting it in neat piles. Then we tied it up in four bundles and headed for home, each of us carrying one bundle. It was a long way home. . . . To make the trip worthwhile, we would carry as much rhubarb as we could carry.

It was hard work and we rested many times before reaching home. When we arrived with the rhubarb, we passed it around, as was the custom in those days. People were many and only a little could be given to each family, but they were pleased and happy with what we gave them.[31]

Wild rhubarb was a favourite ingredient in soup. It was peeled, cut in short lengths, and added to the soup stock, which was often made from bacon rind.

Rabbit and gopher hunts were organized in much the same way. "We are going on a gopher hunt,"[32] someone would say, according to Mrs. Osecap, and they would set off walking along the road to Battleford, a long distance, to the place where gophers were hunted. They carried everything they needed including pots, pans, cups, and large pails for drowning gophers. Mrs. Osecap remembers: "[We] cleaned and cooked the gophers over there, right where we had killed them. Then we would all have a big meal of boiled gophers. It was a nice meal and we enjoyed it. We would then kill more and clean them so we could take them home for the people who weren't able to come with us on the hunt."[33]

Duck hunts took place in the early summer, just before the baby ducks were big enough to fly, and again during moulting season. According to Mrs. Osecap, the women would "wade in the water, walking abreast, scaring the young ducks onto dry land. The men would grab them and wring their necks. The women would catch some in the water, too. Sometimes women would grab garter snakes by mistake. This caused much squealing and some giggling by the spectators."[34] Smoked duck was a welcome dish during the winter months. The feathers were saved for making such useful domestic items as pillows.

Men and boys helped with duck as well as rabbit hunts, indicating that the division of labour was not always sharply marked and could break down in the face of expediency and individual preferences. Marion Dillon, who was raised by her grandparents, remembers her grandfather doing all kinds of jobs about the house:

> He would make sure that Grandma never ran out of firewood. He would also carry all the water Grandma needed to the house. Grandpa would even bake bannock when Grandma was busy at something else or was not feeling well. I used to like the bannock Grandpa baked better than Grandma's. Grandpa also was good at roasting meat over an open fire. It was a treat to eat meat Grandpa had roasted.[35]

Fine Day, a Cree military leader and holy man, and key informant to American anthropologist David Mandelbaum in the 1930s, also described the assistance men gave to women in their tasks. According to Fine Day, both men and women dug prairie turnip — the husband dug when his wife was tired. Men also helped to make maple sugar. The women were far more adept, however, at certain skills. They had a particular way, for example, of cutting bark for boxes. Once Fine Day remembered his grandmother asking his grandfather to cut some bark for her: "When he brought some home it was full of holes and torn in places. She simply threw it in the fire and went to get some herself."[36]

In the early spring, sap was gathered from maple and birch trees, boiled down and "carefully stored away," Dion writes, "as a treat and soother for grandmother's pets later on."[37] Maple sugar time was a gala holiday, but it was also a lot of work, and the help of many was needed. Marion Carter of Seekaskootch Reserve remembers that together the women tapped three hundred trees every spring.[38] Men often participated, cutting and stacking a large amount of wood. The sap was boiled over an open fire all day long, and this required a great deal of wood. The Cree participation in this "industry" was described in the *Regina Leader Post* in the spring of 1884.[39] A few miles northwest of Regina, a group of Cree had about 200 trees tapped and were manufacturing a "very superior maple sugar." A local farmer declared it to be "as good [as], if not superior to the sugar boiled in Ontario." Despite confident predictions that this would be a product the Cree would offer for sale, there is little evidence of the marketing of maple sugar by Aboriginal people in the West.

The list of the resources women drew upon was lengthy. Joe Dion writes that even "the lowly mouse was called upon occasionally, for amid his large stores in the fall he always had some seeds and roots which we gladly stole from the little beggar and used in making nourishing soups."[40] Just under the bark of the aspen or white poplar there is a sweet edible substance that was much enjoyed in the spring.[41] Kinnickinick, which was made from the inner bark of the red dogwood, was cut, dried, and powdered, then mixed with tobacco for smoking. Large quantities of mint were dried to use in tea during the winter.

To a limited extent, Aboriginals sold or traded some of the products they gathered, processed, or manufactured. There was a market for seneca root (an ingredient in patent medicines), for wild hops and wild fruit. Rushes and willows were gathered in the summer months to weave baskets, straw hats, and mats during the winter, and buyers were found for some of these. An important source of income on many reserves was the tanning of hides by women. As one Indian agent reported in 1896, "Tanning of hides by the native process, the product of which may be more properly described as dressed leather, is an industry appertaining to the women, by which the family earnings are, on many of the reserves, considerably augmented."[42] Neighbouring settlers brought their cow hides to the reserves for processing.

There is clear evidence of a time in the early settlement years of the post-1870 West when the host Aboriginal culture and the incoming settlers learned from and required the assistance of each other. Aboriginal women readily adapted to new skills and technology. They did much of the work in the vegetable gardens that each household kept. Marion Dillon remembers that they grew large gardens every year. Amedée Forget, who farmed in the Battleford district in the early 1880s, reports that much care and attention was devoted to the gardens on the reserves. "At any time during the summer you could hardly detect one blade of grass growing between their vegetables."[43] Some had neatly fenced gardens with flower beds, borders of cobble stones, and gravel walks.

Women and children also worked in the grain fields, especially during peak seasons such as haying and harvesting. In 1887 a neighbouring farmer visited the Assiniboine River in southern Saskatchewan and observed the harvest of "the best wheat I had seen this season. It was cut with a reaping machine and there was about twenty men and women, all Indians, going behind and binding it into sheaves, and after them there were papooses or children gleaning or gathering up the stalks and heads that had been left, and binding these up into small sheaves."[44] Mrs. Osecap remembers: "The women helped with the haying. They used a forked stick in place of a hay fork. There were no forks on the reserve at the time. There was maybe the odd fork around, if a man was well-to-do. He was considered rich."[45]

Some women were active in all aspects of the farm enterprise. In the season of 1889-90, for example, it was reported that Widow Sears of Day Star Reserve in the Touchwood Hills had built an addition to her house, summerfallowed five acres, and purchased with her private means a new mower and horse rake.[46]

A wide range of new skills such as milking, butter making, bread making, and knitting were introduced, and, although Aboriginal women responded enthusiastically to these activities, not all advice, or the way in which it was given, was appreciated equally. Instruction was not always systematic in the early reserve years, consisting of what could be given by example from the agent, farm instructor, teacher, missionary, and the wives of these men. Some missionaries and their wives undertook home visits that were intended to encourage methodical, hygienic housekeeping — including mending, sewing, soap making, cooking, and gardening — but were expected to perform these functions to help maintain these institutions. By the late 1880s the wives of many of the farm instructors acquired the official title of "instructress." They held regular classes in "housewifery" and made visits to the homes on the reserves. Knitting and crocheting were taught to reserve women, and many proved adept at these new kinds of needlework, making socks, mittens, and other garments. On reserves with herds of sheep, reserve women learned to card, spin yarn, and weave cloth. The women welcomed new skills and were at times overly anxious to learn. Mrs. Slater, an instructor in the Touchwood Hills, reported in 1891: "Early in the spring the women commenced making butter with so much enthusiasm and success that it was found they were starving the calves, so halt had to be called and the calves were turned out with the cows."[47]

Eleanor Brass from File Hills writes that it was a farm instructor by the name of E.C. Stewart who taught the "miracle of butter" to the women there in the late nineteenth century.[48] Stewart, who was fluent in Cree, arranged milking classes and lectured on the food value of milk products. Every morning and evening in springtime, Stewart would call out *"tooh-toos-ah-poo!"* (milk time) several times until it was heard all over the settlement, and he became known by this name. According to Brass, "the women would come out of their tents and teepees with pails to get their lessons in milking cows. With much laughing and joking among themselves, they became quite adept at mastering this new task."[49] The lesson in butter making that followed delighted the women. For a time before the turn of the century at agencies such as Onion Lake, dairying was listed as one of the main industries, but this activity fell off because of a lack of market and of proper equipment.[50]

The lists of items exhibited by Aboriginal women at prairie agricultural fairs indicates a wide range of new skills. They displayed socks, mitts, petticoats, gaiters, shot bags, drapery, woven carpetbags, quilts, aprons, and dresses.[51] The resourcefulness and ingenuity of plains women, their ability to draw upon traditional talents while adapting to changing conditions, is evident in the material culture of the era. In his study of central (American) plains moccasins in museum collections, Thomas P. Myers argues that women on reservations readily began to manufacture a type of moccasin intended for sale directly to whites that were decorated in the simplest manner possible.[52] They began to produce simplified "Indian" goods for sale. Museum collections attest to the ways in which Aboriginal women readily absorbed new materials, techniques, and new functions for Native art —

incorporating silk floss, wool yarn, stroud, velvet braid, and silk ribbon. In the "subarctic" collection from Manitoba of the late-Victorian-era traveller Emma Shaw Colcleugh, there is evidence of the ways in which Aboriginal women adapted their skills and were influenced by the ready market for their artwork.[53] There are many items of "Victoriana" including picture frames, mat or lamp pads, pillow covers, embroidered New Year's greetings, and wall pockets. Aboriginal women in the Yukon made "gold pokes" in response to the series of gold rushes. On the prairies, women were producing moccasins and other items for sale in the late nineteenth century. Métis trader Norbert Welsh bought "all kinds" of moccasins, which he then sold to the Hudson's Bay Company at over double the price he paid his suppliers. He described many different styles; they were "handsome, embroidered in all colors, and trimmed with weasel fur — ermine."[54]

Often overlooked is the extent to which the knowledge and skill of Aboriginal women was vital to the newly arrived women. There are many examples throughout the Canadian West of Aboriginal women midwives assisting the newcomer women. Ontarian Annie Greer spent her first winter in the West (1893-94) in a log-and-sod hut in the Grandview district west of Dauphin, Manitoba, where she gave birth to her first child; the delivery was assisted by Caroline, the local midwife and doctor, who was also the wife of the chief on the neighbouring reserve.[55] Caroline packed a satchel with herbs, roots, bark, and leaves when she came to Annie's assistance and was credited with saving her life. She refused payment for her services. Caroline further assisted this family by getting them a start in cattle; for several years in the spring she sent down five or six milking cows for Annie and her aunt to milk all summer, enabling them to sell butter in the fall.

Dr. Elizabeth Matheson, who practised medicine in Saskatchewan on the Onion Lake Reserve between 1898 and 1918, was assisted by an Aboriginal midwife (and sometimes two) in the birth of several of her children.[56] In the 1920s, Harriet Sayese Quinney, who was a skilled midwife on the Onion Lake Reserve, assisted Dr. Miller as midwife in the hospital he set up in his home at Elk Point.[57] While the recent immigrants generally welcomed the assistance, they were sometimes hesitant at first about some of the advice given. An Alberta pioneer originally from Belgium, François Adam, recalled the summer of 1892 at Duhamel when his wife gave birth assisted by two Aboriginal women who tented by their house with their children.[58] They made a liquid out of twigs or roots that according to Adam "worked a charm." A few days after the birth, the medicine women were concerned that the child had jaundice and wanted to give it a louse to swallow. The couple refused this treatment, and they did not believe the child had jaundice. In later years Adam was surprised to learn the extent to which this remedy was known in many places throughout the world. Visiting in Belgium, he spoke to an elderly woman long acquainted with his family and asked her, "'Do you know, Kate, what those Indians gave my baby for the jaundice?' Without hesitation she answered, 'Yes, they gave him a louse.' I stood with my mouth open. I could not believe my ears." He later found a similar cure suggested in a book written by a Scandinavian doctor who had studied folk remedies.

There are numerous accounts of the medicinal skills of Aboriginal women who either taught the new arrivals or assisted them in times of illness. In the account books of the European fur traders who preceded the agricultural settlers, there are entries in which it was noted that Aboriginal women were paid a certain amount for their "doctoring."[59] Effie Storer, an early resident of the Battleford district, wrote: "Many of the elder women proved quite adept at diagnosis and in prescribing the correct herb-tea. . . . Lint from the cotton-wood tree and the hairy-fuzz of the anemone seed-pod were frequently called into requisition.[60] A woman born to an early ranching family in Pincher Creek, Alberta, remembers: "If we were sick usually an old Indian woman would help my mother take care of us."[61] A woman settler in the Moosomin district of present-day Saskatchewan in the early 1880s was assisted by an Aboriginal woman when her child became seriously ill. This incident is vividly described in a local history of Moosomin.

The Indian woman took in the situation at a glance. She pushed aside the terrified mother and picked up the ailing child. By signs she indicated hot water from the kettle on the stove. Into it she put a pinch of herbs from the pouch slung around her waist. She cooled the brew and forced some of it between blue lips of the infant. Soon the gasping subsided, and sweat broke to cool the fevered skin. The baby relaxed into a peaceful, natural sleep, cradled in the arms of the crooning Indian woman. . . . That mother to her dying day remained grateful.[62]

Although there is clear evidence of a time when the traditional role and subsistence strategies of Aboriginal women continued, and of a time when cultures mingled and learned from each other, these experiences appear to have diminished as settlement became more dense and government authorities began to more deeply intrude into the lives of Aboriginal people. There were informal means through which Aboriginal women were marginalized. As Pamela White argues, the government, through its official publications, deliberately promoted images of Aboriginal women as "gossipy" and "idle."[63] This is an interesting yet unmistakable inversion of the firmly held belief of the pre-settlement era, that plains women toiled unceasingly and were mere slaves while the men remained abominably lazy. Yet an image of industrious women was not particularly useful any more. The poverty and suffering that characterized early reserve life was largely blamed on women who were now depicted as lazy and intractable. By the early reserve years, government officials were convinced that, like the men, Aboriginal women were "lazy" and "indolent," with plenty of spare time. They did not always see them knitting, dressmaking, or otherwise "usefully employed." Officials seldom acknowledged in their publications that Aboriginal women had difficulty putting their new domestic instruction to use because there was a chronic shortage of raw materials. While women knew how to make loaf bread, for example, they did not have the proper ingredients, ovens, yeast, or baking tins, so they continued to make bannock, despite government attempts to abolish it from the diet.[64] Marion Dillon remembered that they were often short of milk pans, although they made their own, using birch bark.[65] There were no buttons for the dresses women made, unless the instructors purchased them themselves.[66] During a visit to the File Hills in 1891, Inspector T.P. Wadsworth remarked: "Although I was informed that many of the women can knit I failed to see one of them engaged in that useful occupation, and the Agent informed me that he had not any yarn to issue to them this year."[67] Instructress Gooderham reported from the Touchwood Hills that the "greatest drawback in accomplishing much is their extreme poverty, their lack of almost every article of domestic comfort in their houses, and no material to work upon."[68]

Lessons in "housewifery" were to be applied in dwellings that with few exceptions were described as "huts" or "shacks." These were the winter quarters; in summer, reserve residents moved into tents and often shifted campsites. The winter shacks were low, one-storey, one-room log homes. The roofs were constructed with logs or poles over which rows of straw or grass were laid.[69] They were plastered inside and out with a mixture of mud and hay. Some had long rails overhead inside for hanging meat to dry. The clay stoves that were a feature of each of these shacks were built by women. Marie Osecap described how they were built: "They would get four sticks, put some stones on it, the women would then plaster it with mud and hay. They would keep adding stones, plaster it some more. They would then make a hole inside of this stove, where the fire was to be."[70] These stoves were used for cooking, for heat, and for lighting the entire room. The mud chimney, which was always open, also served as a ventilator. Early reserve houses had no flooring, and tanned hide was used for windows. The sleeping places in these homes were seldom more than a bundle of rags on the floor — few had bedsteads or bunks.

Inspectors continually lamented about the state of housing on the reserves. On some there was a lack of suitable timber for housing; and it was also reported with regret that Aboriginal farmers purchased farming equipment and livestock rather than investing in the materials necessary to improve domestic surroundings.[71] Department officials wrongly saw this as a tendency peculiar to Aboriginal people, but farmers everywhere were notorious for purchasing equipment for the farm before attending to their homes and families. The barns, stables, byres and corrals were generally found to be clean and comfortable, prompting Wadsworth to often remark that the animals appeared to be better off than their owners.[72] DIA officials such as Inspector Wadsworth were convinced that Aboriginal women willfully refused to apply their lessons in housewifery.

Women were often blamed in official DIA publications for the slum conditions and poor health that characterized reserve life; their abilities as housewives and mothers were disparaged, as were their moral standards.[73] The systemic causes of poverty were ignored, and, instead, blame was laid upon the supposed domestic slovenliness of Aboriginal women. EuroCanadians believed, for example, that people on plains reserves continued to live in tents in summer because the women preferred this to the work required to maintain a home. An 1880 item in the *Toronto Daily Mail* noted: "[It] is said that the squaws prefer tents to houses as they save work. The interior of a house has to be cleaned; but when the tent floor gets dirty it is only necessary to move to a clean spot, and a shaking of the blanket cleans the walls."[74]

There is little doubt that dirt was a prominent feature of homes on reserves, just as it was in all early prairie homes. Cows and poultry wandered about in the yard next to the houses. If it rained, mud in the yard could be ankle-deep, and the roof dripped liquid mud. Water suitable for drinking and washing was not always readily available, especially in dry seasons when sources dried up and prairie residents had to wait for rain. Sedentary settlement required wells as a source of water, but, on the plains, shallow-dug wells were not as adequate as they were in the eastern provinces. The underground supply was generally below the level that could be reached by a dug well, and getting that water necessitated welldrilling and prior boring with a test auger. This procedure, and the equipment needed for it, was beyond the means of early prairie residents, on reserves or otherwise. In the dry years of the 1880s, water was particularly scarce. Sections of the Qu'Appelle River, for example, were dried up for miles.[75] An 1890 effort to dig a well on the Piapot Reserve was unsuccessful, although they dug down 242 feet.[76] Under such conditions, baths were a luxury, as a well-to-do British woman discovered during a visit to the prairies: "Time was when I thought — with my class — that 'poor people' could at least keep themselves and their houses clean for water was cheap. I know better now."[77] Personal cleanliness was particularly difficult for reserve residents, as one instructor reported, because "they have only the clothes they are wearing daily, and many of them but scantily clad."[78] Few reports of agents and instructors failed to mention that reserve residents lacked adequate clothing and footwear.

Cree author Edward Ahenakew writes that the accusation that the Aboriginal woman was a poor housekeeper was a "hasty judgment":

In the first place, what house has she to keep? Only an extraordinary being could manage to keep her family, herself, and her habitation clean, when that dwelling is a one-room shanty of falling logs, mud-chinked, that has to serve as a bedroom, dining room, play-room and sitting-room all in one. She might scrub every day, and sweep all the time, but it would be impossible to keep that one room neat and clean. It discourages her, and she abandons the effort that had been hopeless from the beginning. It is these shanties that have killed all natural regard for cleanliness, the regard that any right-minded Indian woman had in the teepee life of long ago. Even I can remember how the woman would cut fresh grass each morning to spread over the ground inside the teepee, and the encampments were moved frequently.[79]

There was limited opportunity for off-reserve employment for women. A few worked as domestics, or "hired girls," on farms and homes in the town. Some Indian Affairs officials had such "servants" in their homes. In 1889, Mrs. Hayter Reed was so pleased with the "docile, attentive, good workers" among the girls at the Battleford Industrial School that she hired one for her household.[80] Father Hugonard of the Qu'Appelle Industrial School was active in seeking positions as domestic labourers for ex-pupils of his school.[81] The program was modelled on the "outing system" pioneered at Carlisle Indian School in Pennsylvania in the late 1870s. The goal of the system was to continue the process of removing children from their traditional environment, and placing them in EuroCanadian homes where they could learn English and pick up other practical knowledge such as farm work for the boys and domestic chores for girls. Host families were to provide care and support, and to treat the student as a family member. In the United States, however, this did not always prove to be the case, and the system evolved into a child-labour system, of little educational benefit to the participants.[82] Students worked at menial jobs for which they did not receive fair wages.

In 1891 more than twenty girls were hired out from the Qu'Appelle School, earning from four to ten dollars a month. Some continued to live at the school, while others "lived in." All remained under the control of the principal, who arranged for the terms of service and received the wages. A small sum was sent to the parents, and the rest was kept by the school. It is no wonder that this was a short-lived program. It is unlikely that parents approved of this arrangement. With the change in government in 1896, the policy of supervised out-service was discontinued.[83] Aboriginal women continued to work as domestics, but the practice does not appear to have become a widespread phenomenon. The principal of the Round Lake Presbyterian Boarding School complained in 1911 that there was "a demand for house servants among the farmers and townspeople, and it is surprising that, as there are so many openings for boys and girls in this way, so few are willing to take advantage of them, and there is a disposition on the part of the parents to prevent them."[84]

Female students were outfitted with little of the academic or vocational training that could allow them any role off-reserve besides that of domestic servant. Nor were they trained to work as the teachers, nurses, and clerks who were employed on the reserves or with Indian Affairs. These were segregated schools, and their "half-day" system was distinct from that of EuroCanadian schools. The students performed a great deal of manual labour at these institutions that left little time for academic work. The girls did the cooking and baking, the cleaning, and they made clothes for themselves as well as the boys. If there were few older or "large" girls at a school, the burden of work that fell to them was even greater than for the younger, smaller ones.[85] A 1924 school inspector's report on the Qu'Appelle

Industrial School, which stated that the girls spent half a day in the classroom and the rest of the time at "household economy," might well have applied to an earlier period.[86] They rose at 5:30 to begin work in the dormitories and kitchens right after chapel. "I was unable to see much scientific method in this work," the school inspector wrote. "It seemed to be merely doing the necessary outdoor and indoor chores with no methodical or scientific teaching to develop the sanitary, dietetic, or farm management or animal husbandry. . . . No doubt the girls and boys pick up some routine knowledge of farming and domestic economy in this way but the time for academic work is very sadly cut into."[87] The children read in a mechanical way, and did not understand what they were reading. The parents complained that their children could not speak proper English and knew little else when they left school.

When Aboriginal women expressed interest in continuing their education or training they were given little encouragement. In 1929 a woman in domestic service in Saskatoon wrote Indian Commissioner W.M. Graham wondering if there were any chance for her to train as a nurse. "I'm now going on twenty years of age and feel that I must do something worth while."[88] Graham's reply was: "I do not think it would be possible to arrange for your training in such capacity, and I think it would be more to your advantage to continue in service."[89]

A pass system, enforced after 1885, hampered Aboriginal women in their abilities to seek employment in the villages and settlements. Reserve residents were required to carry passes from their agents, declaring the length of and reasons for their absences. The police were notified if individuals or groups left without passes, and they were sent back.[90] While the pass system applied to both men and women, it is notable the extent to which police and government authorities limited the mobility of Aboriginal women. It is interesting the extent to which there have been greater restrictions on women's mobility globally, and especially in colonial contexts, although these restrictions often served quite different purposes.[91] Often these limitations on mobility were not achieved by direct physical means but through ideological and psychological suasion. In the case of Aboriginal women in Western Canada, formal measures, such as the pass system, combined with powerfully negative images. An 1889 police report from Battleford noted that "a number of squaws were reported by the Indian agent for being in town without passes, and without any visible means of support. They were at once arrested and ordered to go back to their several reserves."[92] It was in 1886 in that town that a person was first arrested under the provisions of the Vagrancy Act for being in town without a pass.[93] Special treatment was reserved for Aboriginal women, as reported in the *Saskatchewan Herald* in March of that year:

It has been an understanding for some time past that no Indians were to be permitted to remain around town or off their reserves without passes. The town was several times cleared of these stragglers, but one squaw always contrived to hide and refused to join in the general exodus. One day last week she dodged the order as usual, and was arrested and taken to the barracks. Locks of hair were cut from her temples — a sort of partial fashionable bang — and she was set at liberty. An hour afterwards there [was] not a straggler in town.[94]

Such treatment, which could only have been intended to humiliate and demean, would not have been tolerated had these been EuroCanadian women. Cutting hair, or the threat to do so, appears to have become routine at Battleford barracks. In March 1888 it was reported, again in the *Herald*: "During the early part of the week the Mounted Police ordered out of town a number of squaws who had come in from time to time and settled here. The promise to take them to the barracks and cut off their hair had a wonderful effect in hastening their movements."[95]

It is interesting that both these reports of women in town occurred in March, which was typically the leanest time of the year for the Aboriginal people of the prairies. In March 1888 in the Battleford district, there were "neither rabbits, prairie chickens, wolves, foxes, nor deer in their former haunts."[96] The women who migrated to the settlements may have been obliged, because of economic conditions, to work as prostitutes, which was about the only form of employment available to them. In an 1883 petition to the prime minister and the minister of the interior, Cree chiefs of the Edmonton district contended that their young women were reduced by starvation to prostitution, a thing unheard of among their people before. Once a proud and independent people, they were now reduced to being "mendicants at the door of every white man in the country," the chiefs wrote.[97] In 1886 it was reported that families camping at Qu'Appelle station and Regina were dependent on prostitution for a living.[98] The pass system was to be enforced, requiring these people to return to their reserves. Officials attributed prostitution to what they insisted was personal disposition or to inherent immorality rather than to economic conditions. One Indian agent was convinced: "The trouble lies in the women seeking other associates than are found among their own people, but who are more aggressive, and they become the victims of their own vanity."[99]

The pass system combined with early campaigns for "conservation" of natural resources to severely limit both the terrain and the products that women were accustomed to relying upon. By the mid- to late 1880s, newspapers like the *Macleod Gazette* and the *Saskatchewan Herald* regularly ran editorials that railed against Aboriginal hunting, fishing, and gathering as rapacious activities dangerous to the environment. Aboriginals were depicted as engaged in the type of "wholesale destruction" that caused the disappearance of the buffalo.[100] Such editorials often emphasized the need to restrict people to their reserves as a means of ensuring the conservation of natural resources. A further rationale for limiting access to natural resources was that being able to live off the bounty of nature at any time of the year made them "lazy" — they did not have to devote themselves to agriculture and plan for the future. As F.C. Gilchrist, Inspector of Fisheries for the North West, wrote in 1893, Native people should not be allowed to fish in the fall, as the practice "has helped to get the natives into a lazy, thoughtless, improvident way to living."[101] In clear violation of treaty rights, the 1893 Game Ordinance of the Territorial government combined with an amendment to the Indian Act to restrict Aboriginal hunting of game.[102] Of course, hunting and gathering activities did not end, but these were increasingly restricted to reserve land. As it was, for the women in plains societies who snared small game, hunted wild fowl, and in some cases fished, these conservation measures must have had an impact on their patterns and activities.

Accustomed to a position of authority in family matters such as how the food resources were to be distributed, women on reserves lost power to the Indian agent. A permit system required reserve residents to receive the written permission of the agent before any grain, hay, cattle, or other resources could be sold. Nor could cattle for home consumption be butchered without the permission of the agent. People were not allowed to determine for themselves when to sell in order to purchase food and clothing. On a visit to File Hills in 1891, Inspector Wadsworth heard numerous complaints from residents that they did not get enough to eat, but they were not allowed to sell any of their crops to buy goods.[103] He found that there were grounds for these complaints, as the agent kept a tight hold upon the crops and the beef cattle, even in the dead of winter when there were few resources to draw upon. Wadsworth visited the home of Mrs. Peepeekesis, widow of the late chief, which he found to be in a deplorable state. She had a son about ten years old, who was in poor health and died shortly after the visit. The inspector found that the bed she shared with the boy consisted only of some hay on the floor with an old tent laid over it, and they had one blanket between them. The woman had been issued no clothing all winter, yet she owned thirty-two head of cattle. That winter, the agent had distributed blankets and clothing only to the able-bodied who assisted him in hauling wood, and the old and the helpless were not able to meet these conditions.

DIA files reveal that there were some agents and farm instructors who abused their positions of authority. In 1882 Chief Crowfoot of the Blackfoot complained that farm instructor John Norrish was exchanging extra rations in return for sexual services. The woman's family was issued a ration ticket for seven when there were only four in the family. Norrish was dismissed from his position.[104] Similar complaints against the farm instructor on his reserve were raised by Chief Thunderchild in 1893.[105] That same year there was a major DIA investigation into allegations made by the chief and councillors of the Hobbema agency that the Indian agent had indecently assaulted a number of women.[106] The agent successfully argued that there was a widespread "conspiracy" to discredit him, and he remained in charge at Hobbema for several more years.

The permit system was enforced on prairie reserves until the mid-twentieth century. This combined with the pass system and the EuroCanadian dominance of the landscape to increasingly restrict Aboriginal women in their freedom and ability to provide for their families. There was also little place for them in the world beyond the reserve. Yet Aboriginal women continued to show resourcefulness and versatility. Eleanor Brass describes how a club was organized on their reserve because they felt they did not have to take "all this abuse and dictation" such as having to ask the agent for their own money to buy groceries.[107]

We would study ways by which we could become independent from the Indian agent. This was rather difficult to do as we had to get permits to sell most of our produce. So we decided to raise the kind of things for which a permit wasn't required. That included garden produce, hogs, and poultry of all kinds.

We brought speakers from the community to talk on a variety of subjects for our projects. We also elected members to head the various departments. Dad was always a good gardner [sic] and therefore he headed the gardening project; Mrs. Helen Ironquil was an expert on poultry.[108]

When she married into the Muskoday Reserve (Saskatchewan) in 1928, Lena Bear (Sayese), a Métis woman, brought a cow and calf with her. She refused to have them branded I.D. (Indian Department) and so was later able to sell them without a permit.[109]

For every story of the successful circumvention of policy, regulations, and the authority of the Indian agent, however, there are many more that attest to the formidable yoke of oppression that characterized reserve life well into the twentieth century. While women had agency, this was constrained and restricted; they may have resisted but were not always successful in their resistance. Clearly oral history, and history written by Aboriginal people, is key to furthering our understanding of the many dimensions of reserve life. In an account of life on the Nut Lake Reserve (Saskatchewan) in the 1940s, the residents described themselves as "prisoners," who could barely survive on the berries, wild meat, and fish on the reserve, and who could not leave without a pass.[110] The effects of the weight of government policy, and many of the other issues raised in this preliminary investigation, are all worthy of further in-depth study. Among topics and possible interpretations simply raised here that should be pursued are the demographics of the early reserve era — for instance, did females outnumber males, and what might be some of the implications of this? To what extent did the "traditional" roles and patterns of women continue, and to what extent were these altered? We know that a major goal of federal policy was to change the role of Aboriginal men and women, but it is not clear to what degree this actually happened. Each of the strategies and industries raised here, such as maple sugaring and tanning, would be topics worth exploring in greater depth. Was there significant interchange between Aboriginal women and the newcomer women? Aboriginal women and the pass system, and the larger question of relations with government authorities, could well be further pursued. Comparisons with northern Aboriginal women, and those of the older provinces of Canada, could provide valuable perspective. Even a cursory glance at annual reports of the DIA for reserves in Ontario suggests that the women of those settlements had greater scope and opportunity to pursue a variety of economic strategies than women on the prairies. Comparisons with other rural women could give rich insight into the similarities and variations of rural life in the West. Debates about farm women mirror those about Aboriginal women to some extent, with some studies portraying content and "empowered" women, and others depicting marginalized and powerless women. Such studies are needed in order to combat the negative images and distorted assumptions that regrettably persist and limit our understanding of the past, which has been impoverished by a failure to recognize and include the part played by Aboriginal women.

NOTES

1. Esther S. Goldfrank, *Changing Configurations in the Social Organization of a Blackfoot Tribe during the Reserve Period* (The Blood of Alberta, Canada), Monographs of the American Ethnological Society, No. 8, ed. A. Irving Hallowell (Seattle: University of Washington Press, 1945).
2. Ibid., 46.
3. Clark Wissler, *Red Man Reservations* (New York: Collier Books, 1938), 239.
4. Marla N. Powers, *Oglala Women: Myth, Ritual and Reality* (Chicago: University of Chicago Press, 1986).
5. Janet Mancini Billson, "Standing Tradition on Its Head: Role Reversal among Blood Indian Couples," *Great Plains Quarterly* 11, no. 1 (1991):3-21.
6. Patricia Albers, "Sioux Women in Transition: A Study of Their Changing Status in Domestic and Capitalist Sectors of Production," in *The Hidden Half: Studies of Plains Indian Women,* ed. Patricia Albers and Beatrice Medicine (Washington, DC: University Press of America, 1983).
7. Ibid., 190.
8. Carolyn Garrett Pool, "Reservation Policy and the Economic Position of Wichita Women," *Great Plains Quarterly* 8 (summer 1988):158-71.
9. Kathleen Jamieson, "Sex Discrimination and the Indian Act," in *Arduous Journey: Canadian Indians and Decolonization*, ed. J. Rick Ponting (Toronto: McClelland and Stewart).
10. Alan Klein, "The Political-Economy of Gender: A Nineteenth Century Plains Indian Case Study," in *The Hidden Half*, ed. Albers and Medicine, 143-73.
11. Beatrice Medicine, "Warrior Women: Sex Role Alternatives for Plains Indian Women," in *The Hidden Half*, ed. Albers and Medicine, 270, 274.
12. Pamela Margaret White, "Restructuring the Domestic Sphere — Prairie Indian Women on Reserves: Image, Ideology and State Policy, 1880-1930" (PhD dissertation, McGill University, 1987).
13. Sarah Deutsch, *No Separate Refuge: Culture, Class, and Gender on an Anglo-Hispanic Frontier in the American Southwest, 1880-1940* (New York: Oxford University Press, 1987).
14. Provincial Archives of Manitoba (PAM), Records of the Church Missionary Society (CMS), Charles Pratt Journal, May 1878.
15. National Archives of Canada (NA), Records Relating to Indian Affairs RG 10, vol. 3687, file 13,698, Frank L. Hunt to Edgar Dewdney, 16 March 1880 (emphasis in original).

16. Glenbow-Alberta Institute, Allen MacDonald Papers, James Scott to Allen MacDonald, 26 January 1880 (emphasis in original).
17. Isaac Cowie, *The Company of Adventures: A Narrative of Seven Years in the Service of the Hudson's Bay Company during 1867-1874 on the Great Buffalo Plains* (Toronto: William Briggs, 1913), 319.
18. N.M.W.J. McKenzie, *The Men of the Hudson's Bay Company* (Fort William: Times-Journal Presses, 1921), 62-63.
19. NA, RG 10, vol. 3745, file 29, 506-4, part 1, Dr. O.C. Edwards to MacDonald, 13 May 1884.
20. *Saskatchewan Herald* (Battleford), 6 February 1889, and Saskatchewan Archives Board (SAB), Annual Reports of the Women's Missionary Society of the Presbyterian Church, 1887-1956, file Hills Board School, typescript.
21. NA, RG 10, vol. 3720, file 23,325, Dewdney to L. Vankoughnet, 20 August 1880.
22. Ibid., vol. 3670, file 10,772, Peter Hourie to MacDonald, 28 December 1883; and vol. 3665, file 10,094, interpreter to Joseph Cauchon, 1 June 1878.
23. Joseph F. Dion, *My Tribe the Crees* (Calgary: Glenbow-Alberta Institute, 1979), 114.
24. Ibid., 116.
25. Ibid., 115-16.
26. SAB, Indian History Film Project, Marion Dillon, 23 July 1973.
27. Ibid.
28. Barry Kaye and D.W. Moodie, "The '*Psoralea*' Food Resources of the Northern Plains," *Plains Anthropologist* 23, no. 82, pt. 1 (1978):329.
29. Dion, *My Tribe the Crees*, 115.
30. Ibid.
31. SAB, Indian History Film Project, Marie Osecap, 3, 11 and 14 February 1974:2-3.
32. Ibid., 3.
33. Ibid.
34. Ibid., 4.
35. SAB, Indian History Film Project, Marion Dillon, 23 July 1973:10.
36. Fine Day, *My Cree People: A Tribal Handbook* (Invermere, B.C.: Good Medicine Books, 1973).
37. Dion, *My Tribe the Crees*, 115.
38. SAB, Indian History Film Project, Marion Carter, 30 July 1974.
39. *Regina Leader Post*, 24 April 1884.
40. Dion, *My Tribe the Crees*, 114.
41. Anna L. Leighton, *A Guide to Twenty Plants and Their Uses by the Cree* (Lac la Ronge Indian Band Education Branch 1983; revised 1986), 18.
42. Canada. House of Commons (CHC). *Sessional Papers*, vol. 31, no. 14 (1896), 290. For an excellent description of this process, see Saskatchewan Indian Arts and Crafts Advisory Committee, *Smoke Tanning: Traditional Indian Method of Preparing Animal Hides* (n.p., n.d.), which describes the smoke tanning of big game hides at Chitick Lake, Saskatchewan, in 1974.
43. Canada. *Senate Journals*. 1887, vol. 2, Appendix 1, Report and Minutes of Evidence of the Select Committee of the Senate on the Existing Natural Food Products of the North-West Territories, 34.
44. W. Gibson, "Homestead Venture, 1883-1892: An Ayrshire Man's Letters Home," *Saskatchewan History* 14, no. 3 (1961):108.
45. SAB, Indian History Film Project, Marie Osecap, 3, 11 February 1974:4.
46. NA, RG 10, vol. 3,845, file 73,406-7, T.P. Wadsworth to H. Reed, 17 February 1891.
47. Ibid., file 82,250-6, Wadsworth to Reed, 9 November 1891.
48. Eleanor Brass, "Miracle of Butter," *Leader-Post* (Regina), 28 June 1960.
49. Ibid.
50. Laurel Schenstead-Smith, "Subsistence and Economic Adaptation in the Onion Lake Agency, 1876-1920" (Master's thesis, University of Saskatchewan, 1983), 149-50.

51. CHC. *Sessional Papers*, vol. 23, no. 12 (1889), 144.
52. Thomas P. Myers, "An Examination of Central Plains Moccasins: Evidence of Adaptation to a Reservation Economy," *Plains Anthropologist* 32, no. 115 (February 1987).
53. Barbara A. Hail and Kate C. Duncan, eds., *Out of the North: The Subarctic Collection of the Haffenriffer Museum of Anthropology* (Brown University: Haffenriffer Museum of Anthropology, 1989), 33-34, 120-21, 213.
54. Mary Weekes, ed., *The Last Buffalo Hunter: As Told to Her by Norbert Welsh* (Toronto: Macmillan Co. Ltd., 1945), 291.
55. Emmy Preston, ed., *Pioneers of Grandview and District* (Steinbach, MB: Carillon Press, 1976), 102-03. Caroline's last name is not provided in this source.
56. Ruth Matheson Buck, *The Doctor Rode Side-Saddle* (Toronto: McClelland and Stewart, 1974), 96.
57. *Land of Red and White, 1875-1975* (Heinsburg: Frog Lake Community Club, 1976), 98.
58. François Adam, "Duhamel," *Alberta Folklore Quarterly* 1, no. 2 (1945):14-15.
59. W.H. Long, ed., *Fort Pelly Journal of Daily Occurrences 1863* (Regina: Regina Archaeological Society, 1987), 128.
60. SAB, Effie Storer Papers, unpublished manuscript, 24.
61. Mabel E. (Johnston) Plante, in *Prairie Grass to Mountain Pass: History of Pioneers of Pincher Creek and District* (Winnipeg: D.W. Friesen, 1974), 409.
62. *Moosomin: Century One Town and Country* (Altona, MB: D.W. Friesen, 1981), 4.
63. White, "Restructuring the Domestic Sphere," 268.
64. Ibid., 134-38.
65. SAB, Indian History Film Project, Marion Dillon.
66. NA, RG 10, vol. 3765, file 32,784, P.G. Williams to Reed, 31 December 1889.
67. Ibid., vol. 3845, file 73,406-8, Wadsworth to Reed, 7 March 1891.
68. Ibid., file 73,406-7, Wadsworth to Reed, 17 February 1891.
69. SAB, Indian History Film Project, Antoine Lonesinger, 21 November 1974.
70. Ibid., Marie Osecap, 2, 11 February 1974.
71. NA, RG 10, vol. 3845, file 73,406-9, Wadsworth to Reed, 8 April 1891.
72. Ibid.
73. White, "Restructuring the Domestic Sphere," 131-42.
74. *Toronto Daily Mail*, 2 March 1889.
75. CHC. *Sessional Papers*, vol. 23, no. 12, 145.
76. Ibid.
77. Mrs. George Cran, *A Woman in Canada* (London: John Milne, 1910), 106.
78. NA, RG 10, vol. 3859, file 82,250-6, Wadsworth to Reed, 9 November 1891.
79. Edward Ahenakew, *Voices of the Plains Cree* (Toronto: McClelland and Stewart, 1973), 112.
80. *Saskatchewan Herald* (Battleford), 5 January 1889.
81. White, "Restructuring the Domestic Sphere," 181-82.
82. Robert A. Trennert, "From Carlisle to Phoenix: The Rise and Fall of the Indian Outing System, 1878-1930," *Pacific Historical Review* 52, no. 3 (1983):267-91.
83. White, "Restructuring the Domestic Sphere," 188.
84. CHC. *Sessional Papers*, vol. 45, no. 27 (1911), 354.
85. Ibid., vol. 36, no. 27 (1901), 402.
86. NA, RG 10, vol. 9136, file 314-11, Inspector John Marshall's Report on the Qu'Appelle Industrial School, 1924.
87. Ibid.
88. Ibid., vol. 9137, file 312-4C, Sadie Bird to William M. Graham, 2 January 1929.
89. Ibid., Graham to Bird, 11 January 1929.
90. CHC. *Sessional Papers*, Report of the Commissioner of the North West Mounted Police for 1887, in *Law and Order Being the Official Reports to Parliament of the Activities of the Royal North*

West Mounted Police Force from 1886-87 (Toronto: Coles Publishing Company, 1973), 88.

91. Ida Blom, "Global Women's History: Organizing Principles and Cross-Cultural Understandings," in *Writing Women's History: International Perspectives*, ed. Karen Offen et al. (Bloomington: Indiana University Press, 1991), 136-37.

92. CHC. *Sessional Papers* (1889) in *The New West* (Toronto: Coles Publishing Company, 1973), 101.

93. *Saskatchewan Herald* (Battleford), 8 March 1886.

94. Ibid., 15 March 1886.

95. Ibid., 13 March 1888.

96. Ibid.

97. NA, RG 10, vol. 3673, file 10,986, clipping from the *Bulletin* (Edmonton), 7 January 1883.

98. Ibid., vol. 3727, file 25,167-2, Hourie to Indian commissioner, 27 May 1886.

99. CHC. *Sessional Papers*, vol. 11, no. 27 (1906), 82.

100. *Saskatchewan Herald* (Battleford), 4 July 1887.

101. NA, RG 18, Records of the North West Mounted Police, vol. 2181, file RCMP 1893, F.C. Gilchrist to W. Smith, 10 November 1893.

102. Chief John Snow, *These Mountains Are Our Sacred Places* (Toronto: Samuel Stevens and Co., 1977), 59.

103. NA, RG 10, vol. 3859, file 82,250-6, Wadsworth to Reed, 9 November 1891.

104. Ibid., RG 10, vol. 3609, file 3,334.

105. NA, Hayter Reed Papers, Chief Thunderchild to Hayter Reed, 15 July 1893.

106. Ibid., vol. 16, investigation into the conduct of Agent P.L. Clink, 1893.

107. Eleanor Brass, *I Walk in Two Worlds* (Calgary: Glenbow Museum, 1987), 36-37.

108. Ibid.

109. Jack Funk, ed., *"And They Told Us Their Stories": A Book of Indian Stories* (Saskatoon: Saskatoon District Tribal Council, 1991), 31.

110. Ibid., 32.

Life in Harmony with Nature

Beverly Hungry Wolf

While young and going to school on the Blood Indian Reserve in southern Alberta, I once gave a book report about choosing to live more simply, closer to nature. My inner self reacted to this book, and I developed a strong yearning for what I have come to think of as "life in harmony with nature." When I married my husband, twenty years ago, we decided to use this as our family theme.

From my Native ancestors I inherited a special closeness to the land. They treated the Earth like a mother. In our traditional Native view of the world, everything is parallel to nature. When a human child is born, it gets its nourishment directly from its mother, just as other animals get nourishment from their mothers. When a child no longer gets its food from its mother, it will get food from its surroundings, and most of this food comes directly from the Earth. The Earth is thought of as Mother because she provides all that we need, and she is deeply revered. Traditionally our people have great respect for women because women create life.

I have seen my Elders receive the first saskatoon of the season. This berry is not just gobbled down; it is taken and held in the air, and a prayer is said. It is then put in the ground as an offering, or as an act of communion with the Earth Mother. When I have picked healing plants with my grandmother, I have seen her put a pinch of tobacco into the ground, praying and giving thanks that this plant was made available so that it could be used for healing. Nothing was taken for granted. It was in this way that my ancestors were able to live in harmony with their surroundings. The Earth as Mother has nurtured all people, in the same way that I as mother have nurtured my own children. This knowledge is part of that special closeness that I feel for nature.

From my tribal grandmothers I learned our ancient legend that tells how the Earth had female origins. They said that long, long ago the Earth was covered by water. Napi — the mythical Old Man of our people — was floating on this water with four different animals. He sent them down, deep under this water, one at a time, telling each one to bring up some Earth. The first three drowned in their attempts, but the fourth one — a female muskrat — managed to come back with a bit of Earth between her paws. Napi then used his magic to make the Earth grow. The male and female powers! When I look at the sources of the various religious functions of the Blackfoot people, I see that most of them were handed down to women. The Okan (Sun Dance sponsorship) was given to a woman who married a Star; when she got lonely, her husband told her she could go home, and with her he sent the Okan. The Beaver Bundle Ceremony was given to a woman who lived with a Beaver and then came back to her husband. The Medicine Pipe Ceremony was given to the wife of Thunder, who was a mortal. One day he asked her if she would like to visit her family, and when she said yes, he told her that she could go and stay with her parents, while he went to his winter home. He told her, "Before you go I will teach you the songs for my pipe and you will teach it to your parents and they will keep my pipe and welcome me back when they first hear me in the spring." The Iniskim is another sacred thing that was given to women. This sacred stone was used for calling buffalo and bringing good luck.

The ceremonies were given by the spirit people to women, and women shared them with men. Women's daily roles were quite different from men's, though they were interdependent. In all our important tribal ceremonies, women play an equal part with men, and most ceremonies would not take place without women. Usually, it is the woman who has the job, morning and evening, of making incense for the bundle; she also has the job of taking the bundle outside every morning and bringing it in every evening. And she has her role to play when it is time to open the bundle. There are specific songs that are sung for her. When it comes time to unbundle the pipe, that, too, is her job.

With the coming of Christian missionaries, the women of my people lost our status as equals. A new faith was forced upon us, and in that faith we women were forever condemned because of some biblical woman named Eve! We were made to feel somehow responsible for the loss of everlasting happiness. The Christian Church teaches that the first two people lived in a beautiful garden named Eden. In this garden was a fruit tree, and the Creator told them they could eat anything in the garden, except the fruit from this tree. Eve then took a fruit from the tree and fed it to Adam. For this they were driven from the garden, and once out of the garden they would know all kinds of hard times. So, women have been given this extra load of guilt to carry. We were made responsible for humans being driven from Eden, where all was peaceful and there was no such thing as sickness, starvation, or strife.

Fortunately, the culture of my ancestors is very strong; our ceremonies for men and women have survived, and in them there is still the understanding that as the children of the Earth Mother we are equals. Life in harmony with nature is still a respected ideal, although nowadays it is hard to live according to that ideal.

For a long time after my people settled on their reserve they managed to prac-tise most of their culture and make a simple living that was close to nature. Each family had its own garden, perhaps a milk cow, chickens, pigs; and they farmed their own fields. From the 1890s until I was a young girl, in the 1950s, Blood families lived without causing much harm to the environment.

Then the government decided that our lives should become "more efficient." They arranged for non-Native farmers to work most of our land, producing consid-erably more than we ever had. Some of the profit from this was given to us — a very small part. Each family was given one big cheque a year, and this money did not last nearly a whole year. Our people no longer went outdoors to work. We didn't grow our own food any more; instead we went to the store.

It seemed that the government wanted to make Native people dependent upon them. We ended up with institutionalized poverty. Limited financial opportunities on the Reserve forced those who stayed to struggle for money to support their families. And, in the process, life in harmony with nature has become harder than ever to locate.

Yet, my people are far more fortunate in our desire for such a life than much of the world's poorer struggling folk. There are many people in the world who have no place to call home, and never will. Some of these people live outside all the time in alleys, under bridges, or in parks. When these people are fortunate enough to find jobs, they have to pay constantly just to have a roof over their heads with no hope of even a little garden to grow their own food. What they don't spend on rent will go to the local grocery store.

The Blood Reserve is our inherited land base, guaranteed by treaty never to be taken away. It surprises me that our politicians have not set up feed lots for cows and pigs, and that there is no place on the Reserve where we can go to buy our own eggs and chickens. It is not only a land base that can grow wonderful food, but it is also a place rich with sacred seeds sown through countless rituals and ceremonies held there by our ancestors, down through the ages. We should learn, again, to be self-sufficient. We should encourage each other again to try growing our own crops, reaping the spiritual harvests, moving back towards harmony with nature. Striving to be self-sufficient develops inner strength and pride. Getting back to being self-sufficient would bring us back to nature, where our ancestors (of all races and tribes) spent their whole lives.

By growing our own food we would help to cut down the amounts of chemi-cals used in the world. We would know exactly what we are eating and where it came from. We would no longer encourage ourselves to buy Big Macs just be-cause they are convenient. We would wonder of what Big Macs are *really* made, knowing that producing and processing just the meat in them causes the destruction of vital rain forests somewhere far from our own homes, not to mention the lives of Native people who live in these forests.

The use of disposable diapers is as popular among Native mothers as among any others. Yet, by using them, we cause great harm to our inherited relationship with nature. When they are dirty, we throw them away someplace, not realizing it will take up to 500 years for each one of them to fully disappear! We're lucky if some neighbourhood dog doesn't fool around with one of them first, maybe later coming by to lick our kids or get a nuzzle. I have heard that these disposable (or, should I say, un-disposable) diapers are the cause of the spread of polio.

Native people seem to suffer a lot from illnesses, many of which are new to us and have no traditional treatments, so we go to clinics and hospital doctors, where we are most often given a drug prescription, which we then faithfully take. This is not life in harmony with nature. This is chemical dependency, part of that same institutionalized poverty that I mentioned earlier. The government fosters this further by paying for all those drugs. It is widely known among Native people that we do not have the best of health care. Some of our doctors just don't care. It's easier for them to give a prescription than it is to really search for the true cause of the illness. As a youngster I would go to the clinic a lot to get out of school. I would tell the doctors my ailments, and each week I would be given a new bottle of pills. Not once do I remember getting a blood test, nor did the doctors ever question my sincerity. It was made very easy for me because I did not have to pay for the medication. Sure, we have ailments that are truly helped by drugs. But I think we've been given far more drugs than our ailments ever required. One of my dearest grandmothers was a victim of this practice. She started to get sick. She was told she was diabetic, and they gave her the medicine for this, which she took for several years only to find that the symptoms did not go away. In the end, we found that she was not diabetic at all, but the drugs had caused a lot of other damage. When I moved off-reserve and had to pick my own doctor, I told him of my distrust of drugs made from chemicals. I was surprised by his answer. He told me I was right to distrust such drugs. He said I could cure an ailment with a pill but I could not guarantee there will be no side effects. Many of our people suffer from chemical dependency because they put all their faith in their doctors. We must remember that doctors are only human and are subject to the same cultural conditioning as other people are. If their culture tells them not to care about Natives, they will treat them accordingly. I know now, however, if we feel that a doctor is not doing the right thing, we have the right to a second opinion.

Speaking only amongst us women, I realize that we have abdicated our position of equality and let men rule us. But I say that we are not powerless! It is now time to reclaim our position. As givers of life, we can reclaim our special closeness to nature and the Earth Mother any time we want it! Think about this, then speak out your feelings. You have an obligation to think about this; you have a right to be heard.

Mothers should teach their sons and daughters from the moment of birth to have reverence for nature and the Earth Mother. We must speak out loudly about healing our Earth Mother. This has to be started in our homes. Instead of trying so hard to live like "white people," let us look to some of our old ways, some of which can still be of use today. Children must learn early about the harmful consequences of living with constant material desires. They must learn that our present "throwaway society" is doomed; that they will be best off learning not to be a part of it. Food, diapers, dwellings, and automobiles; look around you and see how much of these are being wasted.

We mothers should not only teach our children about environmental concerns, but we should also alert our communities. We should campaign that all community decisions be based first and foremost upon their effects on the environment. Our ancestors moved with the seasons, so they did not overuse a piece of land. In those days, they did not own piles of things, but, whenever something had to be discarded, it was offered back to nature. Old tipis were weighed down in the water; children who had outgrown clothes were painted, and then their clothes were tied in a tree or put on a rock as an offering. These are just some of our old ways.

What I have said here comes to me in part from my Blood and Blackfoot grandmothers. Some of my comments about nature are directed to my Native sisters and the Native daughters who are coming after us. But my message is directed to a wider audience as well. It is the same as that of concerned mothers everywhere in the world: As givers of life, we women have a special relationship to the Earth. As mothers, we know what a hard time we have to bring life into the world and then to be responsible for that life, from then on. So we can see how hard the Earth Mother's job is, for she is a much greater giver of life for all of us, including the people of every tribe and nation.

Maybe you think all this sounds like "fancy talk"; you've got no time for it while looking after your kids, cooking for the household, maintaining the daily struggle. But all that effort will be useless if our abuse of nature keeps growing until the Earth Mother stops giving life. Let's learn how to be good to our Earth Mother!

An Examination of Sport for Aboriginal Females on the Six Nations Reserve, Ontario, from 1968 to 1980

Vicky Paraschak

Sport can be defined as a social practice, where human expression occurs within "structured possibilities" (Gruneau 1983). As a social practice, sport creates and confirms a particular subjective reality (Geertz 1983) in keeping with the dominant cultural form. In EuroAmerican society, female participation in sport is trivialized, or devalued, maintaining the masculinized connotations associated with sport (Birrell 1988). This takes shape, for instance, through the small number of sport opportunities available to women in relation to men, and the lack of recognition given to females compared with males. Thus, sport operates as a significant symbolic force in female subordination to males, reinforcing patriarchal values.

Sport is also, however, an area in which values, ideologies, and meanings may be contested (Donnelly 1988). Resistance to the dominant subjective reality may arise, and cultural practices emerge and exist alongside the dominant cultural form, offering alternatives to it. Emergent sport practices need to be examined, to see if they reproduce or challenge the power relations that exist in society (Douglas 1988), since these practices can support, or at least not contradict, other elements within the dominant culture (Williams 1980, cited in Donnelly 1988).

Recent reviews on gender and sport (Birrell 1988), and race relations theories and sport (Birrell 1989), have noted the dearth of information on women of colour. An examination of the literature on Aboriginal women's sport supports this statement. There is a scarcity of research on Aboriginal athletes and sport within North America generally. However, when the issue of gender is considered, the record shows an even greater absence of information on Aboriginal women athletes. Thus, little is written about the "structured possibilities" that exist for Aboriginal women in sport, and/or how closely the power relations underlying these practices mirror those of the dominant sport system.

The absence of women in the literature on Aboriginal sport demonstrates their insignificance within the sport realm. This perception is reinforced by existing

Aboriginal awards for sport achievement, which have in the past failed to recognize female athletes. There are two very different explanations as to why female athletes are largely absent in the literature on Aboriginal sport, and from Aboriginal awards for sport excellence. Perhaps women are not involved in sport. Or, perhaps, there is a systematic bias at work in the reporting and recognition given to Aboriginal women within the sport realm, comparable to that which occurs for EuroAmerican women.

In this paper, I take a first step toward addressing the issue. I present an initial review of the literature on Aboriginal sport, along with an examination of Aboriginal awards for sport achievement, to support the premise that Aboriginal females *appear* to have an insignificant involvement in sport. I then present a case study of women's sport on the Six Nations Reserve, which examines the nature and extent of female involvement in sport from 1968 to 1980. I also include recommendations for further study to help point to some steps that would more fully illuminate the nature of Aboriginal women's sport.

I chose the Six Nations Reserve in Ontario as a case study since previous work on their organized sport system (1964 to 1989) had indicated the ongoing presence of women's sport. The data that I gleaned through their community newspaper, the *Tekawennake*, for the period 1968 to 1980[1] clearly indicates extensive involvement by women in a variety of sports. Sport biographies that could be composed from newspaper accounts also suggest that some of these athletes have had outstanding sport careers. These data lend support to my hypothesis that a systematic negative bias in terms of recognition may be at work in Aboriginal women's sport.

ABORIGINAL WOMEN ATHLETES: AN INSIGNIFICANT PRESENCE?

An overview of sport history conferences and journal articles on Aboriginal sport suggests that Aboriginal athletes within mainstream sport, and at times the literature recording Aboriginal sport involvement, have been marked by racism, exploitation, and ethnocentric distortion (Paraschak 1989, 58). This record may also have been marked by sexism, since only one of the thirty-two articles available for this review pertained to Aboriginal female athletes.

This pattern of omission of Aboriginal women in sport is reflected in overviews on Aboriginal sport completed by Ward Churchill et al. (1979), Zeman (1988), and Oxendine (1988). The historical overview of twentieth-century Native American athletics completed by Churchill et al. focusses primarily on male athletes attending the Carlisle or Haskell Indian schools, without mention of what Aboriginal girls were playing in those institutions. The minimal coverage of female athletes in this review includes a note on Angelita Rosal, who was an international-calibre table-tennis player, and a mention of three "promising" women in track and field

(Churchill et al. 1979, 32). This overview was slightly improved upon in a docu-fiction published on famous Canadian Native athletes, in that one of the twelve chapters dealt with Aboriginal females (Zeman 1988).

A 300-page overview by Oxendine strongly reinforces this pattern of omission. Oxendine's book, which purports to examine the Native American sport heritage from before European contact to the present day, includes a mere five-page section entitled "Sports for Women and Girls" (1988, 22-26). Oxendine briefly mentions female involvement in horse racing, double ball, lacrosse, fastball, and basketball (22, 298-99), then includes an entire section on sport programs at the Carlisle and Haskell Indian schools with no mention of female sport involvement. The fifty-one biographies of famous Aboriginal athletes he provides in his text, from 1890 to the present, were also all male. Women were clearly notable in his book by their absence! After reading these overviews, one is left with the impression that Aboriginal females have not been active or noteworthy in sport.

The few articles that have been written specifically on Aboriginal women in sport dispute the claim that women are inactive or obscure in sport. Craig (1973) and Cheska (1974) both note the traditional involvement of women in ancient tribal games, noting their particular affinity toward ball games such as double ball. They also recognize Aboriginal women's current involvement in the popular sports of basketball, softball, track, and rodeo (Cheska 1974, 23; Craig 1973, 12).

Craig disputes the fact that Aboriginal women are not notable as athletes when she outlines four successful individuals involved in trick riding, cross-country running, and international-calibre basketball and table tennis. She also provides support for the idea that sports involvement is not at odds with an Aboriginal girl's gender identity. As examples of this, she notes that family and friends are very supportive of and interested in female athletes, that female athletes are considered leaders at the Albuquerque Indian School, and that "femininity" does not seem to be an issue for Native female athletes (Craig 1973, 10-11). These claims support the idea that Aboriginal girls have considered sport to be an attractive activity.

Zeman (1988) includes the Firth twins, Sharon and Shirley, among her twelve accounts of Canadian Aboriginal athletes. These athletes participated in four Olympics before retiring from World Cup competition in 1984 (105-06). They received early support from their mother. She encouraged them to get involved with the cross-country ski program in Inuvik (102) even though that involvement took them far from their home over extended periods of time. The Firth twins thus serve as examples of outstanding female Aboriginal athletes who were given support by family during their sporting careers.

When we examine Aboriginal sport awards, we note the perception that Aboriginal females are invisible. The Tom Longboat Award, for example, has been given annually in Canada since 1951 to Indian athletes who display outstanding examples of character, leadership, and "sportsmanship." However, in the first twenty-three years of its existence, only one Aboriginal woman was a recipient: Phyllis Bomberry in 1968 (Littlechild 1975, Appendix F). Similarly, there has been only one female, Angelita Rosal, out of fifty-seven inductees into the American Indian Hall of Fame from its inception in 1972 until 1985 (Oxendine 1988, Table 14.1). The American Indian Hall of Fame honours persons who have brought distinction through sports to themselves and the Indian community (Oxendine 1988, 282).

Several writers (Littlechild 1975; Ballem 1983; Zeman 1988; Oxendine 1988) have stressed the need for Aboriginal role models. The failure of Aboriginal people to identify outstanding female athletes through established awards either supports the hypothesis that Aboriginal females are not active and/or competent in sport, or it points to a systematic bias by Aboriginal people themselves against females in sport. In either case, the lack of recognizable female role models in sport does a disservice to Aboriginal girls who might aspire to be athletes.

The presence of a systematic bias against Indian women has been seen in another realm of Aboriginal life. Research on Aboriginal women in Canadian society has tended to focus on Section 12(1)(b) of the Indian Act, which discriminated against Indian women on the grounds of race, sex, and marital status (Jamieson 1978, 1). In 1985, Bill C-31 was passed, which "provide[s] either first-time instatement or reinstatement to persons who either lost or were denied status as a result of discriminatory elements of the *Indian Act*" (Ontario Women's Directorate 1987, Appendix on Terminology, 1).

Even within an account of this struggle, there is evidence of the importance of sport in the lives of Aboriginal women. Silman (1987) provides several accounts by Aboriginal women of their lives growing up on the reserve. Games and sports were often mentioned as a positive aspect of their upbringing (39, 70, 88). Perhaps the most telling story is told by Mavis Goeres, who became concerned about the loss of status that Indian women faced upon marrying non-Indian men. She stated:

Another thing that hurt me regards my youngest daughter, Susan. She is very, very active in sport, very good in teams. When it came to Indian Summer Games, they said, "You can't play because you're non-status. You're not an Indian." I said, "My God, she's got as much Indian in her as a lot of them here." That's when I really got mad. I think the anger and hurt is what pushed us on, too. It wasn't only happening to my daughter, but to other women's daughters *and* sons. I protested and the *Toronto Star* did a story on my Susan and on Mary (Two-Axe) Early, showing how 12(1)(b) affected both their generations. (Silman 1987, 219)

This account indicates that both sport and sexism have been significant aspects in the lives of some Aboriginal women.

CASE STUDY: FEMALE INVOLVEMENT IN ORGANIZED SPORT
ON THE SIX NATIONS RESERVE, 1968 TO 1980

When we examine organized sport on the Six Nations Reserve, we see that Aboriginal women are indeed actively involved. The Six Nations Reserve, located in southwestern Ontario, is the largest Indian community in Canada (Ontario Native Women's Association 1988, 24), with a population of approximately 7,000 Indians from six different Iroquoian tribes. Women account for slightly more than one-half (52.3 percent) of the total Aboriginal population in Ontario (Ontario Women's Directorate 1987, 6). Accordingly, there would be a fairly large number of women on the reserve from which to draw potential athletes.

A small village, Ohsweken, is located in the centre of the reserve. Approximately 400 people live there. All of the businesses and several of the recreation facilities are located in Ohsweken. The reserve has an arena (opened in 1974), two ball diamonds, a school gymnasium, and a community hall available for various recreational activities (Henhawk 1987).

An analysis of their involvement, focussing on the period between 1968 and 1980, indicates an ongoing presence of Aboriginal females as participants in and organizers of a variety of sports. These athletes participated in an extensive sport system that included both EuroAmerican and all-Indian competitions. In this case study I examine the nature of that participation, in terms of: (1) the variety of sports played; (2) the extent of the sport system; and (3) the sport roles adopted by the women. I then provide some examples of women who have been active in sport on the reserve during this period; specifically, I give brief biographies of women who have had outstanding sport careers.

Data for this case study have been collected primarily from the community newspaper entitled the *Tekawennake Reporter,* which I examined for the years from early 1968 to the end of 1980. The *Tekawennake* is a reserve-based newspaper that began circulation in 1968[2] and was published twice a month during the time I examined it. Accounts of women's participation in sport were consistently included, and there were no derogatory or sexist references made. This pattern is not consistent with newspaper and magazine coverage of mainstream women's sport, which is known to be both scarce and sexist in nature (Coakley 1990, 289-92).

I examined 248 issues of the *Tekawennake*. Over the years, seventy-eight percent (193) of them included information on women's sport. The yearly percentage of issues including women's sport ranged from 100 percent (for the last three years examined) to fifty percent in 1972 (the first time that a sports editor was present). Coaches were usually counted upon to provide information for the sports section during these twelve years. This newspaper data base was supplemented with information previously gleaned from community Recreation Committee files.

VARIETY OF SPORTS PLAYED

The sport involvement of women on the Six Nations Reserve during the time I studied it was far more broad than the existing literature might indicate. According to this literature, basketball, softball/fastball, horseback riding, cross-country running, and lacrosse were undertaken on the reserve. Additional sports, mentioned in newspaper accounts, however, included badminton, baton twirling, bowling (both five- and ten-pin), broomball, figure skating, golf, hockey, karate, billiards, track and field, speed skating, tennis, and volleyball.

Sports for women varied in the length of time they endured and in the participation base that was fostered on the reserve. For example, women participated in softball/fastball, hockey, bowling, and track and field throughout the period under consideration. Added to these sports was figure skating, which maintained a broad participation base from its inception as a reserve-based club in 1975. Other sports — including karate, speed skating, baton twirling, and badminton — were linked to specific competitors and did not appear to have an ongoing participation base on the reserve. Meanwhile, school sports, including basketball, cross-country running, track and field, and volleyball, maintained an ongoing though transient participation base among the school population.

Informal interviews with members on the reserve have shown the presence of other women's sports, too, although not necessarily in the period under consideration. Archery was a very popular sport for both men and women before I began this study. More recently, individual women have been active in professional wrestling, roller derby, barrel racing, harness racing, and professional ballet. There is also a dance studio on the reserve, which has been active for several years, involving both males and females. Clearly, the variety of sports undertaken by female members of this reserve is much greater than has been suggested in the literature.

EXTENT OF THE SPORTS SYSTEM

Existing literature has paid little attention to the sports settings within which Aboriginal women participate, which can be either all-Indian or EuroAmerican in nature. Susan B. Craig (1973) briefly notes the involvement of women athletes at all-Indian schools. And Oxendine indirectly refers to the existence of all-Indian competitions when he notes that the National Indian Activities Association (NIAA) was founded in 1974 to conduct national championships in basketball for Indian teams, both male and female (Oxendine 1988, 299). He also notes the formation of the Iroquois national women's lacrosse team in 1984 (298).

Both of these examples represent a sports setting restricted to Indian participants. This participation base is enforced through membership rules. For example, the letter of invitation for the Open Women's Fast Pitch National Championship of the NIAA in 1980 states: "You must be at least one-quarter degree of Indian blood in order to compete in this tournament. In registering, each applicant must provide positive proof of Indian ancestry and submit documentation" (Kays 1980). Restrictive membership criteria are found in most all-Indian tournaments, including some competitions that make allowance for a set number of non-Indian players to participate on each team.

The majority of accounts in the literature on Aboriginal women's sport note athletes who participate in mainstream sport systems, such as the Firth twins or Angelita Rosal. This may reflect a bias in the literature on Aboriginal sport generally, in that the athletes who are deemed to be "successful" are those who have "made it" in EuroAmerican sport competitions at an international or professional level. This pattern is also evident in Aboriginal sport awards — the two women who had won awards, Phyllis Bomberry and Angelita Rosal, both achieved their success solely within the EuroAmerican sport system.

My examination of the newspaper accounts between 1968 and 1980 revealed a broad system of sport for Aboriginal women on the Six Nations Reserve. Competitive environments consisted of both all-Indian and EuroAmerican settings. All-Indian settings included intra-reserve leagues and tournaments at the inter-reserve, provincial, national, and international levels. Meanwhile, EuroAmerican settings included leagues at the inter-school and regional levels, and tournaments or league championships at the provincial, national, and international levels. It is interesting to note that individual athletes and sports teams often played simultaneously in EuroAmerican leagues and all-Indian tournaments.

School teams tended to compete against other schools on the reserve as well as enter into leagues involving the surrounding communities. In two of these sports — basketball and cross-country running — there was also mention of competitions against all-Indian teams who were not in the immediate vicinity. Only one competitor was mentioned at the university level — Cathy Porter, who played badminton for McMaster University.

Individual athletes participating in club sports on the reserve participated in both intra-club and inter-club competitions. Two examples of such clubs are the Six Nations Figure Skating Club and the Saddle Club. Individual athletes who were involved in clubs off the reserve participated in EuroAmerican events such as baton twirling, speed skating, and figure skating.[3] A karate club, which had both male and female members, existed for only a short while on the reserve.

A number of sports teams were formed on the reserve and then competed as a team in regional EuroAmerican leagues. Examples of this are the Ohsweken Women Warriors in broomball, several teams in softball/fastball ranging in level from Lassies through to Senior B Fastball, junior and senior hockey teams competing in three regional leagues, and both bantam and juvenile girls' lacrosse teams.

Six Nations teams consistently won both regional and provincial league championships. During the period under consideration, the lacrosse teams won three regional and two provincial titles, the hockey teams won four regional league titles, and the softball/fastball teams won nine league titles, nine separate provincial titles, and several league Most Valuable Player (MVP) awards. These teams clearly established a winning tradition.

Softball/fastball teams formed on the reserve would also enter all-Indian tournaments, where they excelled. For example, the Ohsweken Mohawks, a fastball team, not only won the Senior B championship in a EuroAmerican league, but also had members on the winning Canadian Native Ladies softball team and the North American Native fastball championship team in 1979. They subsequently hosted the Canadian Native fastball tournament in 1980. It is interesting to note that softball was the only sport mentioned that was also played at longhouse gatherings and at Indian gatherings celebrating their heritage — both of which are traditional Indian settings.

Individuals from the reserve would often play on other teams in their preferred sports, where, as Aboriginal athletes, they were in the minority. Examples are Bev Beaver and Helen Lickers, who both played on championship hockey teams off the reserve, and Phyllis Bomberry, who played fastball for the Canadian Championship team in 1967 and 1968.

Leagues were also set up for reserve members in bowling, billiards, and golf, even though these leagues usually utilized facilities off the reserve. Bowling was by far the most popular league, with ongoing newspaper reports on the weekly high single and high triple winners, as well as the year-end club champions. Besides the bowling league championships, there was a well-developed all-Indian tournament, as there was for golf as well, both of which began in the 1960s. Competitions in these sports were developed between reserves throughout Ontario, and across Canada and North America. Billiards, on the other hand, remained a local league, and it attracted interested women to the sponsoring bar on a regular basis.

It is clear that a broad system for sport existed. Aboriginal athletes could choose to enter only all-Indian tournaments and local leagues, but more often they participated in non-Indian competitions. Teams from the reserve tended to enter EuroAmerican regional leagues, while individual Aboriginal athletes tended to join a EuroAmerican team or club in order to compete in the mainstream sport system.

SPORT ROLES

The literature on Aboriginal women and sport deals with them almost exclusively in the role of athlete. There is a passing reference in Craig's article to two Aboriginal athletes who returned to coach other Aboriginal women: Pauline Pino, who majored at university in physical education; and Dixie Woodall, who gained international fame as a basketball player (1973, 12). An examination of the Six Nations Reserve, however, shows that women were involved in a variety of roles, including that of athlete, coach, supporter, recreation committee member and executive board member for voluntary sports organizations. Women apparently did not take on the role of referee, a trend that is evident for males as well as females on the reserve. For example, the only umpire clinic that was ever held on the reserve, in April 1987, attracted only two individuals (Six Nations Recreation Committee File: Recreation/Fairgrounds M-Z).

Clearly, most references made in the newspaper pertained to Aboriginal women as athletes. However, female coaches were mentioned for basketball, softball, lacrosse, and figure skating. All of these coaches had first played as athletes in their sport, and several of these individuals were still playing themselves while they coached.

The *Tekawennake* contains many references during the period under consideration to the community support for minor sport. One notable example is the Mothers' Auxiliary for Minor Athletics (MAMAs), which was established to provide support for minor sports. This group of mothers accepted responsibility for hosting officials and visiting teams as early as 1969. They also donated trophies for both boys' and girls' teams, including the two trophies donated in 1978 to the girls' lacrosse team.[4]

The Recreation Committee, which was established in 1964 to co-ordinate and financially support existing sport organizations on the reserve (Six Nations Recreation Committee, 29 December 1964), also included women members during the period of my study. Some of the members were local female athletes, such as Sandra (Hill) Jamieson (on the committee in 1972 and 1975) and Winnie Thomas (1980). Other female members included Claudine VanEvery (1970) and Carolyn Beaver (1979). While female members were in the minority (usually one or two members per eight people on the committee) they remained an ongoing presence on the Recreation Committee. It eventually became a policy of the committee that one of the six members elected from the community must be a woman (Six Nations Council, 19 July 1978), suggesting a sensitivity to the need for both male and female representation.

There was also evidence of frequent women's involvement on the executive boards of both male and female sports organizations during the time of my investigation. Women served in various capacities, including president, treasurer, and secretary, on several different sport organizations. Executive members were often mothers of athletes, although there was also evidence of athletes who accepted administrative roles in their own sports, such as Doris Henhawk, who was secretary for the Bowling Association while still playing in the 1960s.

SPORT BIOGRAPHIES OF SOME PROMINENT
FEMALE ATHLETES

A brief examination of some career highlights of five female athletes from the reserve helps to substantiate the premise that Aboriginal women not only played, but also excelled, in sport. Each of these women was at one time nominated by the reserve for the Tom Longboat Award in recognition of her successful sport career. They were active in sport during the period of my study, although these biographies are not restricted to that time frame.

Bev Beaver was an outstanding athlete in three sports (fastball, hockey, and bowling) in both all-Indian and EuroAmerican sport systems. In fastball, for example, she won the MVP award eight times between the years of 1962 and 1980. In 1979, she was named best pitcher, top batter, and MVP at the Canadian Native championship, as well as all-star pitcher at the North American Native Ladies championship. In hockey, she competed only in the EuroAmerican sport system. She won five MVP awards from 1966 to 1980, and was the top scorer in the league in five different years. In bowling, meanwhile, she maintained high female average or had high triple score for the Six Nations Bowling League in all but one year between 1969 and 1974. She also competed in all-Indian tournaments, and had high triple score in the Ontario Indian Bowling Championship in 1973. She was awarded the regional Tom Longboat medal,[5] as the outstanding Indian athlete of southern Ontario, in 1967 (*Tekawennake,* 20 June 1980, 8).

Ruth Hill was involved in only one sport, fastball, but is notable because of her longevity as a successful pitcher. She began her career competing as a member of the Ohsweken Mohawks fastball team as a teenager. In 1964, she was asked to go with the EuroAmerican Toronto Carpetland team to the World Championship in Florida, where she was named the best pitcher of the tournament. She later pitched for the Syracuse all-Indian Red Jackets in another world championship, where her eighteen strikeouts in twenty-one innings was one short of the women's world record. In 1969, after twenty years of pitching, she still had an average of 13.4 strikeouts per game, and her career continued into 1979, when she pitched at the Canadian Native Fastball Championship (*Tekawennake,* 20 June 1980, 9). She was nominated for the Tom Longboat Award by the Recreation Committee in 1965 (Six Nations Recreation Committee Minutes, 12 July 1965).

Phyllis Bomberry is notable as the first female recipient of the Tom Longboat Award, which she won in 1969. She was a fastball catcher on the EuroAmerican Canadian senior women's softball championship team in 1967 and 1968 (the Toronto Carpetland Senior A team). She was also the top batter at the 1967 championships and the all-star catcher for Canada in 1967 and 1968. She was on the Ontario senior women's championship team in 1967 and 1968 (*Tekawennake,* 17 September 1968) and played with that team when they won the gold medal at the Canada Games in 1969.

Helen Lickers is noted for her successful careers in fastball and hockey. She began playing as a catcher for the Ohsweken Mohawks in 1972. After winning the rookie of the year award, she was recognized as the best catcher in the same regional EuroAmerican league in 1973. In 1979 she was recognized as best catcher and as having the most runs batted in at the Canadian Native Championship, and was named the all-star catcher at the North American Native championship (*Tekawennake*, 20 June 1980, 8). She was a member of the Ohsweken Mohawks, a senior tier-2 women's softball team, when they won the Canadian Native women's softball tournament from 1982 to 1985 (Six Nations Recreation Committee Minutes, 21 November 1985). Her involvement in hockey took place within the EuroAmerican sport system. She was named the league MVP in 1975 and 1976 (*Tekawennake*, 20 June 1980, 8), and, while playing with the Hamilton Golden Hawks Senior A team in 1987, she won the Canadian championship and was involved in an international tournament. That same team won the Ontario championship in 1983 and 1984, and came in third, then second, in the Canadian senior women's hockey championship in those years. She also played to a Canadian championship in 1983 with the Burlington senior women's team.

Helen Lickers has contributed to sport in other capacities as well. She has served as treasurer for the Ohsweken Mohawks since 1985 and was described as a willing volunteer for organizing minor sports tournaments on the reserve (Six Nations Recreation Committee Minutes, 21 November 1985). She was nominated by the Recreation Committee for the Tom Longboat Award in 1985.

Doris Henhawk began her sports career playing second base for the Ohsweken Mohawks, but her notable contributions were made in the years since, when she coached numerous girls in softball. During her playing career for the Mohawks from 1952 to 1962, the team won three Ontario championships in the EuroAmerican intermediate women's competitions. She was also successful as an athlete in the reserve bowling league in 1969 and 1970. In 1976 she had the women's low net score in golf at the North American Indian golf tournament (*Tekawennake*, 8 July 1976).

Doris Henhawk's coaching career has taken place within the EuroAmerican sport system. She began coaching the bantam girls' team in 1973, and in 1974 she, her husband, and another man started minor softball for both boys and girls on the reserve. While serving on the minor softball executive from 1974 to 1983, she coached bantam, midget, and junior girls' teams and won the Ontario rural softball A championships four times. The teams she coached also won their division in the Haldimand women's league for three of those years, and they won the bronze medal at the Ontario Summer Games in 1976. She was assistant coach for the all-star Ontario junior women's softball team, which won a gold medal in the 1985 Canada Summer Games (Six Nations Recreation Committee Minutes, 21 November 1985), and was assistant coach for the Ontario team, which competed at the Canada Games in 1989. She was awarded the Tom Longboat regional medal in 1985.

These five women have had outstanding careers in sport. As athletes, they have competed in both EuroAmerican leagues and all-Indian tournaments, in many cases over an extended period. They have been successful in a variety of sports. As well, some of these athletes have chosen to contribute to sport as volunteers in other ways, such as coaching or serving in an administrative capacity. Their careers lay to rest the myth that Aboriginal female athletes are not worthy of recognition.

RECOMMENDATIONS FOR FURTHER STUDY

My examination of organized sport on the Six Nations Reserve from 1968 to 1980 shows an ongoing presence of Aboriginal females as participants and organizers in a broad variety of sports. These women participated in reserve leagues, organized leagues off the reserve, and national and international tournaments. Their participation occurred in both EuroAmerican and all-Indian contexts, and several women excelled in their chosen sports. My study indicates that Aboriginal women athletes are both active in and worthy of recognition in the realm of sport. The data support the hypothesis that, as for women in the non-Aboriginal context, there may be systematic biases at work against Aboriginal women in sport that lead to a lack of recognition in sport literature and award structures.

Little is recorded about women of colour in sport. In this paper I begin to address that gap by examining the intersection of race and gender as it relates to Aboriginal women in sport. Further research on Aboriginal female athletes is clearly warranted. It would not only contribute to the existing literature on Aboriginal female athletes but would also enhance the study of women in sport generally, which has focussed primarily on the experiences of young, white, middle-class women.

In EuroAmerican society generally, women's participation in sport is trivialized and devalued, in accordance with the patriarchal underpinnings of sport (Birrell 1988, 487). It is not clear yet if the same is true for Aboriginal women. We need to further examine the effect of colonization and the perceptions about "sport" that came along with colonization to better understand the power structure that exists in Aboriginal sport, and this examination needs to be done within the context of the broader Aboriginal cultural system.

The next step required, I think, should be in the form of formal interviews with female athletes on the reserve. Several issues arose in informal interviews during my study, which hold promise for a better understanding of the Aboriginal female sport experience. For example, I found that, in the past, Indian girls who came from a traditional longhouse background were supported in their sport participation, while Christianized girls were dissuaded from participating. It would be illuminating to examine the relationship between religion and sport.

As well, I was told about an ideological belief, held by some Aboriginal people, that they are supposed to be "natural" athletes and thus are expected to be competent in sport without the training and strategy that are integral to EuroAmerican sport. For example, one coach related a story of how she was ridiculed for using signals in softball; she was told that "Natives don't do that." The degree to which this ideology shapes the performance and expectations of Aboriginal female athletes needs to be examined.

Finally, Aboriginal athletes are participating in two seemingly different sport environments — the EuroAmerican and the all-Indian. It would be illuminating to examine these two systems in more detail, to assess the degree to which Aboriginal people, through the creation of the emergent all-Indian system, have transformed sport through resistance, and/or been co-opted into the dominant concept of sport. It is interesting at the outset to note that Indians have often, and perhaps unconsciously, adopted the definition of an Indian created by government and incorporated it into their membership criteria at all-Indian tournaments. Each of these avenues for research should prove fruitful in the ongoing challenge to understand not only mainstream women's sport but also the experiences of those "invisible" girls and women whose stories have not yet been told.

NOTES

1. The timeline for this paper was shaped by the restrictions of the newspaper data base, beginning with the inception of the *Tekawennake Reporter* in 1968, and continuing until 1980, when the long-term editor of the paper retired. This study is premised on the assumption that the newspaper coverage of female sport was indicative of actual sport behaviour on the reserve.
2. In 1971, a woman from the reserve, Carolyn Beaver, bought the newspaper from the Jamiesons, another local couple. She became editor in 1972, and, although she sold the paper to the Woodland Cultural Centre in 1975, she agreed to stay on as editor, eventually resigning in October 1980. The paper did not usually publish in the month of August, and some of the issues were not available for examination (for example, issues from May to December 1977 were not accessible for use during my study).
3. In baton twirling and speed skating, athletes reported in the newspaper were not currently living on the reserve, although they were related to members of the reserve. Figure skaters who joined outside clubs were mentioned during the summer of 1980 (the Six Nations Arena did not operate during the summer months).
4. It would be interesting to assess the uniqueness of this organization by examining the extent to which other community women's groups have chosen to adopt this support role for sport.
5. The Tom Longboat Award winner is chosen nationally; as well, regional Tom Longboat medals are awarded each year.

REFERENCES

Ballem, Charles. 1983. "Missing from the Canadian Sport Scene: Native Athletes." *Canadian Journal of History of Sport* 14, no. 2:33-43.

Birrell, Susan J. 1988. "Discourses on the Gender/Sport Relationship: From Women in Sport to Gender Relations." In *Exercise and Sport Sciences Reviews,* Volume 16, ed. Keat B. Pandolf. New York: MacMillan Publishing Company.

_____. 1989. "Racial Relations Theories and Sport: Suggestions for a More Critical Analysis." *Sociology of Sport Journal* 6, no. 3:212-27.

Cheska, Alyce. 1974. "Ball Game Participation of North American Indian Women." *Proceedings from Third Canadian Symposium on History of Sport and Physical Education.* Halifax: Dalhousie University.

Churchill, Ward, Norbert S. Hill Jr., and Mary Jo Barlow. 1979. "An Historical Overview of Twentieth Century Native American Athletics." *The Indian Historian* 12, no. 4:22-32.

Coakley, Jay. 1990. *Sport in Society: Issues and Controversies.* 4th ed. Toronto: Times Mirror/Mosby College Publishing.

Craig, Susan B. 1973. "Indian Sportswomen." *The Sportswoman* 1, no. 4:10-13.

Donnelly, Peter. 1988. "Sport as a Site for 'Popular Resistance.'" In *Popular Cultures and Political Practices*, ed. Richard Gruneau. Toronto: Garamond Press.

Douglas, Delia. 1988. "Discourses on Black Women — A History of Silence: A Review of Relational Analyses in Education and Sport Literatures." Paper presented at North American Society for Sport Sociology Conference, Cincinnati.

Geertz, Clifford. 1983. "Deep Play: Notes on the Balinese Cockfight." In *Play, Games and Sport in Cultural Contexts*, ed. Janet C. Harris and Roberta Park. Champaign, IL: Human Kinetics Publishers.

Gruneau, Richard. 1983. *Class, Sport and Social Development.* Amherst: University of Massachusetts Press.

Henhawk, Cheryl. 1987. "Recreation on the Six Nations Reserve." Speech presented at Faculty of Human Kinetics Speaker Series, University of Windsor (October).

Jamieson, Kathleen. 1978. *Indian Women and the Law in Canada: Citizens Minus.* Study sponsored by the Advisory Council on the Status of Women, Indian Rights for Indian Women. Ottawa: Ministry of Supply and Services Canada.

Kays, J. 1980. Letter to Six Nations Band Council, 4 June.

Littlechild, Wilton. 1975. "Tom Longboat: Canada's Outstanding Indian Athlete." Master's thesis, University of Alberta.

Ontario Native Women's Association. 1988. "Doctor, Lawyer, Indian Chief." *Newsletter* 9, no. 3:24.

Ontario Women's Directorate. 1987. *Economic Status of Native Women in Ontario.* Report prepared by J. Phillip Nicolson, Policy and Management Consultants Inc., for Government of Ontario.

Oxendine, Joseph B. 1988. *American Indian Sports Heritage.* Champaign, IL: Human Kinetics Publishers.

Paraschak, Victoria. 1989. "Native Sport History: Pitfalls and Promises." *Canadian Journal of History of Sport* 20, no. 1:57-68.

Silman, Janet, ed. 1987. *Enough is Enough: Aboriginal Women Speak Out.* Toronto: The Women's Press.

Six Nations Council. 1978. Letter to Dave Elkins, 19 July.

Six Nations Recreation Committee. 1964. Minutes. 29 December.

_____. 1965. Minutes. 12 July.

_____. 1985. Minutes. 21 November.

_____. 1985. Letter to the Tom Longboat Award Committee, 21 November.

Six Nations Recreation Committee. 1983-1987. File Recreation/Fairgrounds Committee, F-Z.

Tekawennake Reporter. 18 January 1968 to 20 April 1977, and 25 January 1978 to 19 December 1980. Ohsweken, ON.

Williams, Raymond. 1980. *Problems in Materialism and Culture.* London: Verso.

Zeman, Brenda. 1988. *To Run with Longboat: Twelve Stories of Indian Athletes in Canada*, ed. David Williams. Edmonton: GMS Ventures Inc.

Aboriginal Women's Writing and the Cultural Politics of Representation

Julia Emberley

In this discussion, I record, in part, a process of unlearning the colonialist assumptions found in feminist theory and in poststructural methods of interpretation as they are used in the human sciences to examine the cultural productions of Aboriginal writers, artists, filmmakers, and musicians.[1] To write about Aboriginal women's writing, for example, as a self-identified non-Aboriginal raised in a country permeated with the intolerable hierarchies of racism, class exploitation, and gender subordination is to invite a process of unlearning — unlearning colonialist assumptions produced and reproduced in daily life by everything from television to the not-so-accessible university classroom. I concentrate specifically on Aboriginal women's texts and their entry into print culture;[2] however, film apparatuses, musical instruments, and graphic media, as well as languages, constitute an array of technologies that, as Raymond Williams argues, form an integral part of the "material social processes" (1977, 62) of the everyday world.

During the 1980s, Aboriginal struggles for self-determination in Canada continued to take place in the political arena, while a new form of self-determination also emerged in the cultural sphere. Like the struggle of Aboriginal people to gain political representation in relation to the state, their work in the area of culture also involves a struggle in and for representation. The term *cultural politics* is intended to signify the political nature of this struggle in and for cultural representation, and challenges us to rethink the conventional separation between *politics* and *culture*.

Several publications written or edited by Aboriginal women appeared in the 1980s. Aboriginal women guest-edited the special issue on Native women of the feminist quarterly *Fireweed* (winter 1986). Other works by Aboriginal women include: Beth Brant's edited collection of poetry *A Gathering of Spirit: A Collection by North American Indian Women* (1988); Jeannette Armstrong's novel *Slash* (1985); Ruby Slipperjack's *Honour the Sun* (1987); Beatrice Culleton's *In Search of April Raintree* (1983) and *April Raintree* (1984); and Lee Maracle's *I am Woman* (1988). Along with earlier autobiographical works such as Maria Campbell's *Halfbreed* (1983) and Lee Maracle's *Bobbi Lee — Indian Rebel: Struggles of a Native Canadian Woman* (1975), these texts[3] constitute an initial wave of Aboriginal women's writings that are decolonialist and feminist in impulse.

Four theoretical problems emerge in my reading of the cultural politics of Aboriginal women writers. The first is the need to confront racist and colonialist assumptions in the discourses of the human sciences produced by non-Aboriginal feminist theorists, readers, and interpreters of Aboriginal women's writings. The second theoretical problem is the way in which Aboriginal women's writing is contextualized within cultural studies generally and feminist cultural studies in particular. What I argue here is that Aboriginal women's writing emerges out of an experience of resistance to their experience as the "colonized." Indeed, their writing constitutes an important representation of *resistance*. The third theoretical problem raises a set of formal concerns about Aboriginal women's writing. I define this problem by asking such questions as: (1) What constitutes the basis of *difference* in the cultural productions of Aboriginal women writers?; (2) How is our construction of history, conventionally placed both hierarchically above and in opposition to fiction or "story telling," altered by Aboriginal women's writing?; and (3) How does the historical formation of traditions of Aboriginal oral story telling relate to the entry of those stories into print culture? I examine these questions largely with reference to Jeannette Armstrong's text *Slash*. The fourth and final theoretical problem is to ask the question, What are the possibilities opened up by Aboriginal women's writing for articulating a feminism of decolonialization?

These four main theoretical problems indeed cover a wide scope, and so I employ a variety of interpretative strategies to study them. Because I wish to sustain the radical potential of Aboriginal women's writing to challenge conventional ways of seeing, the general format of this study is, in its own way, unconventional. We can never stand outside ourselves on an imaginary Archimedean point with a pretence to objectivity and disinterest. "We" are always, in some way, destabilized subjects. In poststructural theory, the loss of a desire for a full and coherent being, which is to say a stable subject, leaves us open to the possibility of constructing ourselves as subjects, and so empowers us to transform our consciousness as critics. We must therefore transform our own writing practices to achieve a more open and less restricted and formal process of reading, writing, and learning.

This does not mean that we now have an excuse to be unclear about our ideas. It does mean that current forms of academic writing are not "natural." Other ways of writing are needed to examine the experience of Aboriginal women, and so I present my arguments not in an arbitrarily sequential (that is, seemingly coherent) narrative, but as a montage of critical reflections or "images." What holds these "critical images" together is the framework of theoretical problems I have outlined that are worked through the following four sections but that also work these sections in their own complex way.

RESISTANCE WRITING

Literature other than that which fits into accepted aesthetic values of the literary canon is often relegated into trivializing categories, such as "minority" or "ethnic," and these categories sustain the hierarchical assumptions at work in aesthetic valorization, often to the advantage of "white," "male," "heterosexual," and "middle-class" writings. How, then, do we contextualize Aboriginal women's writing? Barbara Harlow's critical study *Resistance Literature* (1987) is helpful here. In this study, she sets out to correct the epistemic violence in literary interpretation, implicitly that of the American New Criticism school, by demonstrating the political affectivity of cultural production as a constitutive part of the network of forces that comprise resistance movements to colonial and neo-colonial practices in Africa, the Middle East, and South America. Political events inform the production of resistance narratives, poetics, and testimonials written by men and women of the "Third World," who are often living in exile, under occupation, or in prison. Harlow states: "Resistance literature calls attention to itself, and to literature in general, as a political and politicized activity" (1987, 28). The "literary text," then, is not merely of secondary importance to political events but is a constitutive element in the political process.

Texts by Aboriginal women demand to be read in the context of *resistance*, in particular, resistance to the structure of internal colonialism in Canada. Using Harlow's critical study as a guide, and using the particular texts mentioned above, I outline three sites of resistance that pertain to Aboriginal women's writing:

(1) The texts resist the normal conventions of literary classifications. Not only do they resist placement in the categories "minority" or "ethnic," but the conceptual borders that line the pockets of genre and voice, fiction and non-fiction, also tear at the seams. This is why I prefer to call these texts "writings" rather than "literature," the latter usually connoting the sense of fiction as non-truth. Writings that we recognize to be works of "imagination" can tell us stories as a way of representing the experience of people excluded from mainstream literature. A poststructural notion of writing also allows for forms of graphic markings to be included other than simply writing as we know it in its colloquial sense. This is particularly relevant for Aboriginal modes of expression.

(2) The writings resist alignment of Aboriginal women with other critical practices such as feminism, for example. Though I have suggested that Aboriginal women's writing is feminist in impulse, the colonialist assumptions in academic feminist theory make it difficult for Aboriginal women writers to align themselves with this

and other dominant forms of feminism. This problem raises important questions about the formation of collective resistance among women when the cultural and political interests and experiences of many women are either ignored, dismissed, or simply taken for granted. Feminist theory in the 1980s became committed to a self-reflective process of examining its own racism and ethnocentrism.[4] However, it failed to consider what Aboriginal women said about their particular concerns within the movement. Attendant to this problem is the inequality between those who are academically privileged and those who are not. Except for a few isolated examples, Aboriginal peoples in Canada have been systematically excluded from attaining higher education and thus entry into the professions. Because of this exclusion, it is necessary that the achievements of such women as song writer and filmmaker Alanis Obomsawin and artist Joanne Cardinal-Schubert, along with many other Aboriginal women writers, musicians, artists, and performers living in Canada, must not go unrecognized. These women are examples of women whose voices were excluded during the 1980s from official (i.e., colonialist) systems of knowledge production.

(3) A third site of resistance that these texts can be said to address is their inscription of an agent of resistance. Both in their characterization and as writing subjects, Aboriginal women are writing themselves and their people into history as subjects to and of their own making. As agents of their own historical traditions, Aboriginal writers in Canada are claiming an unambiguous self-determination to tell their own stories, and are doing it in their own way. Lenore Keeshig-Tobias, editor of *The Magazine to Re-establish the Trickster,* states: "The formation of the Committee to Re-establish the Trickster (CRET) in 1986 arose out of awareness by a group of Native writers to consolidate and gain recognition for Native contributions to Canadian writing — to reclaim the Native voice in literature" (1989, 3).

It remains to be said that the negative critique in resistance writings provokes more than an inkling of resistance on the part of the privileged reader. Though I could meditate on the crisis of the intellectual (in this case the non-Aboriginal academic) and, in so doing, make claims for the representative status of an intellectual vanguard, such a move risks neutralizing the political affects of *agency* — that is, the active part that subjects play in producing resistance and their specific knowledge of what it is that needs to be resisted. This is not to say that non-Aboriginal feminist academics do not have a supplementary role to play in supporting the Aboriginal women's movement. However, for critical theorists, who are trained in the protocols of feminist and Marxist theory, the question remains: How does s/he address the intellectual labour of subjects in resistance to forms of critical practice entrenched in the academic institution? In other words, how does s/he "read" Aboriginal writings of resistance as an alternate form of critical practice, not as un-theoretical or non-theoretical critique, but as writing produced by subjects engaged in critical praxis?

The extent to which Aboriginal women's writing can and does resist colonialist subjectivity and its relationship to the symbolic formation of internal colonialism, when Aboriginal people, too, are subject to the effects of being a colonialist subject, is a complicated question. It is particularly with reference to the representation of Aboriginal people as victims by Aboriginal writers that some of these complications come to light.

WRITING THE "HAPPY BOOK"

A Native man once told a group of writers that we shouldn't write about anger and sadness. He mentioned that angry books, sad stories, full of hate sell to white folks. "They love it when we are fighting and hating each other." He mentioned Alice Walker. . . . But I am not so cynical as to really believe that white people are going to happily plough through the pages of devastation that colonialism has been in the chapters of our lives. But, then, I don't believe "Color Purple" [sic] was a sad story full of hate. (Maracle 1988, 189)

I hurt because in my childhood I saw glimpses of a proud and happy people. I heard their laughter, saw them dance, and felt their love.

A close friend of mine said, "Maria, make it a happy book. It couldn't have been so bad. We know we are guilty so don't be too harsh." I am not bitter. I have passed that stage. I only want to say: this is what it was like; this is what it is still like. I know that poverty is not ours alone. Your people have it too, but in those earlier days you at least had dreams, you had a tomorrow. (Campbell 1973, 9)

The "happy book," like the Harlequin fantasies of mass-market romance, indulges the reader in dreams of unrealized possibilities. Making the dream the reality, transforming conditions of impossibility into possibility, would appear, then, to be the work of the "unhappy book." What is an unhappy book? To a colonialist, an unhappy book contains "sad stories, full of hate," stories that provoke guilt and fear, signs of a dominant culture continuing to deny the originary moment of imperial violence. As a representation of "anti-colonialist" writing, the unhappy book of colonialist invention dramatizes violence, anger, contempt, degeneracy, both in its thematization and in its textual practice. To interpret the writings of Aboriginal women in terms of relations of domination and submission, which the above formulation of the (un)happy book does, displaces the difficulty that Aboriginal writers experience in entering the technology of print culture. That struggle manifests itself in the themes and formal aspects of the writing, which demonstrate that the representation of Aboriginal people as victims is a determination within the publishing industry in permitting publications by Aboriginal writers. The negativity that characterizes these works, then, is symptomatic of the determinations of a colonialist readership and publishing industry. Maracle and Campbell's own determination to represent the negative experience of Aboriginal people at the risk of compromising resistance to that experience in telling their respective stories of victimization is an indication of the ideological contradictions that adhere to the formation of subjectivities resistant to (internal) colonialism.

The subject of resistance in the context of colonialism is not a coherent subject, unified in her or his capacity to resist the determinations to which she or he is subjected. Resistance is itself a process. The process of claiming resisting subject positions by Aboriginal women writers can be interpreted as a practical staging of the deconstructive turn.[5] In a deconstructive analysis, the intolerable hierarchies of race, class, sexuality, and gender contained in binary oppositions such as colonizer/ colonized, inferior/superior, Indian/white, woman/man are overturned when these closed oppositions, in which subjects are contained by a revolving motion of being either one or the other, are displaced. The point to displacing this opposition, taking an *indifferent* position toward either side of the opposition, is to re-articulate open, or alternate, subject positions.

The production of alternate subject positions allows for a diversity of articulations to take place between resisting subjects within and among other social movements. One such alternate articulation involves subjects of resistance in feminist and anti-imperialist struggles.

SELF-DETERMINATION/FEMINISM

Decolonialist and feminist practices represent two discontinuous, however supplementary, struggles: on the one hand, the self-determined, decolonization struggle of Aboriginal peoples living in the geo-political territory known as Canada; and, on the other, materialist-feminist concerns for articulating a theory of gender subordination with a class analysis informed by an anti-racist and anti-imperialist ethico-politics. An articulation between anti-imperialist and women's movements necessitates a theory of gender subordination in post-colonial criticism — criticism directed toward surpassing the colonizer/colonized opposition — which cannot be insisted on too forcefully. However, an understanding of the determinations involved in gender differentiation in indigenous cultures can no longer be formulated in a somewhat elitist lament for the marginality and dispossession of Aboriginal women, their muteness and silencing by dominating patriarchal and racist forces in collusion with a late-capitalist economy. Aboriginal women are not silent. They speak, write, and publish; they scrutinize, assess, and judge for themselves, and because their marginalization and dispossession are real, their refusal to be silent is a struggle that takes place under oppressive and difficult circumstances.

The flourishing of cultural productions by Aboriginal women in Canada is radically transforming the theoretical presuppositions of post-colonialist and feminist critique. In a similar way to which the Arab woman writer Nawal el Saadawi (1980) lifted the veil on the benign paternalism of first-worldist feminism, so, too, Aboriginal women writers have criticized the imperialist assumptions of self-identified — though to a large extent unacknowledged — "first-worldist" feminist practices within Canada.[6]

At the Third Annual International Feminist Bookfair conference held in Montreal in June 1988, Jeannette Armstrong spoke about criticisms she had received from feminists about her use of a man, rather than a woman, as the central character in *Slash*. At a reading session held by Aboriginal women writers during the conference, Armstrong spoke in her own defence, claiming that she used a male character in order to provide a positive and strong image for the men in her community. I have constructed the following feminist interpretation of *Slash* in order to provide an example of the effects of feminism's blindness to the question of racism within the structure of internal colonialism when the specificity of gender and sexism is removed from this larger social context. What might such a feminist critique focus on? The following is a demonstration the limits of which I have demarcated by the use of an indentation:

> The figure of Mardi, a woman activist, in *Slash*, who functions, however from a distance, as Slash's political mentor, recalls Edward Said's observation about the place of Palestinian women, who, with few exceptions, "seem to have played little more than the role of hyphen, connective, transition, mere incident" (1985, 77). The reader learns about Mardi's political involvement only when Slash runs into her at various political rallies and protests. Otherwise, she seems to circulate in the novel as an underground figure, a floating signifier, always at the centre of AIM's (American Indian Movement) most recent political manoeuvres. Eventually, she "disappears," without a trace (Armstrong 1985, 195). As a figure in the novel, she is marginal, and yet, in her absence, she is figured as central to Aboriginal political organization. As a silent figure of mediation who bridges the experience and political involvement of Slash, Mardi's character allegorizes the general position of indigenous women in the struggle of decolonization: their work is central but their recognition marginal.

Though I offer up this interpretation with some conviction of its validity — writing as a "feminist" — there are limitations in it, which emerge in the context of Slash's critical observation of the effects of racism in his relations with Aboriginal women: "There were some things we were too ashamed to even tell. Like all of the white girls laughing at Tony when he asked one of them to dance at the sock-hop. He quit school after that. Also how none of the Indian girls ever got asked to dance at the sock-hops because us guys wouldn't dance with them because the white guys didn't" (Armstrong 1985, 35). A feminist analysis that limits its discussion exclusively to the issue of gender risks displacing the ways in which racism and assimilation are major determinations in the specific uses to which sexism is put at any historical moment.

According to Roger Moody, indigenous women's movements throughout the world have often put "struggles for survival, land rights, sacred places, community-controlled education, and so forth, first on the agenda" before issues that are more directly gender-oriented; however, he goes on to clarify in the next sentence that "there are specifically women's perspectives on all these aims, together with a growing demand for women's participation, at every level of indigenous society" (1988, 242). This observation, though affirming the difference in perspectives between indigenous women and men, does not consider the effects of the imposition of patriarchal values from the dominant colonial power. In Canada, the imposition of patriarchal values occurred during the late nineteenth and well into the twentieth century with the 1876 Indian Act and subsequent amendments, in particular, those contained in Bill 79 (1951).[7]

The question remains: What are the possibilities for articulating the self-determination discourse of Aboriginal women and critical feminist practice? In its contemporary configuration feminist criticism has concerned itself with, among other things, the representation of women, sexual difference, the gendering of subjectivity and the institutions and practices through which the category of "woman" is produced; whereas issues of racism, economic dispossession, cultural autonomy, and self-determination constitute some of the main areas of discussion in anti-imperialist critique. In any attempt to formulate a feminist theory of decolonization, or to word it with a different emphasis, a decolonialist practice of feminism must resist conflating the inevitable tensions, clashes, and contradictions between the values, interests, and aims of the feminist and Aboriginal self-determination movements.

This imperative begs the question, however: Who is in a position to formulate a decolonialist theory of gender subordination? Traditionally, theory has been the preserve of an intellectual vanguard, to the exclusion of "the voices of the oppressed." The current swing to a politics of identity in Anglo-American feminisms with subjective authenticity as the code of legitimation has challenged the role of the intellectual as representative in a hegemonic institution of power: academia — particularly when the intellectuals in question are not members of the underprivileged class, indeed, when their very position within academia makes that membership irrevocable, though not indissoluble. The problem lies, in part, with a conception of theory as a metaphysical game whose principal players — the Floating Signifiers (academics) — would appear to exist in a field of investigation removed from a ground or clearly defined opposition — the Referents (the oppressed). The positing of a fully anti-essentialist discourse, that is, a discourse that purports to be above the concerns of essentialism and authenticity, is no more nor less than the reinscription of what Derrida (1974) criticizes as "the metaphysics of presence," however, in terms of its obverse, the metaphysics of absence. If full presence is not possible, likewise, full absence (vacating the essential and authentic as critical categories) is also, aside from being impossible, undesirable. The solution to the naive framing of presumed unmediated "voices of the oppressed," and the troubling privilege of theory as the exclusive domain of an intellectual vanguard, might be found, I would suggest, in the writings of subjects in resistance. In other words, the popular fictions, testimonials, and poetics of Aboriginal women writers engaged in a critique of colonialism themselves theorize gender and "race" subordination and the epistemological effects of colonial violence.

In the context of the struggle over what constitutes truth, for the intellectual, such a move toward popular writings would demand, as Gayatri Spivak writes, "re-think[ing] the notion that fiction derives from truth as its negation" (1987, 243) so as to destabilize the asymmetric valorization of those textual practices conventionally privileged as disseminators of an "effect of the Real" knowledge as truth. Historical discourse represents one such formation of knowledge credited with official truth-value.

RE-WRITING HISTORY: THE ORAL TRADITION

Official forms of history are received as the definitive word. Written in what Dominick LaCapra (1985) calls a tell-it-like-it-is attitude, official history reproduces an effect of the Real, inscribing its knowledge as *the only possible representation of* truth. *Slash* can be read as a critical reflection on the dominant Anglo-American history of "sixties" Aboriginal politics. *Slash* re-tells the history of Aboriginal politics in British Columbia and Canadian indigenous involvement in the American Indian Movement during the 1960s and early 1970s. Armstrong's use of materialist realism in order to recast and problematize borders of official and unofficial histories provides the material for an intervention into the theoretical problem of history as truth and fiction as untruth.

The distinction between hegemonic inscriptions of history and literature has recently undergone a crisis in interdisciplinary contamination. Under the rubric of a new historicism, a benign exposure to the poststructural critique in literary theory and philosophy has subjected the notion of an unmediated representation of reality to an interpretive turn, or, on another register, a deconstructive turn. Concurrently, despite American New Criticism's orthodox claims to the literary purity of self-contained poetic icons, the historicization of the literary event has become a founding principle of a new cultural politics. Nevertheless, the disciplinary differences between history and literature cannot be wiped away, nor can their discursive differences be absorbed into each other. It is precisely because of the difference between them that they can be used, as Spivak writes, to "critically 'interrupt'" each other, "bring each other to crisis, in order to serve their constituencies; especially when each seems to claim all for its own" (1987, 241).

Alternate critical insights, which would otherwise be ignored, silenced, or suppressed, can emerge in the event of disciplinary confrontations.

In the textual politics of *Slash*, the discursive violence of contemporary Western narrative traditions, in which written history constitutes the most viable representation of truth, is challenged by the trope of Aboriginal oral story telling, which is viewed by Western ethnocentrism as non-truth. The re-presentation of oral story telling, the appearance of "intratextual"[8] stories that interrupt the historical narrative, and the larger historical narrative written in the vernacular, combine to contest the boundaries between oppositions such as oral and written, truth and non-truth, history and fiction.

The following is an example of an intratextual story in *Slash;* it appears like a mini-story within the larger story of decolonialization. It is a story that humorously reflects on the "true" nature of the colonizer's culture:

Once I heard a story, in the early morning, about a woman named Hightuned Polly. She had a dog that she babied like some white women do. She carried it around and made little skirts for it. One time, Hightuned Polly was at a celebration in Omak, during the Stampede Pow-wow. She was staying with some friends in a pow-wow teepee. Her dog got in heat. So all day, there was a big troop of dogs following her wherever she carried her dog. They even sneaked into the teepee under the flaps, while she was inside. Everyone was teasing her as she walked around with fifteen dogs trotting along. Finally, that night, she decided to sew a buckskin pant for her dog, to keep the other dogs from getting to her. Well, in the morning, Hightuned Polly found her dog with many visitors and a hole chewed right through the buckskin. (Armstrong 1985, 19)

There are many ways to read this story: as a story about the effects of tampering with nature or the frivolous effects of imitating the dominant culture; what happens, for example, when the boundaries of cultural difference are crossed, or in this case "penetrated," and imitation becomes a parodic critique by the indigenous culture of the colonizer's culture. The sexual specificity of this story, its irreverent and carnivalesque humour, add to its subversive criticism of colonial culture, in particular to the ways in which so-called primitive cultures are figured as "naturally" prone to sexual licence. The narrative allegorizes the "white man's" attempt to censor, metaphorically, through the use of a buckskin chastity belt what Terry Goldie (1987) aptly describes as the "fear and temptation" experienced by a patriarchal colonial culture in its projected sexualization of indigenous culture. This story can be read allegorically to produce a commentary on the complexities in the articulation of a race/gender analysis.

Armstrong's use of the oral tradition in *Slash* challenges Eurocentric definitions of what constitutes an indigenous literary tradition. Addressing the problem of defining a non-white literary tradition, Ralph Ellison writes: "The notion of an intellectual or artistic succession based upon color or racial background is no less absurd than one based upon a common religious background" (quoted in Gates Jr.

1988, 120). Henry Louis Gates Jr., in his work on Afro-American writers, elaborates on Ellison's critique:

> Literary succession or influence, rather, can be based on only formal literary revision, which the literary critic must be able to demonstrate. These discrete demonstrations allow for definitions of a tradition. Few definitions of tradition escape the racism, essentialism, or nationalism often implicit in rubrics such as "African" or "Jewish" or "Commonwealth" literature. As Ellison argues, "for the critic there simply exists no substitute for the knowledge of history and literary tradition." (1988, 120)

For Gates, "each literary tradition, at least implicitly, contains within it an argument for how it can be read" (1988, xix-xx). The formation of an Aboriginal cultural tradition, then, is not something that exists *a priori* of the texts and oral story telling, written and performed, by Aboriginal people. Indeed, Thomas King cautions the literary critic against too hasty a definition of Aboriginal writings: "When we talk about contemporary Native literature, we talk as though we already have a definition for this body of literature when, in fact, we do not, and, when we talk about Native writers, we talk as though we have a process for determining who is a Native writer and who is not when, in fact, we don't" (1987, 4). The tradition is to be found in the very workings and material effects of Aboriginal cultural practices.

Aboriginal cultural autonomy has been and continues to be intimately tied to the historical and current re-configuration of an Aboriginal oral tradition. The question as to whether "traditional Aboriginal oral story telling" exists or not, to the extent that it is a category that already differs from itself in its recent reception in the forms of transcriptions, taping, translations, and publications, supports a Eurocentric nostalgia for unmediated, closer-to-the-bone, forms of discursive exchange. The circulation of "stories," whether sacred, heuristic, allegorical, or quotidian, under an economic mode of gatherer/hunter production, would obviously differ from their function as cultural commodities under late capitalism. Nevertheless, an oral tradition is being reclaimed, largely through the entry of those stories into print culture as well as through the thematic use of the trope of the oral tradition in texts such as *Slash*.

In her dedication to the novel, Armstrong praises the stories of a friend whose suffering from the violence of alcoholism provided the occasion to take up those stories as weapons, indeed as a strategy, in the war on representation and subjectivity:

We all walk in the shadow of the beast
so we will step lightly
All the stories you used to make laughter
will be told around the tables of your people
And we will be rich with weapons. (1985, 5)

The intratextual stories in *Slash* provide the occasion for a critical reflection on the making of fiction and the unmaking of Eurocentric written history. As much as Armstrong is engaged in re-historicizing Aboriginal political involvement in the sixties and early seventies from an Aboriginal perspective, she is also polemicizing the actual putting-into-writing of Aboriginal history. That the written word disseminates the "truth" of what it means to have a history has become a well-known formulation of European ethnocentrism. Claude Lévi-Strauss, for example, viewed anthropology as a discipline capable of correcting "the absence of written documents in most so-called primitive societies" (1963, 24). With the development of such a discipline, "it is also possible," according to Lévi-Strauss, "to reconstruct the history of peoples who have never known writing" (1963, 24). This ethnocentric bias was responsible for suppressing the truth of Aboriginal modes of "writing," whether oral, hieroglyphic, pictographic, syllabic, torn into the flesh, or woven into textiles — in other words, inscribed in systems other than that of a Roman orthography. The stories within the larger "story" in *Slash* suggest traditional Aboriginal oral "story telling." They entertain, but also unfold, other ways of knowing; knowledge-as-truth in the colonial syntax of history becomes knowledge-as-reading, or interpretation, in the case of Armstrong's "story telling," a re-writing and de-colonization of that official historical truth telling.

In *Slash*, the imposition of European categories of thought as the basis for interpreting Aboriginal cultural traditions is challenged when the central character asserts, "We have our own interpretation as to how we function best" (Armstrong 1985, 223-24). This remark comes at the conclusion to the story when Slash refuses to accept the co-optation of Aboriginal political struggle into the cycle of antagonism and aggression instigated by the state, arguing rather in the discourse of cultural autonomy and self-determination. The very title *Slash* connotes the mark that divides Aboriginal/colonial culture, a mark that embodies the spiritual/emotional/intellectual, as well as the physical, scars of assimilation.

Cultural autonomy allows for the emergence of a tradition that would in turn provide the necessary space for Aboriginal people to think their own insertion, as subjects, into history. The formation of a historical tradition is part of the ongoing cultural and political struggle in and for representation. And it is through the formation of a historical tradition that a politics of "identity" can emerge with cultural and political implications for action made possible.

To return to the specificity of Aboriginal women's struggle in the context of the Aboriginal self-determination movement: the special issue of *Canadian Woman Studies / les cahiers de la femme* (summer/fall 1989), devoted exclusively to the concerns of Aboriginal women and guest-edited by a collective of Aboriginal women, reaffirms a continuum that has not been completely destroyed or obliterated by the Canadian colonial apparatus. Through their grandmothers, Aboriginal women are historizing the reciprocity of relations between Aboriginal men and women, a reciprocity that provides the collective support necessary to resist the divisive sexist and racist pressures of internal colonialism. If the critical project of feminism is ultimately to do away with the need for feminist critique through the transformation of hierarchies of sexism, racism, and class exploitation, then cultural feminism in Canada will have to reinvent itself in the pores of Aboriginal women's struggle for self-determination.[9]

NOTES

I would like to thank those who attended the panel at which I presented this paper for their commentary and criticism, with special thanks to Jeannette Armstrong, Marie Baker, Sue Deranger, Linda Jaine, Beth Perrot, Kim Sawchuk, and Winona Stevens. I would also like to thank Pat Chuchryk for her excellent editorial suggestions in re-writing this paper. I am grateful for the support offered by the Social Sciences and Humanities Research Council of Canada, which enabled the research for this paper. In particular, I would like to thank Peter Kulchyski, whose knowledge of Aboriginal political struggle in Canada was invaluable.

A revised form of this paper has appeared in my book entitled *Thresholds of Difference* (1993).

1. *Feminism* has as many different faces as there are ways of working toward social change. The feminism that I am interested in is materialist feminism. Materialist feminism concerns itself with the study of the material effects of culture in shaping who we are as gendered subjects in the world. The categories of race, class, and gender, how they intersect and affect each other, are central to materialist feminist analyses. For a greater understanding of materialist feminism(s) than I can provide here, I refer the reader to Landry and MacLean (1993).

   Poststructuralism is an interpretive movement that helps us to understand how we remain contained by ideology when we assume our own identities (or subjectivities) to be fixed, singular, and coherent, and reality an immutable force. As Terry Eagleton writes, we conform "to social reality as 'natural' rather than critically questioning how it, and ourselves, came to be constructed, and so could possibly be transformed" (187). I refer the reader to Eagleton's book *Literary Theory: An Introduction* (1983) for further discussion.

2. In English literature studies in Canada, the term *Native* is used with more frequency and consistency than the alternatives *Indian, indigenous,* or *Aboriginal,* the latter two being the desired terms in this volume. The edited collection of essays *The Native in Literature: Canadian and Comparative Perspectives* (King et al. 1987) is an example of a preliminary work that has set the terms of discussion. Terms such as *Aboriginal, indigenous, Indian,* and *Native* carry with them the residue of profoundly colonialist and to a large extent denigrating classifications. At particular historical moments, however, these terms take on positive meanings, especially as "aboriginal" people reclaim language and its empowering capabilities to produce meanings and values for themselves. It is important, therefore, to cite these terms with quotation marks, real and/or imaginary, as a reminder that they are not natural, fixed, canonic, or binding, but that their meaning and value are constructed by the context in which they appear.

   I use the designations *Aboriginal woman* writer as analytical categories to suggest that the body of writing that I am examining is not like any other writing, to the extent that it is a constitutive element of a particular social process in which Aboriginal women (my focus here) and Aboriginal men are struggling for cultural, political, and economic self-determination.

3. This list is intended to be exemplary, not exhaustive. I might also mention the more recent Beth Cuthand, *Voices in the Waterfall* (1989*)*; Heather Hodgson, *Seventh Generation: Contemporary Native Writing* (1989); and Rita Joe, *Song of Eskasoni: More Poems of Rita Joe* (1988).

4. See, for example, Elaine Showalter, ed., *The New Feminist Criticism: Essays on Women, Literature and Theory*, 1985.

5. The principal essay on deconstruction is Jacques Derrida's "Signature Event Context" (1977), in which he states: "An opposition of metaphysical concepts (e.g., speech/writing, presence/absence, etc.) is never the confrontation to two terms, but a hierarchy and the order of a subordination" (Derrida 1977, 195). We could include in Derrida's list black/white, Native/non-Native, man/woman, etcetera.

6. I am referring here specifically to the papers delivered by Lee Maracle and Jeannette Armstrong at the Third Annual International Feminist Bookfair, Montreal, June 1988, published in *Trivia: A Journal of Ideas, Part 2: Language/Differences* 14 (1989). See Maracle (1989) and Armstrong (1989).

7. See Joyce Green (1985) and Kathleen Jamieson (1986) for further discussions on the questions of sex discrimination in the Indian Act, leading up to the amendments of Bill C-31 (1985). See also Sylvia Van Kirk (1980 and 1987) for a discussion of relations between Aboriginal women and colonial men during the fur trade.

    Paula Gunn Allen (1986) makes a general, however compelling, argument that the attack on indigenous cultures by colonialist powers was indeed a patriarchal attack on the accepted position of women as decision makers within indigenous cultures. Gunn Allen uses the word "gynocide" to evoke the forcefulness of this attack on Aboriginal cultures generally and women in particular. For a more detailed account of the Indian Act and Bill C-31, see my *Thresholds of Difference: Feminist Critique, Native Women's Writings, Postcolonial Theory* (1993), especially pages 87-91.

8. I use the term *intratextual* to draw attention to the layering of story telling that appears in *Slash*, when not only is there the larger story written in a realist style, but also there are mini-stories, as it were (either alluded to or written) contained within Armstrong's larger text. These intratextual stories are more representative of Aboriginal oral story telling technique than is Armstrong's overall realist approach.

9. This phrasing has been appropriated from a talk given by Gayatri Chakravorty Spivak at the "Marxism Now" conference in Amherst, Massachusetts, early December 1989, in which Spivak said that Marxism must "re-invent itself in the pores of feminism." I have changed the terms by way of signalling the diversity of articulations between subjects engaged in social change. Those articulations are multifarious and suggest to me that as feminists, critical writers, and activists, *our* struggles are never simply *our own,* but are overdetermined by material social processes that not only contain us but also make possible, through various forms of articulation, resistance to that containment.

REFERENCES

Allen, Paula Gunn. 1986. *The Sacred Hoop: Recovering the Feminine in American Indian Tradition.* Boston: Beacon Press.

Armstrong, Jeannette. 1985. *Slash.* Penticton, B.C.: Theytus Books.

_____. 1989. "Cultural Robbery, Imperialism: Voices of Native Women." *Trivia: A Journal of Ideas, Part 2: Language/Differences — Writing in Tongues* 14:21-23.

Barnett, Don, and Rick Sterling, eds. 1975. *Bobbi Lee — Indian Rebel: Struggles of a Native Canadian Woman.* Richmond: LSM (Liberation Support Movement) Press.

Brant, Beth, ed. 1988. *A Gathering of Spirit: A Collection by North American Indian Women.* Toronto: The Women's Press. (Originally published in 1984, Amherst, MA: Sinister Wisdom.)

Campbell, Maria. 1983. *Halfbreed*. Toronto: Goodread Biographies. (Originally published in 1973, Toronto: McClelland and Stewart Ltd.)

Canadian Woman Studies / les cahiers de la femme. 1989. Special Issue: Native Women 10, nos. 2 and 3 (summer/fall).

Culleton, Beatrice. 1983. *In Search of April Raintree*. Winnipeg: Pemmican Publications.

_____. 1984. *April Raintree*. Winnipeg: Pemmican Publications.

Cuthand, Beth. 1989. *Voices in the Waterfall*. Vancouver: Laraza Press.

Derrida, Jacques. 1974. *Of Grammatology*. Translated by Gayatri Chakravorty Spivak. Baltimore: Johns Hopkins University Press.

_____. 1977. "Signature Event Context." Chapter 8 in *Glyph: Johns Hopkins Textual Studies*. Baltimore: Johns Hopkins University Press.

Eagleton, Terry. 1983. *Literary Theory: An Introduction*. Minneapolis: University of Minnesota Press.

el Saadawi, Nawal. 1980. "Arab Women and Western Feminism: An Interview with Nawal el Sadaawi [sic]." *Race and Class* 22, no. 2:175-83.

Emberley, Julia. 1993. *Thresholds of Difference: Feminist Critique, Native Women's Writings, Postcolonial Theory*. Toronto: University of Toronto Press.

Fireweed. 1986. Special Issue: Native Women. Issue 22.

Gates Jr., Henry Louis. 1988. *The Signifying Monkey: A Theory of Afro-American Literary Criticism*. New York: Oxford University Press.

Goldie, Terry. 1987. "Fear and Temptation: Images of Indigenous Peoples in Australian, Canadian, and New Zealand Literature." In *The Native in Literature: Canadian and Comparative Perspectives,* ed. Thomas King, Cheryl Calver, and Helen Hoy. Oakville, ON: ECW Press.

Green, Joyce. 1985. "Sexual Equality and Indian Government: An Analysis of Bill C-31 Amendments of the Indian Act." *Native Studies Review* 1, no. 2:81-95.

Harlow, Barbara. 1987. *Resistance Literature*. New York: Methuen.

Hodgson, Heather. 1989. *Seventh Generation: Contemporary Native Writing*. Penticton, B.C.: Theytus Books Ltd.

Jamieson, Kathleen. 1986. "Sex Discrimination and the Indian Act." In *Arduous Journey: Canadian Indians and Decolonization*, ed. J. Rick Ponting. Toronto: McClelland and Stewart.

Joe, Rita. 1988. *Song of Eskasoni: More Poems of Rita Joe*. Charlottetown, P.E.I.: Ragweed Press.

Keeshig-Tobias, Lenore. 1989. Introduction to *The Magazine to Re-establish the Trickster* 1, no. 1:2-3.

King, Thomas. 1987. "Introduction: An Anthology of Canadian Native Fiction." In *Canadian Fiction Magazine* 60:4-10.

King, Thomas, Cheryl Calver, and Helen Hoy, eds. 1987. *The Native in Literature: Canadian and Comparative Perspectives*. Oakville, ON: ECW Press.

LaCapra, Dominick. 1985. *History and Criticism*. Ithaca, N.Y.: Cornell University Press.

Landry, Donna, and Gerald MacLean. 1993. *Materialist Feminisms*. New York: Routledge.

Lévi-Strauss, Claude. 1963. *Structural Anthropology*. Translated by Claire Jacobson and Brooke Grundfest Schoepf. New York: Basic Books, Inc.

Maracle, Lee. 1975. *Bobbi Lee — Indian Rebel: Struggles of a Native Canadian Woman*. Ed. Don Barnett and Rick Sterling. Richmond, B.C.: LSM Press.

_____. 1988. *I am Woman*. Vancouver: Write-on-Press Ltd.

_____. 1989. "Moving Over." *Trivia: A Journal of Ideas, Part 2: Language/Differences — Writing in Tongues* 14:9-12.

Moody, Roger, ed. 1988. *The Indigenous Voice: Visions and Realities*, Volume 2. London: Zed Books Ltd.

Newton, Judith, and Deborah Rosenfelt, eds. 1985. *Feminist Criticism and Social Change: Sex, Class, and Race in Literature and Culture*. New York: Methuen.

Said, Edward W. 1985. *After the Last Sky: Palestinian Lives*. With photographs by Jean Mohr. New York: Pantheon Books.

Showalter, Elaine, ed. 1985. *The New Feminist Criticism: Essays on Women, Literature and Theory*. New York: Pantheon Books.

Slipperjack, Ruby. 1987. *Honour the Sun*. Extracted and revised from the *Diary of the Owl*. Winnipeg: Pemmican Publications.

Spivak, Gayatri Chakravorty. 1987. *In Other Worlds: Essays in Cultural Politics*. New York: Methuen.

Van Kirk, Sylvia. 1980. *"Many Tender Ties" : Women in Fur-Trade Society in Western Canada, 1670-1870*. Winnipeg: Watson and Dwyer Publishing Ltd.

_____. 1987. "Towards a Feminist Perspective in Native History." In *Papers of the 18th Algonquian Conference (1986)*, ed. William Cowan. Ottawa: Carleton University Press.

Williams, Raymond. 1977. *Marxism and Literature*. New York: Oxford University Press.

Art or Craft:
The Paradox of the Pangnirtung Weave Shop

Kathy M'Closkey

According to Eric Wolf (1982, 388), "The ability to bestow meaning — to 'name' things, acts, and ideas — is a source of power. Control of communication allows the managers of ideology to lay down the categories through which reality is to be perceived." In this paper I intend to examine how the words *art* and *craft* have affected Westerners' perceptions of things that Aboriginal peoples produce, with particular emphasis on textiles created by women.

Frankly, it has never been clear to me why the choice of medium has determined what has been regarded as fine art for the past 300 years. As a weaver, I view a blank canvas and a blank warp (the threads a weaver works upon) as analogous. Yet, in Western history, one has been elevated to the status of fine art, the other trivialized and demoted to anonymous craft. The classical picture presented by art historians depicts the trajectory of fine art as linear and evolutionary: it parallels the rigid (and erroneous) framework utilized by social scientists in the nineteenth century, which traced the development of humanity as passing through several stages to "civilization."

Few societies have a separate category analogous to our term for *art*. The creation of *art* and its conceptual separation from other activities occurred late in Western history, during the Renaissance. Although conditions of production varied widely in other parts of the world, the distinction between art and craft that originated at the beginning of the Renaissance was applied globally, as Europeans colonized the rest of the world. It is important to understand the role that language has played in distinguishing between what is art and what is not. Our recognition and appreciation of art is shaped by language and cultural conditioning. Meanings are not imprinted onto things by nature; rather, they are developed and imposed by human beings. The power of language, especially when combined with literacy, stamps this knowledge with an authenticity that enlarges as it is perpetuated — reprinted, repeated, and thus rendered as perceived truth. As a powerful discipline, art history authorizes certain representations, such as painting and sculpture, while blocking or invalidating others. As scholars, art historians see themselves in pursuit of knowledge and often fail to recognize their role in creating it. Currently, post-modernists and feminist art historians are deconstructing many of the most cherished assumptions of art history and aesthetics in order to achieve a more balanced view of the history of art (Pollock 1988; Parker and Pollack 1981; Wolff 1983).

Art by women in previous centuries was more than just marginalized; it was rendered invisible. Yet, most Aboriginal and historic textiles are non-representational creations, produced long before the contemporary art world saw fit to redefine *geometric* as *abstraction* and canonize it as the dominant expression in twentieth-century art. An examination of the escalation of the fine arts phenomenon in Europe associated with the demotion of the craftworker's status (particularly as it affected women) is essential in order to understand the effect that the art/craft distinction has had on the perception and subsequent exploitation of Aboriginal production. In this historical review, I present a context to understand the paradox inherent in the production of weaving at the Pangnirtung Tapestry Studio.

HOW CLOTH ART BECAME CRAFT

The needle arts, including quilting and weaving, have a rich history dating back thousands of years. Weaving was nearly a global phenomenon, and quilting was practised by the Egyptians, the Chinese, and the Persians, from whom it was introduced into Europe by the Crusaders (Hedges and Wendt 1980, 14). Both men and women wove and embroidered textiles during the Middle Ages (in Europe) under the auspices of guild membership. Distinctions were noted among different individuals, but no hierarchy existed between arts and crafts.

European tradition dictated that a painter design the main figures in tapestries because painters were the only people capable of *designare*, that is, the ability to draw, compose, and create. During the Renaissance, this ability increasingly required a thorough knowledge of architecture, geometry, perspective, arithmetic, and anatomy (Pevsner 1940, 84). Through their studies of perspective, Renaissance painters laid the foundations of projective geometry in math, mapmaking, and drafting used by architects and engineers today (Mitchell and Stein 1977, 1,445). But the great craftworkers of the fifteenth and sixteenth centuries lacked a key qualification — they had no training in mathematics.

Because the education of painters increasingly differed from that of their contemporaries in the general population, tapestry weavers began to lose their autonomy and eventually their ability to design any portion of a tapestry. Ultimately, all design and colour were rendered in minute detail, and tapestries became "paintings in wool" (Ackerman 1933, 197). Burdened by restrictions, painters and sculptors during the mid-sixteenth century severed their association from the guilds and joined the newly formed art academies, which were headed by nobility (Kristeller 1952). Thus began the institutional separation of art from craft, which reflects the duality concerning mental and manual labour enshrined in Western thought. The Greeks had initiated the separation of intellectual from manual labour by emphasizing mathematics as the first purely intellectual activity, based on the notion that the more mathematics involved in a job, the less manual it was (Sohn-Rethel 1978, 103). But they did not extend it to the realm of art. Painting and sculpture involved manual labour only. The Greeks esteemed poetry and music, and their term for *art* and its Latin equivalent was applied to all kinds of human activity. Painting and sculpture were seen as two of the imitative arts (Kristeller 1951, 504). It was the development of mathematics (most of the early Greek philosophers were also mathematicians) that grew to be an unbridgeable dividing line between mental and manual labour in the West.

The application of mathematical principles in painting dramatically affected the status of the painter. Since artists were able to construct an organized spatial system based on mathematics, they became the quintessential doyens of the Enlightenment. This phenomenon is reflected in Leonardo da Vinci's treatise disseminated in the sixteenth century in which he likened painting to science and depicted painters as god-like since they could illustrate on canvas that which God had created on earth (Clark 1967, 74-75). (The importance of mathematics in the education of painters and its influence on their work are discussed in Baxandall 1972.) Ultimately an intellectual discourse was created between painters and their audiences.

Drawing became the hallmark of "artistic literacy," but it also provided the means to dictate to others what would be produced. The concept of the artist as a unique, outstanding individual developed in contrast to the view that the anonymous craftworker, using only technical ability, executed the specified designs of either a patron or artist. Hence, fine art became primarily an intellectual exercise, whereas the essence of craft production resided in the technical excellence of the completed piece. This distinction between art and craft coincided with the birth of modern capitalism and the emergence of art as a commodity and speculative asset (Hauser 1965).

The fundamental acceptance in Western philosophy of the formal dichotomy between mind and body reflects the ascendency of the visual over other senses. One of the most fundamental divisions in anthropology concerns the separation between literate and non-literate peoples. Literacy (including mathematics) is a major hallmark of civilization. Edmund Carpenter notes in *They Became What They Beheld* (1970) that "when a dominant sense comes into play, the other senses become junk," that "visual values became the mark of civilized man," and that "literacy ushered man into the world of the divided senses" (n.p.). He argues further that sight is the only sense that offers detachment. While this detachment gave literate people enormous power over their environment, it also led to a corresponding unwillingness to become engaged.

The primacy of visual values associated with artistic imperialism inherent in Western art history and aesthetics has shaped and conditioned anthropologists' appreciation of non-Western artifacts. Until recently, textiles have been collected by museum personnel as anthropological remnants of the past. Oversized books featuring "Indian arts" have appeared in the last forty years, but textiles have often been ignored. In *Prehistoric and Primitive Art,* the authors note: "The North American Indian's most distinctive arts are those which are traditional to all great Western civilizations: sculpture, painting, and architecture. His contribution to each of these branches of expression was strong. . . . The Indian was also a superb craftsman or technologist in such decorative or utilitarian media as weaving, basketry, ceramics, and tool or weapon making" (Luis Pericot-Garcia et al. 1967, 190). The authors' distinction represents an unconscious capitulation to the Western art/craft dichotomy. Only sculpture, painting, and architecture are means of expression. Basketry and weaving involve technological expertise and are divorced from expressive and artistic intent.

AESTHETICS

The discipline of aesthetics, which emerged during the latter part of the eighteenth century, canonized the art/craft distinction since it focussed on beauty as expressed only in non-utilitarian objects. The discipline itself comprised the study of beauty and the standards of value in judging beauty. Originally, aesthetics referred to a theory of sensory perception; ultimately, it referred only to sight. Classical aesthetics claimed that vision was superior to the other senses because of its detachment from its objects. (The notion of disinterestedness is central to classical Kantian aesthetics.)

Kant's notion of the sublime applied only to painting and sculpture as non-utilitarian objects and excluded, of course, everything created by human beings working in other media. Regardless of where they were located, nineteenth-century art galleries displayed only fine arts. Articles made by Aboriginal peoples were placed in museums (or in storage) if salvaged at all.

Abbe Batteaux codified the modern system of the fine arts in his treatise published in 1746. He distinguished the five fine arts of painting, sculpture, and architecture (the visual arts), and poetry and music (including dance) from the mechanical arts (Kristeller 1952, 20). The principle common to all arts involved the "imitation of beautiful nature" (Batteaux, cited in Kristeller 1952, 21), that is, realism. By the beginning of the nineteenth century, a number of influential German philosophers including Goethe, Hegel, and Kant had written or published major treatises on aesthetics (Kristeller 1952). Kant himself reinforced the notion of the division of mental and manual labour by presenting it as a transcendental necessity. In his famous treatise entitled *Critique of Judgement*, Kant postulated an absolute opposition between labour and art. He saw labour as a forced, unpleasant activity. Art, on the other hand, was "production through freedom" (Kant 1951, 146). Only "play" (art) could act as mediator to reconcile the formal dichotomy between mind and body, reason and emotion. Otherwise the two impulses were irreconcilable (Sohn-Rethel 1978).

The dualism presented by Kant remains a faithful reflection of the realities of modern capitalism (Sohn-Rethel 1978, 15). The philosophical tradition inherited by Kant and his contemporaries is itself a result of the division between mental and manual labour originating in Greek philosophy — a preserve of intellectuals for intellectuals. The reconciliation of the dichotomy (via art) is itself an intellectual process. Kant's dictum, "The necessary [functional] cannot be judged beautiful, but only right or consistent" (Kubler 1963, 16), provided the kiss of death for crafts.

All crafts suffered a dual penalty, for not only were they equated with manual/functional activities and needs and set off in opposition to art, which symbolized the intellectual and non-utilitarian, but also the status of craftworkers was diminished when a major portion of manual activity was replaced by machines. The creation of art since the Renaissance has occupied the attention of art critics, historians, aestheticians, academics, and artists themselves. The history of craft has been shaped by its exclusion from art history. The fine arts were defined in opposition to crafts: art was everything that craft was not — cerebral, creative, intellectual, individual, non-utilitarian, and European. Crafts were repetitious, mundane, inexpensive, functional, and predictable. Thus was art enshrined theoretically via aesthetics and institutionally through the art academies.

The history of craft in Europe from the end of the eighteenth century is the history of loss of status of craftworkers, through automation, de-skilling, degeneration of the working environment, regimentation, and intense competition — all of which ensured the lowest prices for the owners of productive means and less than living wages for the workers (Thompson and Yeo 1971). There is no doubt that textile production, as with all other practical "crafts," was little respected as a vocation by the upper classes. As an avocation — for example, the gentlewoman and her needlework — it was acceptable. This was the background upon which Aboriginal textiles — created primarily by women — were viewed. Ultimately, Aboriginal handweavers could be perceived as participating in an archaic process compared to de-skilled powerloom weavers.

THE NEGATION OF WOMEN'S ARTISTIC PRODUCTION

During the nineteenth century, crafts were described as being manually produced, decorative, and intellectually undemanding — all negative terms in the world of art. The ideal of realism reigned supreme, and all types of geometric pattern were considered inferior forms of design. The making of art during the Renaissance required the learning of specific techniques and skills within an institutional setting. Because of the organization of the art academies and the adherence of these institutions to social conventions, which prohibited women from enrolling, it was impossible for women to achieve a level of excellence that could equal that of men, regardless of how talented they were. The most important aspect of any artist's training required the attendance at drawing classes,which focussed on the male nude, and women were totally excluded from such classes until the end of the nineteenth century when drawing from the female nude became common.Women did manage to paint, however, and a few became famous. Often they were daughters, mistresses, or wives of famous painters because they were able to learn their skills at home. However, even by the beginning of the twentieth century, there were no biographies of women painters in major art history texts (Parker and Pollock 1981). Women have provided great themes in art (including the muse and her inspirational powers), but as creators, at least according to the records, they were scattered and few.

From the Renaissance onward, and through the process of industrialization, women in Europe and North America were increasingly denied a voice in public life. With few exceptions, women were absent from the spheres of business, politics, religion (except as supplicants), higher education, and, of course, art. Since women's aesthetic impulses could not be concretely realized in a male-dominated field, they created primarily within the domestic sphere. The cult of domesticity, or cult of motherhood, developed about the time when women began to lose their role as producers of essential goods (because of the advances made during the Industrial Revolution).

Prominent nineteenth-century critic and historian John Ruskin (1911) sanctioned the rigid division of roles between women and men. He noted that women's intellect was not for invention or creation: women had taste; men had talent. One of the ways that women failed to measure up was related to their predilection for geometric forms, graphically represented in quilts, coverlets, and Aboriginal textiles. In the early twentieth century, two historians of Neolithic art, Hoernes and Menghin, noted:

The geometric style is primarily a feminine style. The geometric ornament seems more suited to the *domestic*, pedantically tidy and at the same time superstitiously careful spirit of woman than that of man. It is, considered purely aesthetically, a petty, lifeless and, despite all its luxuriousness of colour, a strictly limited mode of art. *But within its limits*, healthy and efficient, pleasing by reason of the *industry* displayed and its *external decorativeness* — the expression of the feminine spirit in art. (Cited in Parker and Pollock 1981, 68; emphasis in original.)

Prior to the publication of these comments about the shortcomings of geometric designs, a cartoon appeared in the *New York Evening Sun* (1913), mocking a current exhibition that featured the introduction of Cubism to America. The cartoon, entitled "The Original Cubist," depicted an elderly woman stitching her patchwork quilt, and it had the following caption: "I tuk the fust prize at the fair last fall" (Dewhurst et al. 1979, 126). Although the drawing disparaged the new art style, it inadvertently acknowledged the long-established use of abstract designs in quilt making.

The fact that no notice was taken of the visual impact of many compelling textiles is proof of the pervasiveness and power of the art/craft distinction itself. Placed on beds or bodies instead of walls, textiles simply were not and could not be "seen" as art — they were located outside the frame of reference created and dominated by the art world. Unfortunately, the way in which art has become institutionalized over the last 300 years has shaped our perception of materials created outside the domain of the art world. Exclusion is a very powerful means of control. The sexual inequality of women (in relation to men) in Western patriarchal societies parallels the artistic inequality of craft (in relation to art). This inequality is underscored by the work of androcentric art historians and is reflected in the cultural hegemony in the West, where art dominates craft.

How ironic that classical aesthetics, which emphasized only sight, generated a severe case of tunnel vision! This trend, unfortunately, has had global repercussions. Since the Renaissance, the creation of "art" was channelled into an extremely narrow (and elitist) path. Entire media were denied; the creation of an artistic apartheid was celebrated by cultural mandarins who perpetuated powerful myths supporting their beliefs. Art became the new religion, and artists the high priests. For the chosen few, their shrines became collection plates. Monetary values acted as a barometer, and measured a very select portion of society's regard for artistic genius. The more I researched the genesis of the distinction between art and craft, the more paradoxical I understood it to be. The growth of this distinction is a great tragedy — catastrophic for all Aboriginal peoples and for Western societies, too.

In one sense, the art/craft distinction was a valid distinction in Europe for a long period of time. This is not to say that European craftworkers chose to relinquish the conceptual element of production. Indeed, it was forced upon them. But the division was unjustly applied to articles that Aboriginal peoples produced, since in Aboriginal societies there was no distinction between the conceptual and the manual. Yes, they were creating in media designated as "crafts," but the conceptual process, the most important aspect of creating, remained intact. In terms of its catastrophic effect, I think the art/craft distinction ranks second to the loss of Aboriginal lands, but it is more insidious. Because of the importance of trade in the earlier years of colonization, many articles fashioned by indigenous peoples were treated as if they were renewable resources and marketed by the pound. Since these were not "raw resources" but finished products often involving hundreds of hours of work, the extraction of surplus was intense. The seeds of underdevelopment were sown in the non-Western world due to rampant depredation by colonial merchants. The words of Mali historian Amadou Hampâté Bâ poignantly summarize the position of indigenous artisans everywhere:

We live in a very curious age. The amazing development of science and technology goes hand in hand, contrary to all expectations, with a worsening of living conditions. Along with the conquest of space has come a sort of shrinking of our world, which has been reduced to its material and visible dimensions alone, whereas the traditional African craftsman, who had never moved from his little village, had the feeling of participating in a world of infinite dimensions and being linked with the whole of the living universe. (Hampâté Bâ 1976, 17)

The biases produced by the fundamental structures of language and philosophical traditions dating back to the origins of Western civilization have undermined the recognition and appreciation of indigenous creativity and aesthetic traditions globally. Many of the world's most "valuable" textiles were produced by the ancestors of some of the poorest people on earth. Thus, aesthetics and economics remain inextricably linked.

TAPESTRY PRODUCTION IN THE CANADIAN ARCTIC

Because the history of craft has been shaped by its exclusion from art history, weaving occupies a nebulous zone in today's art market. Old, rare pieces, such as medieval tapestries or Navajo chiefs' blankets, are "redefined" as art and sought by collectors. Contemporary ethnic weaving, if exhibited at all, is displayed in folk-art galleries or ethnic museums. Only a very small percentage of contemporary weaving would be exhibited in an art gallery as art, especially contemporary weaving by a minority group. Although the art/craft distinction is blurring somewhat in certain art circles today, generally it has not been reflected in the marketing of weaving from the hinterlands.

The recent introduction of tapestry weaving in Pangnirtung, Northwest Territories (NWT), by the Canadian government (and subsidized by it), coupled with a marketing strategy that parallels that of the sculptures and prints, provides a provocative contrast to the usual position of weaving from the hinterlands as functional craft. The social division of labour involved in the production of prints and tapestries is ironic, given the genesis of the art/craft distinction itself. Howard Becker (1978, 863) defines the difference between artist and craftworker as follows: "The person who does the work that gives the product its unique and expressive character is called an 'artist' and the product itself 'art.' Other people whose skills contribute in a supporting way are called 'craftsmen.'" Interestingly, as Marybelle Myers states (1984, 135), the "Inuit don't distinguish between art and craft, but the buying public and especially the professional marketing groups certainly do!"

The Western model of tapestry production at the Pangnirtung weave shop mimics the European tradition that has operated since the Middle Ages. In order to grasp why this idea is important to my argument, it is necessary to examine how woven items were produced in other indigenous societies prior to colonization (and still are produced, the "traditional" way, in many societies today). Several people may be involved in gathering the plant or animal fibres used for weaving, and several people might share in the spinning and dyeing process, but one person is the weaver, and the individual who weaves the textile almost always designs it. The exception to this occurred in stratified societies such as the Inca, where a class of weavers produced textiles designed by a master weaver for royalty. Most weaving by pre-literate peoples continues to require a unique combination and coordination of conceptual, and especially manual, skills, since neither drawings nor other preliminaries are created before weaving begins.

The ability of indigenous makers to solve "problems" concerning such elements as design, colour, and symmetry was developed after years of concentrated manipulation of materials: a selection and rejection of ideas, and a fine-tuned dialectic involving the undivided process of creation and production sustained by each individual. Without a formal mechanism (i.e., a drawing) in place to communicate the design, each indigenous artist was compelled to develop the ability necessary to conceptualize and produce many items necessary for personal and/or tribal use or trade. Hence, the creative process was endemic in all Aboriginal societies. Because of the implicit bias concerning the art/craft distinction, coupled with ignorance regarding the weaving process as articulated in Aboriginal societies, colonizers usually perceived textiles as conservative elements in simple societies; patterns, colours, and techniques rarely deviated from those produced previously. Archaeologist Junius Bird (1963, 49) notes: "The recognition of art in textiles is perhaps obscured by the great volume of past and present production."

The organization of production at the Pangnirtung weave shop provides a provocative contrast to indigenous textile production in other parts of the world. The weaving tradition at Pangnirtung, now twenty-five years old, uses techniques and materials borrowed from indigenous peoples (with the implication of "craft"), yet all Inuit tapestries are sold as art in a few select galleries in North America. How did a handful of weavers on Baffin Island achieve this kind of recognition in less than a generation? Their success parallels that of Inuit soapstone carvers and printmakers whose works have appeared in major art galleries in Europe and North America in the past few decades.

This paradox became increasingly apparent during my two field trips to Pangnirtung.[1] Prior to that period, I had spent several summers in the southwest United States researching and photographing Navajo textiles in preparation for my Master's thesis. I made several visits to the Office of Economic Development in Iqaluit, NWT, and presented my research agenda to the administrators. After viewing my slides from the southwest, Economic Development fieldworkers remarked in astonishment at the quality of Navajo weaving that was maintained without "government supervision."

The Pangnirtung weave shop is one of the most successful workshops ever established in the Arctic. Government-sponsored weaving shops were once located in Broughton Island and Cape Dorset, but currently the Pangnirtung shop remains the only one in continuous operation. It employs approximately twelve Inuit women, who each work forty hours a week, and half of them weave items associated with northern living: scarves, blankets, throws, ties, and the *akujulik*, or "parka with the little tail" (personal notes, Baffin Island field trip 1981) patterned after the traditional *amautik*, the women's winter parka that has a roomy back pouch in which a child can be carried.

Many types of looms are used in indigenous societies, including the backstrap, ground, and upright looms, which are quite different from the floor looms of European invention, which were developed during the Middle Ages. In Pangnirtung, novices begin by weaving the *Pang* braid, or narrow band, on a European-style inkle loom and then graduate to the floor loom to weave larger items such as tapestries. When a weaver feels she is ready to try tapestry weaving, she will begin on a small piece (1 m by 1.5 m). All tapestries currently woven feature figures, some representing Inuit in traditional clothing engaged in various activities "on the land," and others depicting birds or animals (real or imaginary).

Until the early 1980s, any Inuit member of the community who brought a cartoon (a sketch prepared ahead by an artist to communicate the desired design of a work of art) to the shop received $5. If that design was chosen to be woven, the artist received $20. Each time the design was editioned (up to twenty times), the artist received an additional fee. The cost to the consumer for an editioned tapestry escalated by $50 every time it was woven. (For example, many designs have been supplied as cartoons by Malaya Akulukjuk, a woman in her seventies who lived in camp until 1960.) Only the finest wool yarns are used, imported from Ontario and Iceland (the latter used in the scarves and blankets). Every tapestry is "signed" by the weaver in Inuktitut.

In the early 1980s, at the time of my research, full-time tapestry weavers earned approximately $700 a month. The more experienced weavers usually managed two tapestries a month and received about fifty percent of the final price of the piece. Canadian Arctic Producers (CAP) marketed all Pangnirtung weaving, but since the mid-1980s all tapestries are marketed directly to several Inuit art galleries located in large cities in North America. The functional (as opposed to purely decorative) items were shipped to various gift shops. There was a large backlog of orders, and special requests often required up to one year to complete. Sizes range from .75 m by 1 m to 2 m by 2.5 m; costs vary from $775 to $3,600 (1993 prices). A few large rugs (2 m by 3 m) designed by a well-known Ottawa weaver were commissioned, each selling for over $4,000.

Pangnirtung weavers do not spin or dye the wool. Spinning is extremely time consuming and would add considerable cost to each tapestry. Water is scarce (especially in the early spring), and lichen growth so fragile, that dyeing with native plants would be environmentally detrimental; therefore all yarns are imported. Although the articles produced by the Pangnirtung weavers are in high demand the weave shop has run deficits as high as $50,000 annually. The high overhead, including salaries and the cost of materials and transportation, contributes to the chronic deficits of even the most successful workshops. Because of these deficits, and because the government ultimately measures success in economic terms, the future of all workshops in the Arctic is in jeopardy; this is truly unfortunate because the workshops have always fulfilled important social needs in the communities.

THE ORGANIZATION OF THE WEAVE SHOP

As in all other Arctic workshops, weaving is a totally imported activity. Nothing remotely similar was ever done "pre-historically" because loom materials and appropriate fibres were simply not available. The looms used in Pangnirtung are totally unlike the portable backstrap and upright looms used by indigenous peoples in many other parts of the world (e.g., Mexico, Central and South America, India, Indonesia, and Africa). Pangnirtung weavers use floor looms made in Quebec that are fashioned after European models invented during the Middle Ages. These floor looms are the most expensive looms available, but they are preferred because the foot treadles on them allow the weaver to work much faster than on more traditional looms, where a great deal of the work must be done with the hands. In addition, a twenty to twenty-five metre warp may be put on the loom and a number of pieces woven on it before the addition of another warp is necessary. When one weaves on a more traditional hand-operated loom, usually only one item can be woven per warp. The more "primitive" the loom, the slower the process. Weaving is a slow process with any kind of loom, but weaving time with a floor loom is fifty percent faster than with a hand-operated one.

The production of each Pangnirtung tapestry involves a social division of labour. The weavers use full-scale cartoons, which are pinned behind the warp threads, to copy exactly the artist's design (just as the European tapestry weavers did during the Renaissance). During the 1970s, designs in the form of cartoons were purchased from local Inuit, or rejects from the printshop were used. More recently, drawings are purchased from Inuit artists employed making drawings for the printshop. The earlier works by villagers were frequently altered by the workshop managers to render a design suitable for weaving. However, when a design is provided by a recognized artist, changes are seldom made. Koreula de Patie, manager in the late 1980s, noted that the quality of the designs would improve when artists were drawing potential tapestry patterns because they would incorporate more design and detail than many of the villagers would. The workshop manager decides how large each tapestry should be (variation in size is necessary in order to provide a broad price range for the marketplace), and she carefully enlarges each drawing to scale. Currently, twelve full-time and five part-time weavers work at the tapestry studio. Each weaver decides which design she would like to use for weaving a new edition. The weavers choose the colours from the yarns ordered by the weave-shop manager. Sometimes the weavers' colour choices are too subtle, and the manager encourages them to use brighter colours. And when an additional copy of a tapestry is produced by a different weaver, she may decide on colour changes. The current manager is an Inuit woman and former weaver at the studio; previous to the current manager, it was necessary to have an interpreter on the premises.

Five of the Pangnirtung weavers at the co-operative have small table looms at home and weave mini tapestries (30 by 40 cm). These are sold to local residents and tourists who visit Pangnirtung. Here too, the designs come from artists in the community. Colour changes may be made as each design is re-woven.

Over the years since its inception, the weave shop's success has greatly fluctuated. Because the Inuit women had no traditional background in weaving, the quality of the work varied directly with the professional training and standards of the manager who was in place. There was a period in the mid-1970s when piece after piece piled up in CAP's warehouse — technically there was nothing wrong with the tapestries, but the designs were poorly chosen, the colours were unsuitable, and the edges were finished inappropriately with a long macramé fringe. Because the weave-shop manager imports all wool, she has control over the colours available to the weavers. The edges are now finished with a Swedish braid technique that is much more suitable to the pieces; consequently, the finished tapestries look very "slick" and professional. During the 1980s, the fortunes of the weave shop changed when a new manager made the decision to opt out of CAP marketing. Twelve galleries were hand-picked in North America to handle only the tapestries, and this action greatly enhanced the acceptance of the tapestries as "fine art" (see: Lindgren and Lindgren 1981; Stuart 1972).

All items produced in the Arctic and marketed elsewhere must conform to the highest artistic standards; otherwise the consumer will not be interested. Because of high overhead and transportation costs, and to avoid exploiting the Inuit economically, prices remain elevated. Craft items (as distinct from "art"), including handsewn pieces, have never returned a decent amount to the producer. Only by working in a subsidized shop and producing the finest-quality items can individuals make any money at all. But all these subsidized workshops are under extreme economic pressure, and closure remains an imminent possibility. Sadly, the economic future of the individual Inuit artists is therefore also at risk.

CONCLUSION

Weavers in pre-literate societies (and in many Aboriginal societies today that are literate) weave without drawings and create directly on the warp; that is, individuals are compelled to master the entire process. During the Middle Ages, drawing became the equivalent of artistic literacy, and it has played *the* central historical role in the training of an artist. Its supreme importance has affected Westerners' perceptions concerning Aboriginal production, has shaped terminology, and has consequently skewed an appreciation of the fundamental processes concerning the creation of *art*. Scholars of classical art history have successfully constructed an ideology promoting the notion that "true creativity" is the exclusive domain of the conceptualizer, that is, the artist responsible for the image. And the term *artist* was denied to all Aboriginals because they created functional articles in media categorized as crafts.

Regardless of the medium, individual expression is an essential ingredient in producing a work of art. But, in the Pangnirtung weave shop, the works of art are produced by more than one individual (co-operation must occur) and a curious paradox results when the process is explored in reference to the art/craft distinction. Does the social division of labour in the Arctic weave shops militate against individual expression? (Yes!) Or is there a trade-off, where the loss of individual expression is balanced by the role of these workshops in offsetting Inuit unemployment, which is endemic in the North? Or does it really matter that individual expression is lost, when the production of art constitutes meaningful activity for many Inuit? These are questions worth pondering. And it is important also to understand that the capitalist marketplace provides its own constraints, which often remain hidden. The classification of Pangnirtung tapestries as art, combined with sophisticated marketing strategies, masks the reality of production at the weave shop. Given the social division of labour, in which the conceptual component is provided by artists, the weavers are defined as technicians who execute artists' designs by providing (manual) labour. Without an understanding of how things were made in pre-capitalist societies, coupled with an awareness of the historical construction of categories such as *art* and *craft*, it is difficult to recognize the constraints operating in the creation of art in indigenous societies that are shaped by capitalist relations.

NOTES

Certain portions of this paper were published as part of my paper entitled "Some Ruminations on Textile Production by the Navajo and Inuit," in *Papers from the Third, Fourth and Sixth Navajo Studies Conferences* (Window Rock, AZ: Historic Preservation Department, The Navajo Nation, 1993).

1. Funded by Northern Studies Grants, September 1981 and September 1982.

REFERENCES

Ackerman, Phyllis. 1933. *Tapestry, the Mirror of Civilization.* New York: Oxford University Press.
Baxandall, Michael. 1972. *Painting and Experience in Fifteenth Century Italy: A Primer in the Social History of Pictorial Style.* Oxford: Clarendon Press.

Becker, Howard S. 1978. "Arts and Crafts." *American Journal of Sociology* 83, no. 4:862-89.

Bird, Junius B. 1963. "Technique and Art in Peruvian Textiles." In *Technique and Personality,* ed. Margaret Mead, Junius B. Bird, and Hans Himmelheber. New York: Museum of Primitive Art.

Carpenter, Edmund. 1970. *They Became What They Beheld.* New York: Ballantine Books, Inc.

Clark, Kenneth. 1967. *Leonardo da Vinci: An Account of his Development as an Artist.* Baltimore: Penguin Books Ltd.

Dewhurst, C. Kurt, Betty MacDowell, and Marsha MacDowell. 1979. *Artists in Aprons: Folk Art by American Women.* New York: E.P. Dutton, in association with the Museum of American Folk Art.

Etienne, Mona, and Eleanor Leacock, eds. 1980. *Women and Colonization: Anthropological Perspectives.* New York: Praeger Publishers.

Hampâté Bâ, Amadou. 1976. "African Art, Where the Hand has Ears." *The UNESCO Courier* (29 February):12-17.

Hauser, Arnold. 1965. *Mannerism: The Crisis of the Renaissance and the Origin of Modern Art, Volume 1: Text.* New York: Alfred A. Knopf.

Hedges, Elaine, and Ingrid Wendt. 1980. *In Her Own Image: Women Working in the Arts.* New York: The Feminist Press.

Kant, Immanuel. 1951. *Critique of Judgement.* New York: Hafner Press.

Kristeller, Paul Oskar. 1951. "The Modern System of the Arts: A Study in the History of Aesthetics (I)." *Journal of the History of Ideas* 12:496-527.

———. 1952. "The Modern System of the Arts: A Study in the History of Aesthetics (II)." *Journal of the History of Ideas* 13:17-46.

Kubler, George. 1963. *The Shape of Time: Remarks on the History of Things.* New Haven: Yale University Press.

Lindgren, Charlotte, and Edward Lindgren. 1981. "The Pangnirtung Tapestries." *Beaver* (autumn):34-39.

M'Closkey, Kathleen. 1985. "The Institutionalization of Art with Two Internal Colonies: A Comparison of the Inuit and the Navajo." Master's thesis, University of Windsor.

Mitchell, James, and Jess Stein, eds. 1977. "Mathematics and Civilization." *The Random House Encyclopedia.* New York: Random House, Inc.

Myers, Marybelle. 1984. "Inuit Arts and Crafts Co-operatives in the Canadian Arctic." *Canadian Ethnic Studies* 16, no. 3:132-53.

Parker, Rozsika, and Griselda Pollock. 1981. *Old Mistresses: Women, Art and Ideology.* New York: Pantheon Books.

Pericot-Garcia, Luis, John Galloway, and Andreas Lommel. 1967. *Prehistoric and Primitive Art.* New York: Harry Abrams, Inc.

Pevsner, Nikolaus. 1940. *Academies of Art, Past and Present.* Cambridge: Cambridge University Press.

Pollock, Griselda. 1988. *Vision and Difference: Femininity, Feminism, and the Histories of Art.* London: Routledge.

Ruskin, John. 1911. "Of Queens' Gardens." In *Sesame and Lilies: The Two Paths and the King of the Golden River.* New York: E.P. Dutton.

Sohn-Rethel, Alfred. 1978. *Intellectual and Manual Labour: A Critique of Epistemology.* New Jersey: Humanities Press.

Stuart, Donald. 1972. "Weaving at Pangnirtung, N.W.T." *Craftsmanslash: L'Artisan* 5:16-17.

Thompson, E.P., and Eileen Yeo. 1971. *The Unknown Mayhew.* London: Merlin Press Ltd.

Wolf, Eric R. 1982. *Europe and the People without History.* Berkeley: University of California Press.

Wolff, Janet. 1983. *Aesthetics and the Sociology of Art.* London: George Allen and Unwin (Publishers) Ltd.

Voices through Time

Betty Bastien

One of the major roles of Indian women has been to maintain "tribal identity" for their children and their children's children. Tribal identity is based on the collective experience, in which relationships are characterized by the interdependencies of self with others, in which partnership is the basis of life and the force through which life is strengthened and renewed, and in which children experience themselves as tribal people rather than as individuals. The collective experience is strengthened and renewed in ceremony, where children are empowered with the knowledge of the sacredness of relationships, which itself comes from the knowledge that tribal people are connected, in a web, to all of creation. Within this web, a Native woman gives her child unconditional love as she receives it from Mother Earth. She teaches her child a reverence of and a profound respect for all creation, because everyone in creation participates in a manner that perpetuates and strengthens life. Father Sun teaches woman that life grows in the web of creation. In raising her child, a Native woman teaches that responsibility lies in nurturing and renewing the relationship with all creation. This is ceremony — the direct processes of relationships and the obligation to renew these relationships (Peat 1994, 66-68).

It is important to note that tribal identity among tribal peoples has been effectively negated by the oppression of Indian people in the process of colonization. According to Remi Clignet (1971), who draws on the works of Memmi, Fanon, Mannoni, and Freire, a feeling of self-hate is perpetuated among any oppressed people. As explained by the "universality of culture" theory, oppressed people actually try to emulate their oppressors in an attempt to gain equality (1971, 307), and this emulation of the oppressor's culture comes about through the process of assimilation. In Canada, assimilation of Indians has been imposed through the education system, which has promised us upward mobility within the context of Canadian culture. However, in reality, the education of Native children has instead been a systematic assault on Indian culture, and the result has been the continued failure of Native children. Thus, the system only reinforces feelings of inferiority (Davis and Zannis 1973, 127-28).

Within the framework of assimilation, the oppressor presents the illusion that the members of the oppressed group will be awarded the privileges enjoyed by their oppressors. However, the experience of tribal people has been just the opposite; instead, we have systematically been excluded from institutional change, that is, amendments to the Indian Act, and the entrenchment of self-government in the Constitution. Canada's legislation, policy, and procedures are all designed to exclude Indian people, though the official claim is to integrate us.

This paradox is intrinsic to the Indian Act itself, which governs and administers the daily processes that structure the lives of Indian people. This act is based on the principles of civilizing and assimilating Indian people into mainstream society; however, it does so while keeping us separate through its definition of status and a system of apartheid. The institutional processes are subtle but pervasive in their destruction of the interpersonal relations of tribal people.

The process of institutionalized cultural genocide has had a critical effect on the development of our collective "sense of self," which can be measured by observing the experiences of several generations of our people. In our interaction with a society laced with racism and cultural annihilation, we have gradually lost our vitality, spontaneity, and creativity. This process can be compared with the insidious but progressive erosion of the ecological systems on our planet and the destruction of the ozone layer.

To understand the devastating aspect of this cultural annihilation is to understand the significance of tribal identity. Native American anthropologist Alfonso Ortiz (1969) describes tribal identity "as a feeling of rootedness, of belonging to a time and place" (cited in Beck and Walters 1977, 5). Vine Deloria Jr. (1973), Native scholar, author, and lawyer, speaks of the "self" as the source of meaning and purpose to life itself (cited in Highwater 1981, 169-72). One's sense of tribal identity allows for a perception of reality; and a strong sense of tribal identity brings alive, with vitality and inspiration, the expectations, desires, and purpose of life for Indian people. As Indian women, we have traditionally held the responsibility of providing our children with a sense of belonging to a time and place. However, the process of colonization has made this task difficult. Undoubtedly, without the strength of tribal women, many of our people today would not have survived culturally. Indian people within a tribal context would cease to exist. It is time to acknowledge the importance of Indian women as a source of strength in maintaining the continuity of traditions through difficult times. Indian women, because of the strength of our vision, have forged a reality that interprets the experiences of our children, in turn giving them strength to maintain the vision and to pass it on to their own children.

Traditionally, ceremony gave tribal children self-concepts that were not separate from, but connected to, a community of both human and non-human spirits. Tribal children were never abandoned or neglected, and they did not suffer from alienation or apathy. Today, as Indian women struggle to balance traditional roles and the dominant society's expectations of us, many of our children find life meaningless. The rate for suicide among Native youth is up to six times higher than the national rate for the same age group (under the age of twenty-five), and Indian women experience violence at intolerable levels. These issues are directly related to oppression — oppression of a group of people with a different world view from that of the oppressor. Indian people have survived only because of the strength of our tribal identity, which provides the courage to continue to face a new day with hope. Our children are our hope. We must not forget. We must never forget our role as women in teaching children the context in which to introduce themselves, and to place themselves within the centre of the universe.

I am your relative; my father is Sun, the source of life; my mother is Earth, who provides life with nourishment; my grandmother Moon, who provides light when there is darkness; and my grandfather is Morning Star, providing the guidance to a new day. (anonymous)[1]

NOTES

1. These powerful words were said at a conference I attended, entitled "Our Circle of Wellness: Prevention of Substance Abuse," in Albuquerque, New Mexico, 22-24 May 1990.

REFERENCES

Beck, Peggy V., and Anna L. Walters. 1977. *The Sacred Ways of Knowledge and Sources of Life.* Tsaile, AZ: Navajo Community College Press.

Clignet, Remi. 1971. "Damned If You Do, Damned If You Don't": The Dilemma of Colonizer-Colonized Relations." *Comparative Education Review* 15, no. 3:296-312.

Davis, Robert, and Mark Zannis. 1973. *The Genocide Machine in Canada: The Pacification of the North.* Montreal: Black Rose Books Ltd.

Deloria, Vine, Jr. 1973. *God is Red.* New York: Grosset and Dunlop.

Highwater, Jamake. 1981. *The Primal Mind: Vision and Reality in Indian America.* New York: Harper and Row.

Ortiz, Alfonso. 1969. *The Tewa World: Space, Time, Being, and Becoming in a Pueblo Society.* Chicago: University of Chicago Press.

The Changing Employment of Cree Women in Moosonee and Moose Factory

Jennifer Blythe and Peggy Martin McGuire

In this paper we examine the changing employment patterns of Cree women living in Moosonee and Moose Factory, two predominantly Cree communities on the south shore of James Bay in northern Ontario. Moose Factory is situated on an island in the Moose River. Moosonee is located nearby on the western bank of the river. The data came from a research project on women and work conducted in 1984 under the auspices of the Research Program for Technology Assessment in Subarctic Ontario (TASO), McMaster University. Three principal investigators teamed with a group of Cree women to administer a series of surveys and interviews with women aged fourteen to ninety.[1] Our aim was to contribute to a baseline profile of the region and to understand how the work and family roles of Aboriginal women in northern Ontario have been influenced by socio-economic change.

The decisions women make about how to support themselves and their families depend in part on their ambitions, values, and abilities, but their choices are constrained by environmental and social considerations. Women who live in small towns in northern Ontario find a limited range of jobs available. Gender, ethnicity, and education further restrict choice, and, in addition, women face ethical decisions about balancing personal goals and the economic advantages of certain jobs against the non-financial needs of their families. In this paper, we review how these constraints have influenced the employment choices of women of different ages in the two communities. By looking at choices along two axes — historical change and maturational change — we can compare some of the conditions of choice faced by young women with those of their elders. In order to understand the context of the choices being made, we briefly refer to two approaches used by writers to conceptualize change in northern communities — Marxist theory and modernization theory. More central to our argument, however, is the concept of stake in family and community, which gives us a framework for investigating the shifting perceptions of family responsibility in relation to community cohesion.

HISTORICAL TRENDS

The Hudson's Bay Company established a settlement on Moose Factory Island in 1673. A trading post has existed there permanently since 1730, and there was a well-established, settled population by 1800. Moosonee also began as a trading settlement, but it dates only from 1902 when Revillon Frères established a post there. Local Cree traded with the companies, trapping in the winter and setting up temporary encampments near the posts in the summer. Some Aboriginal people, often the progeny of Company servants and Cree women, were permanent employees of the companies. Jennifer Brown (1980) has written extensively about the lives of these Company wives in the eighteenth and nineteenth centuries. In this paper, however, we concentrate on employment in the twentieth century, the period experienced by the oldest of the women living in the two towns. During this time, as trapping families left their mobile life in the bush and settled in the communities, the inhabitants' concept of community changed from a focus on people to a focus on place.

The fragile economy of the communities of Moosonee and Moose Factory has always restricted job opportunities. Until the early 1930s, the two communities had only a small permanent population, consisting of Company employees and their families. Numbers increased when Cree people moved into the settlements in search of relief in the periods of famine and poor hunting that characterized the early twentieth century. Also, in the summers, trappers came to sell pelts and get supplies for the next season, and men found casual work helping to unload the yearly supply boats. A few Cree women found employment as well, and others made leather goods or snowshoes for sale at the posts. Most older women who lived this life remember a childhood spent on the land, learning women's work from their mothers and a modicum of men's skills from their fathers. Although they specialized in tasks that were considered women's, they also had enough knowledge to provide themselves with necessities when the men were absent on extended hunting or trading trips.

The late 1920s and the 1930s were a period of economic stagnation. The world price of furs fell, and the fur companies ceased to give the trappers advances for the winter season. Cree families had the choice of remaining in town, hoping for government relief or casual employment, or of returning to the bush with inadequate supplies. It was their misfortune that the Depression coincided with the decline of game and a shortage of food animals brought about by a combination of natural cycles and overtrapping by outsiders. Some families settled permanently in town at this time, finding employment when they could. The most enterprising among them supplemented their food supply by growing potatoes as well as by fishing, preserving geese, and gathering wild foods. In spite of the hard economic times, a few Cree women who grew up in the Depression recalled happy, if hardworking, childhoods, but they had fathers who were employed for at least part of the period, and they had energetic mothers who gardened, fished, and salted geese. Among families who decided to trap, people sometimes starved or succumbed to minor illnesses from hunger. One woman explained how influenza and hunger combined to kill her mother and three brothers in a single winter. A few families settled on the reserve at French River, where the Indian agent introduced goats and encouraged people to grow potatoes. Surplus potatoes were sometimes sold to logging camps down the railway track, but the farming project was never very successful.

While the towns remained small in the 1930s, their character began to change. There were tentative plans to establish a port at the mouth of the Moose River, and the railway was extended from Cochrane to Moosonee to service it. The plans for the port were cancelled, but the railway made the town less isolated. More permanent institutions were established at Moosonee as the government began to pay more attention to the area. A small hospital was built, and an Indian agent and a police officer were sent to the communities. A residential school, Horden Hall, was established on Moose Factory Island. A few Cree women who had settled on the island with their families now were able to find work as cleaners, kitchen help, and laundry workers. However, the economic situation was still desperate. In 1932, the Hudson's Bay Company moved its headquarters to Winnipeg and closed down its farming operations. Ship building and maintenance also ceased. Men from families with many years of service with the Company found themselves unemployed. In 1935, Indian Affairs records reported: "Many of the members of this band [Moose Band] were employed as servants of the Company, but no work is now attainable since the Company has removed its headquarters. Consequently they are now almost destitute depending on the Government for aid" (PAC 1935).

After the Second World War, both communities grew. A reserve was established on Moose Factory Island, and men found work constructing new houses. At this time, tuberculosis had reached epidemic proportions in the James Bay area, and a large hospital was built on the island. This led to increased employment for women. While the professional staff came largely from southern Ontario, there were a considerable number of unskilled jobs that could be filled by local people. Indirectly, the hospital also stimulated a local crafts industry. Patients, particularly Inuit, occupied themselves with various crafts during their long hospitalization and sold them to hospital staff. Cree women working at the hospital also began to produce moccasins and other leather and beadwork articles for sale. After they retired from hospital work, some of these women continued to make crafts as a means of supplementing their pensions.

In the 1950s, work associated with the construction of a Canadian Forces base and the DEWLine early-warning radar system became available for Cree men in Moosonee. A few of their wives also found employment as the town grew. The populations of both communities increased rapidly as people from settlements on both the east and west coasts of James Bay came to find work, to seek medical attention, or to be near children who were attending school. Unlike French River, the new reserve on the island soon attracted a large population. Other migrants, mainly from the east coast of James Bay, settled in tents on lands belonging to the Anglican Church. A squatter settlement also grew up in Moosonee to the south of the old town.

In Moosonee, in particular, the period of relative prosperity did not last long. In the 1960s, eighty percent of the indigenous inhabitants were on welfare. The southern section of town was occupied by squatters, who lived in tents and sub-standard buildings. Here, lack of sanitation and inadequate nutrition characterized a community that was both sickly and demoralized (Bucksar 1968, 15). Eventually, two government reports led to local changes, which included the establishment of a local government body in 1968 — the Moosonee Development Area Board — and the extension of services to the squatter settlement. As well, the James Bay Education Centre was created to provide adult education courses, and the school system was improved. A new public school was built, and a local high school was established on the site of the Canadian Forces base, which had closed in 1975. As the passenger service of the Canadian Northern Railways, dubbed the Polar Bear Express, became more frequent, tourism began to develop in the area. Provincial government offices were established in Moosonee, and the Department of Indian Affairs set up an office on Moose Factory Island. All these new institutions provided jobs, and, while the unemployment rate in the two communities remained high, the number of persons permanently on welfare drastically decreased. In particular, a significant number of jobs became available for local Cree women in offices and the service industries.

WORK PATTERNS OF CREE WOMEN
IN THE TWENTIETH CENTURY

There are no accurate census figures for Moosonee and Moose Factory. The population of the towns is mobile and official statistical data are generally agreed to be extremely inaccurate. However, we estimate that the two towns had a combined population of approximately 3,000 to 3,500 in the mid-1980s. About eighty percent of Moosonee and eighty-five to ninety percent of Moose Factory residents were Cree. Most non-Aboriginals were temporary migrants from southern Ontario, though a few were permanent residents. Most members of the Moose Band lived on the reserve on Moose Factory Island. Members of other bands and those without band status lived in the off-reserve portion of the island where the hospital, a Hudson's Bay Company store, some government offices, and the school were located. Moosonee had a more urban appearance than Moose Factory. There were more stores, offices, and institutions, and the population was more heterogeneous. The non-Cree population was larger than that of the island, and the Cree population included members of a variety of northern Ontario bands as well as a considerable number of people without band status.

While it is impossible to assess with accuracy what proportion of the adult Cree women then living in the community completed our questionnaire, we estimate that it was between one quarter and one third. The sample was not random. The Cree interviewers made extensive use of personal and family networks in collecting the data, and it is probable that unemployed and less educated women are under-represented. However, we believe that the sample is a large enough portion of the population to reveal significant trends.

The type of employment that Cree women took during their working lives depended on two variables: age and level of education. These overlapped — different jobs were possible or desired at different periods in women's lives; and, of course, different jobs were available according to the amount of education attained. Before the 1960s, formal education was not a factor because only unskilled jobs were available anyway. In the 1970s and '80s, jobs became available that required more education, the older women in our study typically had little education, and the younger women had had more opportunity to acquire education; consequently, the better jobs were filled by the younger women. Of course, age and education level did not explain an individual's employment pattern entirely. Local networks and personal characteristics were also important factors. Nevertheless, certain patterns were evident in the employment histories of Cree women of different ages and educational backgrounds. Our sample included thirty-four older women (those over sixty); thirty-six middle-aged women (between forty-five and sixty); sixty-one mature adult women (from thirty to forty-four); and 115 young women (between fourteen and thirty), all but thirty-two of whom were between twenty and twenty-nine. The various categories were set up to target: (a) retired women; (b) women with adult families; (c) women with school-aged children; and (d) women who had either no children or small children.

In our discussion, we refer to two common theoretical models — Marxism and modernization theory. Marxist feminist theory suggests that the status of women declines with modernization and industrialization as the family is absorbed into the general system of cash payment for labour performed and production for exchange rather than use (see, for example: Leacock 1981; Rapp 1975; Bourgeault 1983). Some modernization theorists, on the other hand, have suggested that women acquire more status when they leave the domestic realm and enter the marketplace (see, for example: Boserup 1970; Tilly and Scott 1978; Armstrong and Armstrong 1978). The Marxist model, which emphasizes the separation of domestic and public realms under capitalism, can help us understand the changes that the older women faced as their labour became relegated to the home as separate from the workplace. The modernization theory, which emphasizes individual attainment of status through modernization, can help us understand the struggles of younger women to enter the public workplace. Neither model can completely explain the intergenerational changes faced by the women included in our data. While both Marxist and modernization theories are inadequate to explain the effect of colonialism and industrialization on women's lives in the two remote northern Ontario communities, both can provide some understanding. The Marxist model has some value for understanding effects on the lives of older women, while the modernization theory model is more relevant to the situation of younger women. We also discuss the position of women of all ages in terms of the concept of "stake in family and community," to provide a framework that will emphasize the perceptions and strategies of Cree women themselves in dealing with rapid change.

WOMEN OVER SIXTY

As the Cree people became enmeshed in the fur trade, and became increasingly involved in and dependent on the marketplace, change proceeded to some extent along lines suggested by the Marxist model. When we examine the changes in the lives of northern Aboriginal women that came with missionization and the fur trade, including attempts by missionaries to reorganize families according to a nuclear, patriarchal model, it is clear that women suffered some loss of autonomy in their family and community responsibilities.

In northern Ontario, the Cree economy has been affected by the fur trade since the seventeenth century. The men of some Aboriginal families had a long history of employment with the trading companies. The notion that men be primary wage-earners and senior partners in their families developed among them as a result of European influence. Yet, in most families that continued trapping in the bush, considerable autonomy remained with the women. The flexible complementarity of gender roles traditionally enjoyed in Cree families became eroded after women's unpaid work in the home became less valued than work outside the home. This did not occur until the Cree became urbanized.

Most Cree women over sixty in our sample had retired or were working in the home during the period covered in our study. The majority had begun their lives in the bush, migrating into town permanently from the 1920s to the 1950s. They recalled their childhoods in detail and the ways in which they were taught the various skills that had prepared them for life on the land. Their informal education stressed independence, self-reliance, and flexibility. Life in small groups fostered co-operation and continuity between generations, and children learned easily from their elders. Their families trapped in winter, and some recalled living on Charlton Island or at Hanna Bay in summer when they or members of their family worked for one of the companies. A few women had lived permanently in the settlements, and, while the lives of these women had been less subject to contingency than those who had lived in the bush, the sophistication of life in town in the early twentieth century should not be exaggerated. Game food was important in their diets, and women fished and gathered berries. In fact, a few had married trappers and managed to adapt themselves to a nomadic existence.

The work that women did as trappers' wives was both essential and respected as complementary to that of their husbands, but, when trapping families moved to town, the expectation was that men rather than women would be employed; and work for money was highly valued. Nevertheless, the notion that employment for wages was more highly valued than other ways of earning a living, for example, the selling of crafts, that men should be employed, and that men's work was more valuable than women's, probably influenced the self-concept of those who grew up in the bush less than it did the more urbanized, younger women.

Some older Cree women had never worked outside the home, but when a bush-oriented couple moved permanently into town from the bush it was common for both husband and wife to seek work. Those women over sixty had little education, usually no more than a year or two at a mission school where they were taught religion and literacy in Cree. Those born to Company families were bilingual, but the majority spoke only Cree. However, neither the English language nor formal education was essential for getting a job in town. Practical skills were the criteria for employment from the 1930s to the 1950s. Cree women worked as domestics either at the hospital or the residential school (Horden Hall) and some remained in these jobs until they retired in the 1960s and 1970s. There is no evidence that these women associated low social status with these jobs. Their sense of personal competence came instead from their mastery of traditional skills and from their experience of dealing with contingency, and so they were not greatly affected by EuroCanadian measures of social prestige.

In 1984, the problems of these older Cree women were related not to their employment but to the adequacy of their income from transfer payments. Most received only Canada pension, which was minimal, and some of those, particularly widows, were forced to live in substandard housing. The cost of living in Moosonee and Moose Factory was (and is) high, and these women sometimes suffered considerable hardship. The more fortunate lived with a married, employed child or grandchild. A number of them had taken up crafts while working at the hospital and since retirement had marketed them through the Homemakers Cooperative (in Moosonee) or the Cree Cultural Centre (in Moose Factory). They specialized in leather items and were the first generation to adapt traditional items to the tourist market. In terms of rate per hour, the return on crafts was very low, but for these women the expenditure of time was worth the effort because there were few other ways of earning money. For some, making crafts had social as well as monetary benefits. Those who attended the Cree Cultural Centre, either to work on crafts or sell, found it a place to meet friends and neighbours. A few older women who were still fit did find other ways of supplementing their income from transfer payments. One woman reported that she sold homemade bread from her house; another explained how she and her husband made doughnuts to raise money for particular projects; while a third said she tanned hides to sell to craftswomen. These women still exhibited the enterprise and tenacity that they had shown when they migrated to town, but some of them were isolated from the extended family support that they would have enjoyed in a nomadic hunting community. Those who lived alone were especially marginalized in the money-oriented community because of their low incomes and because the focus of co-operation had shifted from the community to the household.

WOMEN FROM FORTY-FIVE TO SIXTY

A few Cree women between forty-five and sixty had lived in the bush, but the majority had spent their youth in town or passed some years in residential school. Women from Company families and those who migrated as children to Moosonee or Moose Factory in the 1930s and '40s had attended local schools, while those who arrived after the war had likely attended one of the residential schools in the James Bay area. Some younger women arrived with their parents in the 1950s when low fur prices coincided with an effort by the Canadian government to create housing and educational programs for Aboriginal people. Schooling had been made compulsory, and some parents had settled in town so that their children would not have to go to residential school. A few came to stay near relatives who were long-term patients in Moose Factory Hospital. Spending more time in town than their elders had done enabled the majority of middle-aged women to complete grade six. A few had earned some high school credits from outside the community, and several had taken advantage of courses offered by the James Bay Education Centre when it opened. Whatever their educational background, however, women under sixty were fluent in English.

Middle-aged Cree women had more experience of life outside the James Bay region than the older women had. Several had left northern Ontario for a time when the Canadian Forces base closed and their husbands were transferred to similar employment elsewhere in Canada. Some had worked in factories or service industries in the south. They gave a variety of reasons for returning: they liked the town; they missed their relatives; their husbands wanted to hunt. But it was evident that their commitment to their community was high and they were glad to be home.

The erosion of women's autonomy and the shifting of the focus of their labour to the home as suggested in the Marxist model is evident for the middle-aged women of our study. Their greater urban experience had exposed them to EuroCanadian values so that they perceived paid employment differently from the way their elders had. Despite their greater opportunities for employment, less than half of our sample of middle-aged Cree women were employed. Many married women had large families with children still in school. However, other factors than family responsibilities influenced whether married women sought employment. Educational qualifications were not necessarily the main criteria. Women who worked outside the home were often not much more qualified than the ones who worked only as homemakers.

A decisive factor determining whether a married woman looked for paid work was the nature of her husband's employment. The rate of employment among middle-aged men was high in Moosonee and Moose Factory compared with the rate for younger age groups, and the husbands of many middle-aged women had been employed for several years by the hospital or other institutions and businesses in the two communities. A few Cree men owned businesses themselves. Some had recently retired with pensions. It was the wives of these men with steady incomes who were most likely to have jobs. So women who were employed were not usually the only wage-earners in their households, and married working women usually lived in households with a relatively high standard of living.

Conversely, Cree women whose husbands were not employed or who followed a strategy of sporadic part-time and temporary employment did not work outside the home at all. This pattern suggests that those women over sixty and those from forty-five to sixty had different attitudes to work from each other. When older Cree couples moved into town between 1930 and the 1950s, both husband and wife sought work. At certain times, little work was available to either partner. Men and women worked where they could in order to survive. In contrast, middle-aged women in 1984 thought of their husbands as the primary wage-earners. They usually did not work if their husbands were unemployed, presumably because they felt that this would undermine his role. If he were working, they could work too. Since the jobs they took were generally less lucrative than those of their husbands, they did not threaten their husbands. Both men and women valued men's work more than women's work, but men who were securely employed did not feel the need to assert their authority by discouraging their wives from seeking employment.

Among single, widowed, and divorced middle-aged women, there was considerable variety in education and employment. It is notable that the divorced women were the most educated in this age range and had taken upgrading and professional courses to increase their employability. The pattern of employment among married women suggests that the notion that men were the primary wage-earners had been internalized by middle-aged Cree. It is possible that older divorced women had developed successful careers that threatened this primacy. Our study indicates that women's success in employment became a factor in the deteriorating gender relations among younger people.

Prior to the 1980s, only domestic work had been available, and the older women in the study did not think of domestic work as low status. Some of these women had worked for many years at unskilled jobs before acquiring the qualifications that fitted them for their present jobs. In the 1980s, jobs were more varied not only in type but in terms of prestige. A few middle-aged women still worked in unskilled jobs, although not by preference. More worked in relatively skilled jobs in stores and offices. Others worked as nursing assistants and Cree language instructors. It would appear that married women felt that work outside the home was an option rather than a necessity and so could reject low-paid, low-prestige employment.

Many women who worked at home did in fact earn money. Middle-aged women spent more time than other women producing crafts for sale and made a wider variety of goods. While the older women specialized in moccasins, middle-aged women knitted, made clothing and bead jewellery, carved, and dressed Indian dolls. As well, they made a variety of leather goods. As the generation intermediate between the older women who remembered life on the land and the younger people who were essentially urban, they still knew the techniques of leather working, and they also added other items, gleaned from a variety of cultural sources, to their repertoire. Women who were employed in full-time work did not make crafts for sale unless their work was so poorly paid that they needed a supplementary income. A few particularly skilled women had also been temporarily employed as craft teachers by the James Bay Education Centre. These women were also interested in the business development of Aboriginal crafts, both as a means of earning money and as an expression of Cree identity. One woman's long-term work in this field, though usually voluntary, was in fact intensive and time-consuming enough to be termed a career.

Many middle-aged women were more active in voluntary work and community affairs than women in other age groups, and those who were most involved had above-average education for their age group. Employed women tended to be more involved than those who worked at home, although there were notable exceptions. Two homemakers were on the Moose Band Council and were also involved in a variety of local projects and national organizations.

The situation in Moosonee and Moose Factory for middle-aged women in our study did not necessarily involve a drastic devaluation of women's work as much as it did an over-valuation of men's employment. Middle-aged couples had reached an accommodation in which men were the major wage-earners and women contributed to family and community welfare in many ways. There was no indication that middle-aged women in the community felt demeaned if they were not employed. They valued the work they did, and unlike their husbands they did not feel the moral imperative to be employed. Yet, the value placed on men's paid employment clearly did cause problems when men became unemployed. Men had become possessive of their prerogative of being "breadwinners."

WOMEN FROM THIRTY TO FORTY-FOUR

More than half of the Cree women between thirty and forty-four had been born and educated in Moosonee or Moose Factory, and few had ever lived in the bush. Consequently, peers rather than parents and elders were the significant influences in their lives. The majority spoke English as a first language, and a minority could not speak Cree at all, indicating a growing generation gap. Almost all women in this age group had completed public school, and perhaps half had one or more years of high school. A minority had completed grade twelve, and some had taken college courses. Like the middle-aged women, some had experience outside their communities. They had attended high school either in North Bay or Timmins, and some had also worked in southern towns.

Many of these women expressed an interest in taking job training, but those who had large families or children too young for day care found it difficult to attend school unless they had relatives who could help. In spite of these barriers, a number did complete upgrading or vocational courses that qualified them for the jobs they had when they were interviewed. Some of these women took courses at the James Bay Education Centre day care. Though there were very few courses available at this institution, it did provide an opportunity for some local women to gain qualifications when family commitments kept them in the community, and it had day-care facilities.

The effects of increased education on employment were notable among women in their thirties and early forties. Proportionally, more women in this age group had jobs than in the older age groups. About half of our sample were employed. Their jobs included administrative and clerical work in offices, stores and educational institutions, child-care and health-care work, skilled and unskilled work in catering, and domestic work. Office work was the most frequently cited kind of employment; domestic work was the least frequently cited.

About a quarter of our sample classified themselves as homemakers, who did not have paid employment outside the home. Some of them intended to get outside work or return to school when their children were older, and some cited the expense and difficulty of finding child care as reasons for not seeking employment. Others clearly preferred to stay at home, and some stated that their husbands preferred this too. As among the older and middle-aged women, married women in this age group usually did not seek employment unless their husbands were employed; however, the sample did contain a few couples in which the wife rather than the husband had a job, indicating the beginning of a new trend. There were a number of families in which neither husband nor wife was employed, though in some of these cases the husband worked seasonally or took temporary or part-time jobs when available. Few made crafts, and those who did made bead jewellery rather than leather goods. As among the older women, craft making provided a supplementary income.

The employment pattern of single women aged between thirty and forty-four was similar to that in the sample of middle-aged women. Divorced women in this group had more education and more-responsible jobs than other women in this same group, while jobs held by other single (i.e., never-married) women ranged from highly skilled to never employed. Both married and single women took part in community affairs. While the older women in the sample were involved in church and local government activities, women in this age group were more involved in community services, including entertainment and sport.

In general, the women in this age group had characteristics that are transitional. Attitudes to work were often similar to those of middle-aged women. But the community offered women of this age group more opportunities for rewarding paid work at a time when employment options for men were diminishing, a trend that became even more marked in the youngest age group.

WOMEN FROM FOURTEEN TO THIRTY

Young Cree women were clearly oriented to the small towns rather than the bush. Although some had worked, studied, or lived with their parents in other Ontario towns, most had spent their lives in Moosonee or Moose Factory. Many did not speak Cree at all, or did not speak it well. As well, values had changed, and, while some young women enjoyed excellent relations with their elders, they tended not to seek information about Cree culture from them. Rather, they took college courses, which certainly indicated a lack of communication between generations.

The under-thirties were the most educated age group in our sample, and, though some of them had finished only grade eight, most had completed grade ten, and an increasing number had completed grade twelve. The establishment of Northern Lights High School in 1975 in Moosonee meant that young people could now complete high school without leaving home. Some had taken college courses or other job-training courses, and a few had been to university.

The belief of modernization theorists that women's status improves with the growth of capitalism is somewhat supported by what we observed in Moosonee and Moose Factory. Some studies of northern women suggest that women's work has maintained more continuity than men's work and that women have often been able to find more stable employment than men. The latter is true at Moosonee and Moose Factory, but only for younger women and only after men had been defined as primary wage-earners and women as just contributors to the household economy. Economic changes in the 1970s made a considerable number of jobs available in areas traditionally considered the province of men.

Despite their higher education and greater opportunities to find work, these young women displayed more employment-related conflicts than women in the older age groups did. They faced various problems: whether they should look for a job; whether they should return to school; how they could best accommodate the demands of work and family at the same time. Having slightly more opportunities for employment than their male counterparts created difficulties too. They responded to the challenges in different ways, depending on temperaments, abilities, and social circumstances.

A large proportion of our sample in this age group had some kind of employment, but we found a difference between the older and the younger women in the study in the kinds of jobs taken. Women in their teens and early twenties sold fast foods, and worked in stores or as waitresses. These jobs had low pay and inconvenient hours, provided little opportunity for initiative, and were characterized by a high staff turnover. Young women often worked in a variety of jobs for short periods, and the work was often temporary, part-time, or seasonal. These women took these jobs because they lacked specialized training and because many employers regarded young women as "bad risks" and would not employ them for more stable jobs. Also, many young Cree women at this stage in their lives had not decided what further training they wanted and were simply marking time. Some were working out conflicts between work life and home life. Slightly older women tended to take more-stable jobs or work at home.

As Lynda Lange (1988, 31) points out in a study of Dene women, it is assumed that "unemployment" as a status did not exist in pre-contact times, whereas women who stay at home today are relegated to that category. Lange's data also suggest that contemporary young indigenous women face different evaluations of work and competence that are influenced by outsiders than did their grandmothers, and that they have lost autonomy while men have gained authority. However, the question of whether the young women in our study as a group have gained or lost autonomy, in comparison with women in the older age groups, is complex. Some enjoyed more independence than their mothers, some less, depending on their opportunities for employment.

Certainly, the attitude of young women to employment differed from that of other groups. The younger women in Moosonee and Moose Factory were much more likely than the middle-aged women to regard employment as a desirable state. When the oldest women first sought employment, practical competence and willingness to work hard were more important than formal qualifications. Moreover, they did not think of paid domestic work as implying low social status. Middle-aged women avoided such employment but saw work in the home as rewarding. For young women, both having paid work and a particular type of employment were important. In fact, for many young Cree women, identity had become bound up with employment. Getting a good job was associated with getting a good education. Women who had gained employment after upgrading their qualifications by returning to school derived considerable satisfaction from their achievements, while those with little education found it difficult to get any job at all. For some, unemployment had to do with a lack of self-esteem and personal skills, both of which prevented them from undertaking a serious job search or re-entering school. These women felt powerless to improve their situations.

More than men, women considered their non-working lives and their relationship to their families when they looked for jobs. They perceived themselves as the primary care givers to their children. Some believed that their employment was less important than that of their husbands. We observed that, as with elderly women, the decisions that young Cree women made about their careers were highly influenced by their domestic situations — what they did about their working lives was closely related to the needs of their children and especially to the employment and attitudes of their husbands.

Because of their unemployment or their inadequate employment, many young men were not in a position to support a family, and so young women were cautious about marrying them. Some Cree women did leave school to marry, but, on average, women in this age group settled late into permanent relationships. Marriage was more likely to end in divorce for young women than it was for women in the older age groups. Social life without a partner was difficult, and a man provided protection against unwanted attention by others, but many women preferred to be single anyway, even though they might have had children to care for. A large number of women in their late twenties were still unmarried.

Conflicts often arose between husbands and wives when wives worked outside the home. They were no longer conforming to the model of the husband as "breadwinner," and husbands would often respond by increasing authority at home, attempting to undermine both the monetary and non-monetary contributions of their wives. In 1984, many young women felt that Cree men expected to be the "bosses" in family decision making and that women were to be subordinate. Some young women, particularly those whose lack of education precluded their finding work, were forced to accept the men's evaluation. However, employment opportunities for qualified women since the late 1960s allowed some women to assert their independence.

Of the young women who were married, about half had full-time employment or had employment that was more stable than that of their husbands. Some of the young women worked while their husbands were unemployed or combined various strategies of part-time, temporary, and seasonal work. These men sometimes had higher annual incomes than wives who were employed in offices, but their earnings were irregular and unreliable, which was stressful — women could not rely on their husbands for regular support for themselves and their children.

Some young women were not employed. A few said that they preferred to work at home while their children were young or noted that their husbands preferred them not to work. Others thought of themselves as unemployed and said that they wished they could find work, and cited lack of child-care facilities or insufficient qualifications as reasons for their failure to find a job. For all young women with children, seeking work outside the home was problematic, since a job had to pay enough to offset the cost of child care.

While an increasing number of young women completed school, and some attended college or university before they married and/or had children, many left school early and discovered only later that they required further qualifications to find satisfactory employment. As they became more mature, women often reassessed their lives. From their mid-twenties, they started to return to school to prepare themselves for better jobs. The James Bay Education Centre provided general upgrading as well as specific courses in business studies, social work, early childhood education, and nursing. As among women in the older age groups, some of these women did not have the academic background to follow through with upgrading, became discouraged, and dropped out. Others, with more years of schooling, were successful in completing programs.

The decision to return to school was never easy. A woman had to find someone to babysit her children, and she had to reorganize her life to include assignments and reading. If she were married, the decision was even more difficult if she did not have the support of her husband. Some men did accommodate themselves to their wives' ambitions. Others felt threatened by a wife's relative success in employment. Some men saw their wives' steady jobs as emphasizing their own inability to provide.

Sometimes the decision to return to school was taken after a divorce as part of a long-term career strategy. In other cases, divorces resulted from women going back to school or work. Husbands who felt threatened attempted to confine their wives to the domestic sphere. Some women gave up their ambitions for the sake of family harmony. Others rebelled against the restrictions their husbands placed on them.

After completing their training, women tended to work in full-time, long-term positions. The majority had office jobs, and the most successful were beginning to move into administrative positions. Single (either divorced or never-married) mothers saw their jobs as a means of providing their children with the stability that a regular income could bring, and they found that life as a single was less stressful than the economically less predictable and sometimes more repressive lifestyle of married women. They also felt that the experience of completing their courses and finding work had provided them with the self-esteem and confidence that they had previously lacked and that sustained them in facing the problems of balancing personal relationships and a career. As among the older women in the study, it was notable that some of the most educated women with the best-paying jobs in the community were single.

STAKE IN FAMILY AND COMMUNITY

Both modernization and Marxist theories of change under capitalism are somewhat useful in describing changes in Moosonee and Moose Factory. However, they both have limitations. Both assume a separation of public and private, or domestic, spheres of work. To the Marxist materialist, the separation of the two domains becomes more pronounced with colonialism. The modernization theorists believe that the two domains become less pronounced in some situations. In our case study, both cases have occurred: Some women "modernized" and maximized their status, but they did so within a system in which their "domestic role" was already devalued. However, any attempt to use public and domestic distinctions consistently to explain women's work, and their perceptions of that work, fails. The women in our study did not perceive the two domains as being in themselves real factors in making choices. The public/domestic distinction is meaningful to EuroCanadian culture but was less so in earlier Cree economy and contemporary cultural evaluations. Married middle-aged women were prepared to let their husbands take the lead in acquiring money, but this did not mean that they were not active outside the home in other capacities. In addition, the distinction cannot be used in explaining status differences. Although attempts are still being made to discover cross-cultural correlates of status, there is still no generally accepted definition of what status is, or what the indicators of it should be (see, for example: Sanday 1973; Whyte 1978; Hendrix and Hossain 1988). While paid employment had become an important aspect of self-identity for some young people, Cree women tended to evaluate individuals by competence, and this comprised a range of factors including the ability to function in both family and community.

We believe that it is more helpful to analyze our data in terms of stake in family and community than to use a public/domestic distinction. Both the family and the community are recognized as sets of affiliations that people make with one another. The family need not be a "domestic" unit; indeed, family (as among the Cree of Moosonee and Moose Factory) might extend throughout the community as a network of bonds that have real economic and political consequences. Among the Cree in Moosonee and Moose Factory, it is the women who are responsible for creating meaningful ties; they are meaningful because they represent an investment in community through family and support family through community. And women must now do this within the constraints of their jobs, so it is the women and their families who must decide where the boundary between family and community will be.

In the bush, family and community overlapped considerably in terms of work. Marriage and the sustenance of children were community responsibilities because they were vital to the long-term survival of the whole group. People expected that a newly married couple would take a few years to work out relations of interdependence, and community members were available to mediate when problems arose. Older Cree women regard the contemporary towns with some alarm, because they see conflicts developing between family networks and impersonal institutions (for example, schools), which have taken some of the work roles away from the family and the community.

Young Cree women do not have the high community commitment that their grandmothers once had. Nor do they have the sense of overlapping family and community responsibilities that can easily bend to accommodate work responsibilities. They are faced with an urban context that blends into a southern infrastructure, and they must "carve out" family and community niches for themselves. This is an enormous problem only partly solved by education, and young women are not quite sure what their community of influence is, what the boundaries of the family are, and which sets of expectations about competence they should obey — their elders' or their teachers'. They suffer the identity consequences of "unemployment" because the worth of work is being set outside both family and community. They are no longer sure that the family will be able to aid them in working out the maturation of a marriage with underemployment and low self-esteem now to deal with. The role models that were once effective do not relate to the contemporary situation. The older Cree feel that the young people are almost outside their influence.

As they mature into their twenties and thirties, many of the women are responding to the new challenges. Some reject the "bossing" of the men, wanting to establish their autonomy in the workplace as well as in the home. Some are social entrepreneurs, challenging other women to help them re-establish community life. Many are encouraging their children to get a solid education, to establish a career, to reinvest family into community. This may mean using the institutions in a new way, one that will serve local ambitions rather than alienate family and community members from each other. They are very concerned about economic development and about reinvesting income locally through small businesses and tourism. They place high value on recreational facilities and programs that might give youth some direction, competence, and identity.

SUMMARY

Life in Moosonee and Moose Factory has rarely been easy for women, or for men, for that matter. In half a century, the communities have changed from settlements built around the fur trade to small towns whose inhabitants work in government offices, schools, hospitals, small businesses, and in the tourist industry. Changing values linked to changing economic conditions have caused differences to develop between generations of women. Economic conditions have caused problems for younger people because of an imbalance of opportunities for skilled employment for women and men, and because there simply are not enough jobs for everyone.

When the older women in our study (those sixty and over) were girls, they worked together with men as equals in family and community. The women in their middle years (those between forty-five and sixty) had the task of redefining roles, bringing traditional expectations of women's contributions into the town-based cash economy. As men's work became more valued than women's work, women had to express their contributions through family and community leadership. The youngest women faced an urban environment, a public education, and increasing expectations of and opportunities for their own employment outside the home. They also had more difficult tasks than the oldest women had faced in keeping family units together, as the pre-conditions for gender complementarity were disappearing.

Women in all age groups expressed a sense of crisis as occurring in early adulthood or late middle years. These seemed to be crucial times for making decisions about life paths and integrating family and community roles. These crisis points are conditioned not only by environmental factors, but also by women's own life and family cycles.

In this paper, we have described the study we conducted to understand how the work and family roles of Aboriginal women in Moosonee and Moose Factory have been influenced by socio-economic change. We have concluded that the concept of stake in family and community is more helpful for understanding the range of responses that Cree women in Moosonee and Moose Factory have had to career and family options than are Marxist or modernization theories. These women regarded community as an extension of family and their stake in community as a reflection of their models of family, even over the generations. Marxist theory can explain the environmental changes and pressures, and modernization theory can in some cases describe adaptive change, but neither takes into account a woman's own expectations for continuity in change. Women "invest" in their communities as they have been taught to by their families, creating the conditions for their own environments in the best way they can. Aboriginal women across Canada have "modernized" their communities and are trying to revitalize their families, slowing the impact of the damage caused by urbanization and developing capitalism. They are doing this not by rejecting development but by trying to influence the conditions of development so that they and their children will have choices in the type of family and community they will have. Community — the kinship of people as well as public economic and political power brokerage — must be reconstituted to provide a network of support for these choices.

NOTES

1. The three principal investigators were Jennifer Blythe, Peggy Martin Brizinski, and Sarah Preston. We were assisted in data collection by a number of Cree research assistants in the summer of 1984. Analysis of data was performed by Blythe, Martin, and Preston, and much of the material included in this paper is contained in our jointly written report, "I Was Never Idle: Women and Work in Moosonee and Moose Factory" (1985). We would like to thank Sarah Preston for permission to use her material, including material on the early history of the towns and on women over sixty. However, we as authors are responsible for any inaccuracies that might be contained in the paper. Field work in Moosonee and Moose Factory was funded by a Social Science and Humanities Research Council Strategic Research Grant.

REFERENCES

Acheson, Ann W. 1980. "The Kutchin Family: Past and Present." In *Families: Ethnic Variation*, ed. K. Ishwarin. Toronto: McGraw Hill Ryerson Limited.

Ager, Lynn Price. 1980. "The Economic Role of Women in Alaskan Eskimo Society." In *A World of Women: Anthropological Studies of Women in the Societies of the World*, ed. Erika Bourguignon. New York: Praeger Publishers.

Armstrong, Pat, and Hugh Armstrong. 1978. *The Double Ghetto: Canadian Women and their Segregated Work*. Toronto: McClelland and Stewart.

Blythe, Jennifer, Peggy Martin Brizinski, and Sarah Preston. 1985. "I Was Never Idle: Women and Work in Moosonee and Moose Factory." Research Program for Technology Assessment in Subarctic Ontario (TASO), Report No. 21, McMaster University, Hamilton, Ontario.

Boserup, Ester. 1970. *Woman's Role in Economic Development*. London: Allen and Unwin.

Bourgeault, Ron G. 1983. "The Indians, the Métis and the Fur Trade: Class, Sexism and Racism in the Transition from 'Communism' to Capitalism." *Studies in Political Economy: A Socialist Review* 12:45-80.

Brown, Jennifer S.H. 1980. *Strangers in Blood: Fur-Trade Company Families in Indian Country*. Vancouver: University of British Columbia Press.

Bucksar, R. 1968. "Moosonee and the Squatters." *Canadian Welfare*. Ontario: Canadian Welfare Council 44, no. 5:15-16.

Cruikshank, Julie. 1976. "Matrifocal Families in the Canadian North." In *The Canadian Family Revised,* ed. K. Ishwarin. Toronto: Holt, Rinehart and Winston of Canada, Limited.

Hendrix, Lewellyn, and Zakir Hossain. 1988. "Women's Status and Mode of Production: A Cross-Cultural Test." *Signs: Journal of Women in Culture and Society* 13, no. 3:437-553.

Klein, Laura F. 1980. "Contending with Colonization: Tlingit Men and Women in Change." In *Women and Colonization: Anthropological Perspectives,* ed. Mona Etienne and Eleanor Leacock. New York: Bergin and Garvey Publishers, Inc.

Kruse, John A., Judith Kleinfeld, and Robert Travis. 1982. "Energy Development on Alaska's North Slope: Effects on the Inupiat Population." *Human Organization: Journal of the Society for Applied Anthropology* 41, no. 2:97-106.

Lange, Lynda. 1988. "The Changing Situation of Dene Elders, and of Marriage, in the Context of Colonialism: The Experience of Fort Franklin, 1945-1985." In *Northern Communities: The Prospects for Empowerment*, ed. Gurston Dacks and Ken Coates, Boreal Institue for Northern Studies No. 25. University of Alberta: Boreal Institute for Northern Studies.

Leacock, Eleanor. 1981. "History, Development, and the Division of Labour by Sex: Implications for Organization." *Signs: Journal of Women in Culture and Society*. Special Issue on Development and the Sexual Division of Labour 7, no. 2:474-91.

Matthiasson, John. 1979. "Northern Baffin Island Women in Three Cultural Periods." In *Occasional*

Papers in Anthropology: Issues on Sex-Roles in Changing Cultures, ed. Ann McElroy and Carolyn Matthiasson. Buffalo, NY: State University of New York.

McElroy, Ann. 1975. "Continuity and Change in Baffin Island Inuit Family Organization." *The Western Canadian Journal of Anthropology* 5, no. 2:15-40.

Public Archives of Canada (PAC). 1935. Records relating to Indian Affairs, RG 10, vol. 3,034, file C57044.

Rapp, Rayna. 1975. "Anthropology." *Signs: Journal of Women in Culture and Society* 4, no. 3:497-513.

Sanday, P. 1973. "Toward a Theory of the Status of Women." *American Anthropologist* 75:1,682-1,700.

Tilly, Louise A., and Joan W. Scott. 1978. *Women, Work, and Family.* New York: Holt, Rinehart, and Winston.

Whyte, M.K. 1978. *The Status of Women in Preindustrial Societies.* Princeton, N.J.: Princeton University Press.

Youssef, Nadia Haggag. 1974. *Women and Work in Developing Societies.* Population Monograph Series No. 15. Berkeley: University of California, Institute of International Studies.

The Exploitation of the Oil and Gas Frontier: Its Impact on Lubicon Lake Cree Women

Rosemary Brown

The greatest strength [of the community] is in the traditions from the old people, . . . [and] respect for each other, . . . but this is breaking down. The bible camps help.

This observation was made during the summer of 1987[1] by a Lubicon Lake Cree woman in her forties. Her statement reflects the complexity of the inter-related changes wrought within Lubicon Lake Cree society when their hunting, trapping, and gathering mode was transformed into one based upon wage labour and transfer payments. This transformation was brought about by the exploitation of the oil and gas frontier on traditional Lubicon lands beginning in the late 1970s. The complexity of these changes can best be understood by analyzing traditional Lubicon Lake Cree society as an articulation (or interconnection) of economic, social, political, and religious structures (or roles and relationships) shaped by ties to the land.[2] When ties to the land were ruptured by oil and gas activity, the traditional economic base was destroyed and consequent and interrelated changes took place in economic, social, political, and religious structures. Some of these initial changes triggered others as the Lubicon Lake Cree created strategies such as the land-claim struggle to protect their families and community from the ravages of imposed "development." Underlying many of these strategies was the persistence of traditional ideological structures related to stewardship of the land and to the maintenance of the social fabric of Lubicon Lake Cree society.

In this paper I present a brief historical overview of Lubicon Lake Cree society and a discussion of the economic, social, political, and spiritual changes experienced and perceived by Lubicon women since the late 1970s. I argue that the exploitation of the oil and gas frontier was a negative and stressful experience for Lubicon Lake Cree women and that, as roles and relationships changed, so did the bases upon which egalitarian relations existed between Lubicon Lake Cree women and men. Furthermore, I argue that articulation of modes of production, a Marxist analytical framework in which reproductive roles are usually subsumed under production, does not adequately explain the perceptions and actions of Lubicon Lake Cree women in what was a rapidly changing and fluid situation. These perceptions and actions, specifically the focus upon the impact of alcohol abuse on the community and the increasing participation in Pentecostal bible camps, are more readily accounted for only when the centrality of women's roles in biological and social reproduction is taken into account.

BACKGROUND: TRADITION AND CHANGE

In 1988, the Lubicon Lake Cree Nation consisted of 457 members, most of whom lived at Little Buffalo Lake, located ninety-five miles northeast of Peace River in northern Alberta.[3] Until the early 1980s, the Lubicon Lake Cree were a traditional boreal-forest hunting, trapping, and gathering society whose members engaged in a complex web of interlocking social, political, and economic roles and relationships shaped by the dependence of the Lubicon Lake Cree on the land and its resources. Within this traditional society, Lubicon Lake Cree women performed many important roles in the production of use and exchange values, in ritual ceremonies, and in decision making. They controlled the distribution of the products of their labour as well as game meat brought into the camp or home, and their productive and reproductive roles were compatible. These factors can be interpreted to indicate that gender relations within traditional Lubicon Lake Cree society were generally egalitarian (Sanday 1974, 198; Rosaldo and Lamphere 1974, 12; Sacks 1974, 190; Leacock 1980, 9-10).

With the advent of imposed and intensive exploitation of oil and gas deposits on traditional Lubicon land in the late 1970s, the Lubicon Lake Cree began experiencing the latest in what Brody (1981, 1987) refers to as a series of "cumulative" frontiers: economic (fur, timber, energy resources); political (administration of the Indian Act); and ideological (churches and schools). These frontiers have served as points of articulation or contact between the Lubicon Lake Cree and the capitalist mode of production.

For example, during World War Two, several parallel and at times related processes began to effect some structural modifications in Lubicon Lake Cree society. The Lubicon had been bypassed during Treaty Eight negotiations in 1899 because of their isolation from major waterways, and hence they had never signed a treaty with the federal government. In 1939 they were officially recognized as an Indian band and promised a reserve, which they never received. A chief was elected, emergency transfer payments became available to band members, and some children were sent off to residential school for their education. Some band members began working for farmers who moved into the area, helping them to clear their lands and to harvest their crops.

A more sedentary lifestyle evolved when the Lubicon moved to Little Buffalo in order to send their children to the Baptist school built in the 1950s. Once they were there, the women remained in Little Buffalo with their children for most of the year, while their husbands continued to trap in the bush. Some minor oil and gas activity was carried out, and jobs opened up at the school and on the roads in the 1970s.

These changes had occurred slowly, however, and had left intact the traditional relationship of the Lubicon Lake Cree to their land, including the hunting, trapping, and gathering mode based upon the land. Kenneth Bodden, a scientist working with the Boreal Institute, wrote in a court affidavit (1982, 21):

It is evident from the large amount of meat harvested . . . and from the value of the fur sales . . . that traditional lifestyles, based on trapping, hunting, fishing and gathering, provide the residents of Little Buffalo Lake with cultural, economic and social benefits that make subsistence activities attractive despite encroachment of alternative lifestyles.

Despite increased opportunities to engage in wage employment, the community has maintained a close and economically viable contact with their natural environment and its resource base.

Intensive exploitation of the oil and gas frontier, on the other hand, placed the oil companies and the provincial government in direct competition with the Lubicon Lake Cree for their land. Between 1973 and 1978, the province built an all-weather road connecting the community of Little Buffalo to Peace River. The province then issued licences to multi-national oil companies to explore for and develop oil and gas resources on traditional Lubicon lands. Between 1979 and 1986, over 400 oil wells were drilled within a fifteen-mile radius of the community, and, between 1980 and 1984, 4,053 miles of seismic roads were built (Ryan 1986).

The overall impact of such development was to rupture the ties between the Lubicon Lake Cree and their traditional lands. Large areas of land were removed from Lubicon control for drilling and storage sites and camps. Access to "private" roads was regulated; haying fields, berry patches, and trap lines were destroyed. Fishing streams were blocked off, and more trap lines as well as cabins were destroyed by fire. Fur bearers were driven from the area, as were moose and smaller game animals.

As a result, the wildlife and the habitat required to sustain wildlife dropped to a critical level by the end of 1982 (Factum of Appellants 1982, 32). The number of moose killed for food dropped from 219 in 1979 to nineteen by 1983. Average income from trapping during the same period dropped from over $5,000 per trapper to less than $400 (Lubicon Lake Cree Nation 1989b, 11). The traditional hunting, trapping, and gathering mode of the Lubicon Lake Cree had been virtually destroyed.

CHANGING ECONOMIC STRUCTURES: DISSOLUTION OF TRADITIONAL PRODUCTION RELATIONS

The destruction of their traditional hunting, trapping, and gathering economy meant that Lubicon families no longer served as units of production in which men and women performed complementary roles to produce food and other products for their families' use, and sufficient furs, hides, and leather goods for the market. Instead, families became units of consumption, with the income to purchase goods limited to transfer payments and the few paid jobs that were created in the community. Ninety-five percent of the community became dependent on transfer payments by the mid-eighties as compared to ten percent in the early eighties (Ominayak 1987).

During this transitional process, women experienced a decline in the practice of many traditional productive skills, a shift to paid labour or welfare, changes in housing and household technology, changing diets and methods of food preparation, and growing incompatibility between productive and reproductive roles. Very few women, and virtually no women under the age of thirty, continued to snare small game, tan hides, dry meat, manufacture leather items, or do beadwork as a way of producing either use or exchange values. Those women who did, continued to control the distribution of items made or the income from items sold, but in general they had less to distribute because there was less game meat and hide available. One activity in which many women did continue to participate, often collectively with other female family members and children, was the gathering and processing of berries.

Meanwhile, many of the men continued to hunt at least on a part-time basis, and many women said that their brothers and sons were still taken into the bush to learn how to hunt and trap with fathers, uncles, and grandfathers. In other words, many boys were still being socialized to be hunters, but it was within a context where hunting provided game meat as a dietary supplement, not as a mainstay. In addition, trapping was no longer capable of providing a future for families growing up in Little Buffalo.

Women developed a variety of strategies in response to the destruction of their traditional hunting, trapping, and gathering economy. These included engaging in paid labour, obtaining education and job training, and gaining control over welfare income. Some of the women on welfare who had husbands who abused alcohol asked for the family's welfare cheque to be made out to them, a strategy sometimes suggested by the band office. Several people in the community used the food bank in Peace River and bought clothes and other items second-hand.

All of the women who worked outside the home were employed within the community, except for one woman who in 1987 had worked cooking and cleaning at a nearby camp for oil-industry workers. Jobs within the community were found in the school, the health centre, the band office, and the band store. Women worked as secretaries, cooks, bookkeepers, cleaners, social workers, teaching and counselling aides, and store clerks. A few babysat in their own homes, and a few sold crafts. Although a few women worked as construction workers on band housing in the early eighties, no women worked on housing in 1987 and 1988.

Women said that they sought work outside the home in order to pay bills, get away from welfare, or in some cases to pursue certain occupations. Of those women who were not working, several were continuing their education or hoping to do so, either at the high school in Little Buffalo or at the Cadotte Vocational Centre, twenty kilometres away.

Women, whether or not they worked outside the home, continued to be responsible for a wide variety of tasks associated with the household. These included food preparation, cooking, cleaning, laundry, and child care. These tasks were strongly affected by changes taking place in housing and household technology associated with the introduction of provincial and federal housing programs in the 1970s and 1980s, and the installation of power lines after the road was completed in 1978. Electric lights replaced candles and lanterns; electric ovens and stoves replaced wood-burning ones; electric wringer washers replaced scrub boards; electric radios took the place of those operated by battery; freezers were used instead of the muskeg for preserving meat; and televisions, VCRs, and telephones came into the community.

While these new appliances made some tasks easier for Lubicon Lake Cree women, it must be noted that changes in household technology often increase expectations as to how much work women can do and so in effect place more demands upon women. Lubicon Lake Cree women now had larger homes to clean, and, because they did not have running water, they still had to haul water for housecleaning, cooking, laundry, and bathing. Furthermore, the introduction of electricity and the building of the road created demand for a wide variety of electrically operated consumer items, automobiles, and four-wheel-drive trucks. As a result, Lubicon Lake Cree women and their families were further integrated into the cash economy as they purchased these goods and became responsible for power and telephone bills, and monthly car payments.

The existence of the road made it easier to go into Peace River to purchase not only general consumer items but also food supplies. Easier access to a shopping centre, as well as the decline of opportunities for hunting, trapping, and gathering, led, in the late 1970s and early 1980s, to a significant decrease in the ratio of bush food to store-bought foods in the diet of the Lubicon. Before the late seventies, most diets consisted of game meat prepared in a variety of ways, bannock, berries, garden vegetables, and a few store-bought items such as flour, tea, oatmeal, and some tinned goods. After the early eighties, as less game meat became available, most Lubicon diets consisted of a much larger percentage of store-bought foods such as cold cereals, eggs, bacon, sausages, bread, packaged macaroni and cheese, hot dogs, baloney, candy, soft drinks, potato chips, and a wide range of tinned foods. A small band-operated store carrying these goods was established in Little Buffalo in the mid-1980s. While convenience foods were easier for women to prepare, they were usually less nutritious and not as easy to share as traditional foods. Furthermore, the task of shopping was now added to women's responsibilities, as well as the need to supply the family with sufficient food from what was often a welfare income.

Although women continued to be responsible for child care, this responsibility was no longer compatible with the jobs women held (except for babysitting) or the educational upgrading some women were engaged in. Women had always relied upon other women for child-care assistance, but this assistance had always been rendered on the basis of reciprocity. Now, however, women had to pay others, including relatives, for looking after their children. The fact that other women were also working or upgrading cut down on the number of women available for babysitting. So did alcohol abuse among some women. The tension that had arisen between productive and reproductive roles was revealed in the replies that twenty-eight women made to a question about who was better off in the community today — men or women. A quarter of the women replied that the men were better off because they were not responsible for the children and therefore were more free to do what they wanted to do. One woman stated: "I have said to my husband I wish I was you so that I didn't have to look after the children. Men think women are supposed to stay in and look after the kids and think that women don't work." Another said: "When a woman separates she can't find work to support the kids because there is no babysitter. If a man leaves he can find work because he has no one to look after."

Some of these changes in economic roles and relationships undermined the basis upon which egalitarian relations between men and women had existed in the past. Sanday (1974, 198), for example, argues that one crucial factor to assess in determining the status of women is the balance between male and female contributions to production. With the destruction of the traditional Lubicon hunting, trapping, and gathering mode, families and hunting groups ceased to be units of production within which women's economic roles were complementary to those of men. Either both husband and wife became dependent upon the state for welfare payments, or both worked at paid jobs that bore no relationship to each other, or one stayed at home while the other worked outside the home. And, while hunting remained important as a supplement to family incomes, the tanning of hides did not. Most men who worked at paid jobs still tried to hunt, but no women who engaged in paid work also tanned hides. Furthermore, the jobs women held — as teaching aides, cooks, health-care workers, office workers, bookkeepers, store clerks, or social workers — all fell within the purview of what in the rest of Canada has been traditionally referred to as women's work.

Rosaldo and Lamphere (1974, 12) point out that not only the tasks associated with women's roles in production but also their degree of control over the product of their labour affect their status. Lubicon women still controlled their own incomes — whether they were wages or transfer payments. As always, however, control was conditioned by family needs. The significance of women being able to control the product of their labour, however, had been related to their ability to distribute that product, as well as the meat that husbands brought back into the camp. It was through this distribution that social ties had been built and that women had ensured a reciprocal exchange of goods and services. Several women stated that, while it was easy to share when moose meat formed the basis of their diet, it was much more difficult to share tinned goods when the amount of store-bought food one could purchase was limited by one's income. In other words, store-bought food could not be used to cement social and ritual ties in the same way that moose and other game meat had. The very fact that, ultimately, women and their families were now dependent upon the state, rather than on each other, undermined the basis for mutual co-operation and sharing.

Another factor to consider when determining the status of women in a society is the relation between their productive and reproductive work (Sacks 1974, 190). All of the paid jobs held by Lubicon Lake Cree women, except for babysitting, were of necessity performed outside the home, thereby increasing the gap between the private familial domain and the public one. As a result, women could no longer combine child care with productive work, nor for a variety of reasons could they assume that relatives were available to look after the children. If they could find sitters, they were now expected to pay.

CHANGING SOCIAL STRUCTURES: WEAKENING OF TRADITIONAL TIES AND BONDS

Related to the changes in economic structures arising from imposed oil and gas activity were changes in social roles and relationships between wives and husbands, parents and children, elders and youths, and among families in the community. The 1980s witnessed an increase in marital conflict and breakdown among all age groups, except in marriages where the wife was over fifty. The reasons cited most often for marital breakdown were the increase in alcohol and wife abuse, which in turn were attributed to the fact that men did not have productive work. Some women felt that there "would be less [drinking] if the men had jobs and more self-respect."

Changing patterns of socialization of, and expectations for, children were also connected to and resulted from the shift in productive activity. It was now the school that was to prepare children for the future on the basis of a curriculum designed to integrate children into the wage-labour economy. This increasing reliance upon the school for the education of children was paralleled by the decline in bush skills learned by girls and younger women, and to a lesser extent by boys and younger men, from their parents. Play among children also reflected the shift in the mode of production and related changes. Girls still played with dolls, but, except for that, children were no longer socialized through play to take on traditional economic activities and roles. Meanwhile, new agents of socialization — television and VCRs — have been introduced into the community. While providing hours of entertainment, they are exposing children (and adults) to the sex-role stereotyping and consumerist attitudes that pervade television and video programming and advertising.

As for the relationship between Elders and youths, when seventeen women in their twenties and younger were asked about the values they learned from their parents, only six mentioned respect for the Elders. However, fourteen out of eighteen women over the age of thirty who were asked the same question mentioned respect for the Elders. Among the comments were: "The young don't listen"; "They laugh at the Elders"; and, "They don't help the Elders without being asked." This loss of respect was linked to the loss of traditional economic roles in which the young learned from Elders as well as to an increase in alcohol abuse among the young. Also, the Elders found it difficult to prevent the young from drinking.

As for relations among members of the community as a whole, many women mentioned increasing gossip, increasing tensions, and less co-operation and sharing. Two women connected these changes to the increase in alcohol consumption: "People got along a long time ago but not today, because of the drinking"; "If you start helping people who have been drinking they won't leave you alone." The comments of a few other women revealed that relationships were becoming increasingly commercialized as opposed to being based upon reciprocity and mutual need. One now had to pay for favours such as rides into town or the fetching of water and groceries: "Nobody does anything for free; . . . even for water I have to pay ten dollars or they'd want the gas; . . . even to go to the store I would have to pay."

It was the issue of drinking, however, and the problems associated with alcohol abuse, that permeated almost every conversation. Drinking was identified by women as being responsible for an increase in marital conflict, the breaking up of homes, and numerous fatal accidents. Perhaps the most poignant response to a question about changes within the community came from the young woman who said that "more people [were] dying in accidents because of alcohol." She had lost three cousins and an aunt in alcohol-related accidents. Nine different alcohol-related accidental deaths after the opening of the road and one alcohol-related suicide were mentioned during the interviews. The impact of these deaths extended far beyond the immediate families involved because, as another woman stated, "not everyone drinks, but because everyone is related, everyone is affected."

Women employed a variety of strategies to deal with the isolating effects of the social changes they were experiencing. For example, many were taking special care to maintain social ties, especially within the extended family. There were several instances of sisters having chosen to live in very close proximity to each other, and many examples of constant visiting and assistance with child care on a short-term basis. Women organized birthday parties to which all family members were invited, and they drove around the community with their children to share birthday cake with others. Female cousins and sisters travelled with each other to social functions outside Little Buffalo. Extended family groups would travel into town together to do laundry, or shop for groceries, or into the bush for summer camp or berry picking.

Women were concerned about alcohol abuse, too, and they spent a lot of time talking to young people about it in order to discourage them from drinking. A few mothers took their children to AADAC (Alberta Alcohol and Drug Abuse Commission) meetings held during the summer of 1988 in order to influence them not to drink, and many took their children to bible camps for the same reason.

Women also developed ways to deal with husbands who drank and/or were abusive. These ranged from talking to their husbands when they were sober, asking other relatives to talk to their husbands, leaving husbands temporarily, leaving them permanently, fighting back, and drinking with them. Most women who left their husbands, or who needed advice or someone to talk to, went to other female relatives for support. One key point that emerged was that several of the larger family groupings had one woman to whom several different female relatives usually turned.

When I began this research, I did not expect to find this focus upon alcohol abuse. I assumed that women would speak of the loss of their productive roles in the same way that men spoke of their loss of hunting and trapping. The court affidavits prepared for the 1982 court action by male Elders (albeit with input from women) identified the loss of hunting and trapping and the scaring away of game as the most significant change in the community. This was also true in my 1987 interviews with men, although these men also referred to some of the issues discussed by women in 1987 and 1988. Most women, however, in interviews and discussions in 1987 and 1988 identified alcohol abuse as the key change in the community after the late 1970s.

At first, this difference between men's and women's perceptions appeared inconsistent with an articulation of modes of production analysis with its emphasis upon productive roles as articulated in Marxist theory. As Hartsock (1983, 237) points out, however, Marxists often use the term *production* in a way that obscures women's reproductive work. She argues that if Marxist frameworks are to be truly Marxist, they have to take into account what people do. If what women do revolves around reproductive as well as productive activities, these activities have to have a central position in modes of production analysis in the same way that productive roles do. Women's reproductive work in Lubicon Lake Cree society involves not only the bearing and raising of children, but also the building and maintenance of social ties that in the past had helped to ensure co-operative relations of production. They had built and maintained these ties through the reciprocal exchange of goods and services, social activities, and the transmission of cultural skills and values such as sharing and respect for Elders. Women and the rest of Lubicon Lake Cree society relied heavily upon these ties.

Alcohol abuse directly affected women's reproductive roles, both biological and social. Alcohol abuse was associated with the increase in marital discord, wife abuse, and family breakdown; the fact that children were on the loose and/or neglected; that young people were dying in accidents; that community co-operation and sharing had decreased; and that Elders were no longer listened to. It was because women defined themselves "relationally" that the process of rapid social change was such a negative and stressful one for them.

CHANGING POLITICAL STRUCTURES: SEPARATION OF PUBLIC AND PRIVATE SPHERES

Innumerable changes also took place in political structures during the time when the Lubicon mounted a massive campaign for the settlement of their land claims.[4] This struggle involved community members in a whole range of non-traditional political activities. Most of the women interviewed had actively supported the land claim. Many had participated in meetings over the years, several had attended court hearings in Calgary and Edmonton in the early 1980s, and many went to the 1987 Buffy Sainte Marie concert, held in solidarity with the Lubicon, in Calgary. Others had participated in rallies and protests connected to the Lubicon boycott of the 1988 Olympic Games in Calgary, and one female Elder visited support groups in Europe. Women also allowed anthropologists and media to interview them and participated in the making of videos and films. When the Lubicon set up roadblocks for a week in October 1988 in order to assert jurisdiction over their traditional lands, many women spent hours at the main blockade, while others prepared food for the numerous supporters who came to Little Buffalo at this time.

In order to undertake their land-claim struggle, the Lubicon Lake Cree created new structures, such as the Cree Development Board, which dramatically increased the scale of decision making within the community. According to the chief, the board was set up to provide representation for all members of the community, including those not counted as status Indians by the Department of Indian and Northern Affairs. The board incorporated the elected band council and the chief. The chief explained that because family groups were traditionally represented by senior male hunters, representatives to the Cree Development Board were the male heads of families. Women were not therefore directly represented in structures outside the extended family. Women had always played, and continue to play, an important part in decision making in the context of the extended family, and so they did have a voice. Although not organized as a group, they expressed their views at community meetings and within their families. This is evident in an analysis of some of the concrete provisions the band sought in the land-claim negotiations. Besides the demands for economic development funds that would enable the band to re-establish ties to the land, for vocational training and for job creation, the community sought a range of recreational facilities for the youth in the community, a laundromat, and a combination day care and nursing home for the Elders, all concerns directly connected to women's reproductive roles.[5] The need for a child-care facility reflected the fact that increasing numbers of women were seeking paid work outside the home or were training to do so and that productive and reproductive roles were no longer compatible. The fact that the day care would be combined with a nursing home for the Elders also demonstrated a commitment to respect and care for the Elders within the community, and a commitment to continue the traditional relationship between the Elders and youth — one of cultural transmission and guidance. As well, it was hoped that recreational facilities would provide young people with constructive alternatives to drinking. In fact, stated repeatedly was the belief that with a reserve in place the Lubicon would have a mechanism for keeping alcohol out of the community.

Leacock (1980, 9-10; 1981, 135) identifies women's part in decision making in their society as a factor related to status. In Lubicon Lake Cree society at the time of my interviews, traditional lines of communication, which had always allowed women's voices to be heard, did not always function, leading to some feelings of alienation and frustration. Factors interfering with communication were the loss of respect for Elders, the increase in alcohol abuse among both men and women, and the increasing number of single-parent families headed by women.

CHANGING RELIGIOUS STRUCTURES: MECHANISMS FOR RE-KNITTING SOCIAL TIES

Traditional religious or spiritual roles and relationships also changed as Lubicon Lake Cree society shifted from one mode of production to another. The Lubicon Lake Cree had already been exposed to alternate religious traditions on a sporadic basis through contact with missionaries in the interwar years. Exposure increased in the 1940s when some children were sent away to residential schools, and in the 1950s and 1960s after the Baptist-run school and two churches were built in Little Buffalo. As long as the Lubicon were connected to the land through hunting, trapping, and gathering, however, they retained their own traditional beliefs, their rituals connected to healing, midwifery and hunting, and the Tea Dance Ceremony, in which women played an important role. The death of a key spiritual leader in the 1970s, easier access via road to a range of medical services in Peace River, and the rupture of Lubicon ties to the land after the late 1970s combined to produce a decline in the number of tea dances held, the end of midwifery, a decline in the practice of traditional healing and the rituals connected to hunting, and an increasing lack of awareness of traditional spiritual knowledge among women under thirty.

Spirituality was still important in women's lives, however. Many women in the community, especially those who had experienced personal losses and who were keenly worried about their children and grandchildren, found support and strength in prayer, attendance at church, the annual pilgrimage to Lac Ste. Anne, and/or participation in bible camps.

Of significance was the fact that growing numbers of women (twenty-two in 1988) were participating in Pentecostal bible camps. Women usually attended with other family members, including husbands. Women said that they went because they liked the music, because they liked to see people, and because they wanted to learn more about the bible and how to act. Another woman, when asked if she drew strength from the bible camps, replied, "Yes, I could not have gotten through the time after _____'s death without it." This is not an uncommon response, according to some of the literature on Pentecostal movements: "Behavioral patterns in the new Church are based on the same norms of reciprocity and mutual aid inherent in the relations among kin and fictive kin. . . . Pentecostalism flourishes where 'traditional supports have been eroded without provision of . . . resources for individuals to cope independently with life crises'" (Glazier 1980, 2).

CONCLUSION

The imposed and intense exploitation of the oil and gas frontier on traditional Lubicon lands in the late 1970s ruptured Lubicon ties to their land and transformed their traditional hunting, trapping, and gathering mode of production into one based on transfer payments and wage labour, which in turn brought about many inter-related changes in economic, social, political, and religious roles and relation-ships. These changes were often negative and stressful for Lubicon Lake Cree women. They undermined the bases upon which generally egalitarian gender rela-tions had existed in the past, and they adversely affected women's reproductive roles, both biological and social. By recognizing the centrality of women's repro-ductive roles and the social values associated with these, modes of production analysis is able to account for not only women's experiences of change but also their perceptions and their responses. Their responses to rapid social change evolved within the context of a vision of the future based on a settlement of the land claim. A settlement would enable the whole community, women and men, young and old, to re-establish their connection to the land, even if on a different basis than in the past. This connection would provide the Lubicon Lake Cree with the capacity to control the direction of future change and to ground change in tradition, especially the values related to social relationships. Because of women's significant role in social reproduction, it is their testimony that speaks directly to the difficulty of maintaining traditional values and the social fabric of Lubicon Lake Cree society when ties to the land have been ruptured and the way of life destroyed. At issue is how long women will be able to do so without a just settlement of the land claim.

POSTSCRIPT 1995

Multi-national resource companies continue to exploit the oil and gas frontier. Against the express wishes of the Lubicon community, Unocal built a sour gas plant about three kilometres from the proposed reserve boundary during the summer of 1994. To make matters worse, since 1988 when the Alberta government gave Daishowa Inc. a licence to harvest trees in an area that covers almost the entire traditional territory, the Lubicon have had to fend off clear cutting on their lands. The Lubicon Settlement Commission of Review, an independent and non-partisan body, reported in March 1993 that the federal and provincial Conservative governments had not negotiated in good faith for a land-claim settlement. Current negotiations by the Liberal government are being stalled by the Alberta government. Meanwhile, in the early 1990s, the federal government attempted to undermine the land claim by creating a new band (the Woodland Cree Band), which some Lubicon members have joined. Suspicions about provincial attempts to split the community arose in 1993 when members of one family group attempted to join the Woodland Cree, and again, more recently, during current negotiations, when the same family tried to create another new band.

These moves to undermine the political settlement and to divide the Lubicon have added immeasurably to the stress, strain, frustration, and exhaustion under which community members live. Because of their important position in maintaining social relations within the community, Lubicon women continue to bear the brunt of social dislocation. Some remain involved with the Pentecostal movement, while others have re-affirmed and strengthened their participation in traditional spiritual ceremonies. Lubicon women have attempted to counteract the impact of social dislocation in other ways, too. One example is the creation of the Lubicon Lake Nation Women's Circle in 1992. Their goals were to strengthen community ties and to support the land-claim struggle. As of the fall of 1995, however, the Circle is inactive.[6]

NOTES

1. This paper is based upon interviews carried out with thirty-eight Lubicon Lake Cree women during the summers of 1987 and 1988 and one week in the fall of 1988, as well as documentary research.
2. The theoretical framework of articulation of modes of production was drawn from the work of Rey (1973, 1975, 1979) and Meillassoux (1972, 1975).
3. Details about the history of Lubicon Lake Cree society are available elsewhere (Brown 1990; Lubicon Lake Cree Nation 1989b).
4. Details of the land-claim struggle are to be found in Richardson (1989) and Lubicon Lake Cree Nation (1989b).
5. The Lubicon Lake Cree Nation's negotiating demands are analyzed in Lubicon Lake Cree Nation (1989a).
6. For more information, please read John Goddard's *Last Stand of the Lubicon Cree,* and the PhD dissertation of Dawn Hill, McMaster University.

REFERENCES

Bodden, Kenneth. 1982. *Statement of Kenneth Bodden in Ominayak et al.* v. *Norcen Energy Resources Limited,* 15 September 1982, in the Court of Queen's Bench of Alberta Judicial District of Calgary.

Brody, Hugh. 1981. *Maps and Dreams: Indians and the British Columbia Frontier.* Vancouver: Douglas and McIntyre.

_____. 1987. *Living Arctic: Hunters in the Canadian North.* Vancouver: Douglas and McIntyre.

Brown, Rosemary. 1990. "Rupture of the Ties that Bind: Lubicon Lake Cree Women and their Society." Master's thesis, University of Calgary.

Caulfield, Mina Davis. 1981. "Equality, Sex and Mode of Production." In *Social Inequality: Comparative and Developmental Approaches,* ed. Gerald D. Berreman. New York: Academic Press.

Factum of Appellants. 1982. *Ominayak* v. *Norcen et al.,* Alberta.

Glazier, Stephen D. 1980. *Perspectives on Pentecostalism: Case Studies from the Caribbean and Latin America.* Washington, D.C.: University Press of America.

Goddard, John. 1991. *Last Stand of the Lubicon Cree.* Vancouver: Douglas and McIntyre.

Hartsock, Nancy. 1983. *Money, Sex and Power: Toward a Feminist Historical Materialism.* Boston: The Northeastern Series in Feminist Theory.

Hill, Dawn. 1994. "Spirit of Resistance of the Lubicon Lake Cree." PhD dissertation, McMaster University.

Leacock, Eleanor. 1980. "Montagnais Women and the Jesuit Program for Colonization." In *Women and Colonization: Anthropological Perspectives,* ed. Mona Etienne and Eleanor Leacock. New York: Praeger Publishers.

_____. 1981. *Myths of Male Dominance: Collected Articles on Women Cross-Culturally.* New York: Monthly Review Press.

Lubicon Lake Cree Nation. 1989a. *Analysis of Federal Government's January 24, 1989, "take-it-or-leave-it offer."*

_____. 1989b. Band Prepared History.

Meillassoux, Claude. 1972. "From Reproduction to Production: A Marxist Approach to Economic Anthropology." *Economy and Society* 1, no. 1:93-105.

_____. 1975. *Maidens, Meal and Money: Capitalism and the Domestic Community.* Cambridge: Cambridge University Press.

Ominayak, Bernard. 1987. Interview.

Rey, Pierre-Philippe. 1973. *Les Alliances de Classes*. Paris: Francois Maspero.

_____. 1975. "Les formes de la decomposition des sociétés precapitalistes au nord Togo . . ." In *L'Agriculture Africaine et le capitalisme*, ed. Samir Amin. Paris: Editions Anthroposidcp.

_____. 1979. "Class Contradictions in Lineage Societies." *Critique of Anthropology* 4, nos. 13 and 14:41-60.

Richardson, Boyce, ed. 1989. "Wrestling with the Canadian System: A Decade of Lubicon Frustration." *Drumbeat: Anger and Renewal in Indian Country*. Toronto: Summerhill Press, Assembly of First Nations.

Rosaldo, Michelle Zimbalist, and Louise Lamphere, eds. 1974. Introduction to *Women, Culture and Society*. Stanford: Stanford University Press.

Ryan, Joan. 1986. Some Lubicon Lake Cree Statistics, 1980-1986. Unpublished.

Sacks, Karen. 1974. "Engels Revisited: Women, the Organization of Production, and Private Property." In *Women, Culture and Society*, ed. Michelle Zimbalist Rosaldo and Louise Lamphere. Stanford: Stanford University Press.

Sanday, Peggy R. 1974. "Female Status in the Public Domain." In *Women, Culture and Society*, ed. Michelle Zimbalist Rosaldo and Louise Lamphere. Stanford: Stanford University Press.

Gender and the Paradox of Residential Education in Carrier Society

Jo-Anne Fiske

Studies of the colonial educational system imposed upon North American indigenous peoples have focussed on three issues: cultural conflict arising from the imposition of a "moral" education designed to "civilize" Aboriginal peoples; the failure of schooling to assimilate Aboriginal workers into the paid labour force; and the unintended development of political leadership among male graduates of mission schools (see, for example: Fisher 1977; Knight 1978; Miller 1987; Iverson 1978). At the same time, however, these studies have paid scant attention to the implications of formal schooling for women's social and economic placement in the home community. Significantly, they have neither explored the ramifications of gender differences in the educational process and its outcomes, nor charted the linkages between school attendance, on the one hand, and family and kinship organization, on the other.

In this paper I analyze the significance of residential schooling for Carrier women of central British Columbia who attended the Lejac Residential School, a facility financed by the Canadian state and operated by Catholic congregations. I trace the contradictory outcomes of formal schooling for students over the course of six decades, between 1922 and 1984. I argue that the process of education subverted the social goals of the Catholic missionaries who ran the residential school. The aim of the federal government and the missionaries was to train female students to become farm wives, members of nuclear households resident in reserve communities. Their education included primarily "domestic sciences," reading, arithmetic, and religious instruction. Since the missionaries clearly intended that the girls become "Catholic" wives and mothers, submissive to male authority, all school activities were subordinated to religious instruction and ritual. Today, however, Carrier women are employed in a variety of vocations and professions and are active in community and interband politics as they struggle to maintain their

Carrier identity and to regain control over their lives. I argue that their formal education provided the skills necessary for women's political participation, while traditional Carrier values, in contradiction to Catholic precepts, encouraged their emergence in the public and political realm.

I used a variety of research methods to gather data on the residential school. I searched official records of the government and Oblates of Mary Immaculate. From the fall of 1979 to May 1980, I interviewed twelve former students and five former teachers, members of the Sisters of the Child Jesus (reported in Fiske 1981). These lengthy informal interviews, held in respondents' homes, as well as conversational exchanges in casual gatherings, were the most valuable sources of information on school experiences. A second period of field work, which was undertaken between 1983 and 1985, opened up further insights into the paradoxical consequences of residential schooling. Concentrating on women's political involvement, I gained new data about and understanding of the effect of schooling on adult experiences, in particular on community leadership. The data I present here contain verbatim quotes from interviews held during both periods of field work.

THEORETICAL FRAMEWORK

This analysis of gender and education is based on a theoretical framework that focusses on three distinct political forces that shape women's strategies of survival and social mobility: (1) the philosophy and practices of colonized education experienced by the Carrier, with specific concern for gender ideology; (2) the historical transformation of family organization and female productive and reproductive roles; and (3) the sexual politics of the home community. As students, girls were subjected to patriarchal authority that paid scant heed to their specific needs and aspirations. As young adults, they were excluded from the formal political structures imposed by church and state upon their communities. Therefore, in order to understand the contradictory experiences and outcomes of indigenous women's education, we need to look at the gendered nature of power relations at each stage of female experience as women confront the constraints and options afforded in the process of colonization.

Colonial education is typically viewed as a cultural invasion: "The invaders penetrate the cultural context of another group, in disrespect of the latter's potentialities; they impose their own view of the world upon those they invade and inhibit the creativity of the invaded by curbing their expression" (Freire 1970, 150). Colonial curricula ignore, contradict, and deny the students' culture; their language is forbidden and their daily life is structured according to the foreign moral precepts of the colonizers. Official control remains in the hands of the church and state elite. The philosophy and practices of the educators are couched in paternalistic terms; the colonizers assume a moral and intellectual superiority that carries with it the mandate to advance indigenous society by improving the morality of future generations.

Colonial education is, of course, but one facet of imposed change. In fact, it is designed to support and augment economic and social transformation enforced on the indigenous community as a whole. Universally, colonial educators have struggled to eradicate indigenous family and kinship structures so that marital and parental relationships will conform to European gender roles (cf. Altbach and Kelly 1978). In Canada, this process has historically been, and still is, aided by the state. Federal legislation known as the Indian Act intrudes into all family relations by granting the minister of Indian Affairs, through his agents, the right to determine inheritance of personal property, post-marital residence, and access to land and housing.

Colonial education is also designed to support foreign notions of social order and leadership. Not only is education rigidly hierarchical and grounded in the assumption that social progress is to be achieved by inculcating notions of obedience, duty, and obligation, but it is also premised on a European Christian assumption of male superiority. In the process of colonization, the church and state have introduced new models of leadership to indigenous peoples. In Canada and elsewhere, missionaries of the Catholic Church have sought to impose a theocratic order designed to augment the priests' powers. To this end they have established local political hierarchies that explicitly excluded women and that were empowered to uphold Catholic notions of patriarchy (Fiske 1981, 90-92). The state has followed a parallel route: under the Indian Act, women were excluded entirely from political participation; they could neither hold office nor elect office holders.

Colonial processes are, of course, shaped by dialectical relations. Harsh interventions are resisted as the colonized perfect strategies of rejection and subversion. Schooling is no exception: students develop effective strategies to retain their cultural identity and to rebel against severe authority (King 1967; Haig-Brown 1988). Indigenous communities manifest diverse responses. Even while parents and community leaders recognize the potential benefits of academic and vocational instruction, they protest against unwarranted cultural loss and the wholesale social disruption created by the residential mission schools. Enforced use of English and the concomitant loss of Aboriginal language, for example, provoke anger and resentment as the elderly become unable to communicate with the students returning from school. A lack of practical skills necessary to traditional economies among the young (e.g., fishing, trapping) generates further intergenerational tensions and gives rise to disillusionment and resistance (Fiske 1981; Haig-Brown 1988; Miller 1987).

The diversity of community responses is in part shaped by the gender division of labour and the indigenous gender ideology. Women and men may be served differently by the removal of young children to residential schools. Women find themselves caught between their desire to gain new skills for themselves and for their children, and sacrificing their children to a foreign control that is often cruel (Fiske 1981; Miller 1987; Haig-Brown 1988). Yet the absence of their children from home may release women from reproductive tasks, freeing them for productive labour. At the same time, industrial and agricultural schools, which depend heavily upon student labour, require an adolescent student body — girls and boys who normally would be engaged in productive and reproductive labour at home or in the labour force. Strict sexual segregation in the school also means that students return home with different skills that may affect their re-integration into the community. Furthermore, changes in economic opportunities and state intervention alter the community's needs for and perceptions of formal schooling.

PHILOSOPHY AND PRACTICES OF COLONIAL EDUCATION

Until very recently, Canadian Indian residential schools were viewed by state and church as a key mechanism for colonization and acculturation of Aboriginal peoples. The federal government saw them as essential to altering the Aboriginal economic order and to assimilating Aboriginal peoples into the dominant society; the missionaries saw them as necessary to transforming the Aboriginal moral order and to creating a segregated Christian society. Residential schools emerged at the same time as reserves were established for the Aboriginal populations (Patterson 1972, 70). From 1830 through to the turn of the century, the federal government steadily increased its support for residential schools, hoping that gradually the Aboriginal population would be either absorbed into the labour force or resident in self-sufficient agricultural reserves (Miller 1987, 3).

Residential schools were a joint enterprise of state and church. The Canadian government negotiated with missionary societies regarding the location and administration of the schools. The state limited its involvement to providing funds and land, while the missionaries provided teaching staff, hired industrial assistants, and managed the schools' farms, which were expected to become self-sufficient. Wherever possible, residential schools were isolated from Aboriginal communities. In the expectation that once they were familiar with EuroCanadian values and vocational skills students would abandon their own culture, parental visits were discouraged. During their annual ten months of residency, the students had virtually no contact with the world beyond the school's border; they spoke English, ate EuroCanadian foods, and played EuroCanadian games and team sports (Gresko 1986; Haig-Brown 1988; Miller 1987).

In British Columbia, the Catholic educational strategy relied exclusively on residential schools, preferably ones isolated from Aboriginal and EuroCanadian communities. The Catholic missionaries considered residential schools essential instruments to block the transmission of Aboriginal culture and to prepare students for life in a segregated community dependent upon subsistence agriculture (Knight 1978, 253).

Lejac Residential School, which opened in 1922 and closed in 1972, was one link in a chain of mission schools operated throughout British Columbia by the Oblates of Mary Immaculate, a French Catholic mission order that predicated its mode of missionization upon a reactionary, patriarchal pastoral idealism. In their view, the route to "advanced civilization" lay in the establishment of self-sufficient, patriarchal nuclear families (Fiske 1981, 92). Hence, extended families and corporate kinship organizations were to be eradicated. The Oblates considered the matrilineal kinship system of the Carrier (which entailed membership in one's mother's clan and succession to positions of rank held by her or her siblings) to be a degraded state, the outcome of "looseness of morals and absence of social re-straint" that would have to be abandoned before its adherents could "become thor-ough Christians" (Morice 1902, 23). The priests also objected to women holding traditional positions of power. Among the Carrier, women as well as men acquired noble titles and were eligible to inherit a chieftainship provided they had adequate wealth to validate their claims. Ideally, the converted would dwell in autonomous, theocratic villages governed by an ecclesiastically controlled political hierarchy. The residential school, it was thought, would assure the perpetuation of the Catho-lic community and provide an educated male elite to lead it.

The patriarchal philosophy of the Oblate agenda was reflected in their school organization and educational practices. School principalships and vice-principal-ships were reserved for Oblate priests. Orders of nuns were secured for classroom teaching, health care, and daily domestic management. By example as well as by their teaching, the religious sisters reinforced the patriarchal values of EuroCanadian society. The Sisters of the Infant Jesus who served at Lejac, for example, had no formal teachers' training. Rather, they had received an education that stressed religion and domestic sciences at the expense of academic knowl-edge. In all aspects of their work and social relations they were subordinate to the male administration.

Like other missionary bodies, Protestant and Catholic, the Oblates stressed the importance of religious and moral education at the expense of classroom stud-ies. The religious and moral instruction was shaped by negative assumptions about the psychology and character of Aboriginal girls. While moral education was deemed essential for all students, the Oblate priests held it to be particularly neces-sary for girls, as the following statement indicates: "I also consider a school for the Indian girls a far greater benefit here than a school for the boys. Both would be required, . . . but the girl's [sic] is undoubtedly the most required. In vain would we teach the boys so long as the girls are ignorant and wicked" (Oblate Fathers, Records, James McGuckin, OMI). Since the girls, more than the boys, had the onus of sexual morality placed on them, they faced a greater number of rules and more stringent demands upon their behaviour. Notions of correct modesty dictated the girls' dress and behaviour. They wore unbecoming uniforms, were denied personal adornment, and were subjected to standard hair styles. Sexual segregation was enforced rigidly. All social activities, routine chores, and, where possible, lessons, were undertaken separately. The classroom was divided into a "girls' side" and a "boys' side"; it was considered a serious offence merely to glance across the room. Communication between girls and boys was forbidden; even sisters and brothers were prohibited from speaking to one another.

The Oblates imposed a severe routine intended to inculcate habits of obedience, cleanliness, and punctuality. Daily activities were strictly regulated; routine bell ringing marked the change in activities. Infractions of established rules and alleged disrespect met with disciplinary measures ranging from a loss of privileges to corporal punishment. Like the daily routine, the students' lessons were repetitive and highly structured. At Lejac, as at all of the Oblates' schools, the students rarely spent more than two hours in the classroom (Haig-Brown 1988, 54ff). The curriculum was limited to the basic and "concrete" study of primary arithmetic and reading as a result of prevailing notions of Native mentality: "In academic subjects the Indian child advances most satisfactorily in subjects that might be described as 'imitative,' as for example, reading, writing and very primary arithmetic" (Dunlop 1946, 17). Aboriginal culture was ignored at best, denigrated at worst. All instruction was in English, and use of the Aboriginal language brought swift and harsh punishment.

State and church were united in their goal for female education: to train future farm wives. Thus the girls spent at least half of each day performing domestic chores, which in the official records is categorized "domestic sciences." Upon arising each day, the girls performed routine cleaning tasks. Each afternoon all the girls retired to the sewing room. Here, following the appropriate prayers, the young girls mended socks, sewed on buttons, etcetera, while the older girls at their sewing machines set forth to make all the required school uniforms. Each year the items numbered in the hundreds. For example, in the school year 1927-28, the girls completed "293 dresses, 191 aprons, 296 drawers, 301 chemises, 600 pairs [of] socks" (PAC, Lejac Quarterly Report, 31 March 1928). Similar inventories of the girls' production are intermittently recorded throughout 1924 to 1946 (PAC, Lejac Quarterly Report, 1924-46).

Although the government's practice was to provide girls with only a domestic education and literacy to grade eight, it supported the Oblates' frequent requests to retain girls long after their formal studies were completed. The church, ever cognizant of its self-assumed moral obligations to protect girls from so-called vices of frontier and indigenous societies, frequently requested that they remain at school until a marriage was arranged for them. Hence, it was not uncommon for girls to stay at Lejac until they reached eighteen or twenty years of age. The presence of young women was an important advantage for Lejac; they became a full-time un-paid source of labour, assisting the sisters in the nursery and infirmary and taking charge of the kitchen.

Although the government and Oblates agreed on a common educational prac-tice, they frequently differed on what was appropriate for the girls' future. The government favoured their assimilation into the work force, and the church fa-voured their permanent residence, as wives, on a reserve. Both were content that they had fulfilled their moral and social obligations to the female students. Neither questioned the limits of the education offered; rather, they appeared to share the view of one principal who, in 1938, stated, "As far as the girls are concerned there is not much more that can be done. They already are taught all the branches of domestic science" (PAC, Lejac School Registers). The girls, however, did question the limited course of studies and regretted the poor quality of instruction. They enjoyed learning and chafed at the imposed routines and mundane labour. In her memoirs, one former student recalls, "I found that I wanted to learn. I like to read; I even liked arithmetic and spelling. Sometimes I found myself wishing that we did more studying" (Moran 1988, 43). Girls found that their aspirations for future work and careers could not be fulfilled with their limited education, a situation later described by one as "criminal negligence; . . . it was criminal what we weren't allowed to do" (Fiske 1981, 44).

When the federal government agreed to provide financial support for Lejac, it anticipated that with time the school would become self-sufficient. State enthusi-asm for Indian education, however, had diminished by 1922, and the federal gov-ernment became more and more hesitant to fund Indian education. Consequently, not only were the pupil subsidies meagre, remaining at national rates set some twenty years earlier, $125 per pupil per annum, but the Oblate principal was de-nied funds for hired labour and routine maintenance (Oblate Fathers, Records, Lejac School Diaries; PAC, Lejac School Registers). In the face of insufficient endowments, the girls' domestic work was critical to survival of the school. As the farm was extended so was the range of the girls' chores. In regimented work par-ties the girls alternated in the kitchen, laundry, and bakery. Eventually the girls assumed responsibility for making cheese and butter, and preserving fruits and vegetables.

Despite the barriers facing girls, they did spend more time in class than the boys. Because of the demands of farm labour, boys attended classes irregularly, while the majority of girls received regular, albeit minimal, instruction. Not only were girls in class more frequently than boys, but it appears that both boys and girls also developed discrete strategies of resistance and accommodation that in turn affected the course of their school experiences. While the boys chose to be openly defiant of routines, the girls chose to be more subtle in their relationships with the sister. They soon learned, "You could get away with murder if you were a teacher's pet." Girls formed friendships with the more compassionate sisters and chose to be "good" in order to earn favours or to avoid punishment for breaching minor rules. Other girls chose to be obedient because it was easier to withdraw and "turn off" the nuns and priests. Some, shy and awkward, were submissive because, in their words, they "didn't want to stand out," or "didn't want to be noticed." These sentiments contrast sharply with those of the men who recall, as boys, "We wanted them to know we were still 'wild.'"

The contrast between compliant female behaviour, with its more subtle forms of resistance, and the outright challenges of the boys had some positive ramifications for the girls. In an effort to maintain amicable relations with the girls, the sisters tended to treat their pranks with determined good humour rather than punishing them, and rewarded their good behaviour with small privileges. It comes as no surprise, therefore, that on average the girls were more successful than the boys. More girls than boys completed grade eight. Between 1943 and 1948, when boys were released as farm labourers, no boys advanced beyond grade six, while sixteen girls were able to do so. Two years later, the government permitted the Oblates to offer secondary classes, and again it was girls who enrolled.

There is some irony here, for the school's practices were not intended to favour the girls' classroom instruction. Neither were the Oblates primarily concerned with maintaining a large female enrollment. Rather, given their reliance on student labour, they were often desperate to find and to keep boys capable of strenuous farm labour. The reasons that the school failed to do so lie as fully in the changing Carrier socio-economic order and community responses to the school as in the school itself.

REASONS FOR ATTENDANCE

The Carrier had first requested an industrial school more than a quarter of a century before Lejac had opened. With EuroCanadian settlement in the Nechako Plateau, the Carrier had diversified their economic strategies. Their Aboriginal seasonal round of fishing (primarily salmon), hunting and trapping large and small game, and foraging vegetation first had been adapted to the requirements of trapping and fishing for trade and had been altered again with increased opportunities for wage or contract labour. From the turn of the century, the Carrier had enjoyed relative prosperity consequent upon wage and contract labour associated with railroad and agricultural expansion. Nonetheless, they recognized that, with continuing depletion of natural resources, which threatened their trapping and subsistence production, and with increasing EuroCanadian settlement, they would need the benefits of formal schooling.

Despite the Carrier's stated desire for educational facilities and their conviction that literacy would lead to social equality, responses among them to the school

varied and affected girls and boys differently. Some families who occupied prominent positions within the villages, in particular positions endorsed by the Oblates,
strongly supported the school (Oblate Fathers, Records). Changes in family organization and the diversification of productive tasks affected school enrollment.
The shift of winter activities from extended family settlements to individually
owned trap lines encouraged parents to enroll their children. Without the burden of
young children at home, women were free to undertake a variety of productive
tasks. They spent longer and more profitable periods on the trap line or at the lake
shore where they fished. With men routinely working away from the community,
women assumed sole responsibility for livestock or other farm work. Women also
sought opportunities to earn cash. They joined the men in freighting goods, providing railroad ties for the newly constructed railroad, and clearing land for the
white settlers.

Family dislocation also influenced school enrollment. Several Carrier communities were devastated by the 1918 Spanish influenza. In consequence, infants
were handed over to the school to be cared for by the sisters and older girls. Older
children who were not needed for their labour at home were sent to residential
school by widowed parents or other relatives who were unable to provide well for
them. Girls in particular were sent to school, often to remain there year-round until
they were adolescents.

Of course, not all parents wished to send their children away; emotional ties
and dependence upon children's contribution to the family economy made many
reluctant. Some parents complied only when urged or coerced by the Oblate priest;
others refused entirely, hiding their children when the priests came for them, a
source of frustration that led one priest to complain to his superiors: "The month of
September was spent in collecting children from the camps, . . . the parents doing
nothing towards their education unless coaxed and threatened" (Oblate Fathers,
Records, Joseph Allard, OMI). Carrier parents were more reluctant to part with
sons than with daughters, apparently feeling that their sons' economic contributions were vital to the family subsistence (Oblate Fathers, Records, Allard). Mothers often refused to part with their very young sons. Local families assisted their
sons' escapes and hid others from the priest. Families departed early for the trap
line to avoid enrollment. Thus, on average, boys entered school at the age of ten
and remained for no longer than three or four years (PAC, Principal's Report, 1944).

The government exacerbated this situation by discharging boys before the
school-leaving age of fifteen. Either at the request of their guardians, who required
the boys' labour, or in order to evade state financial responsibility for impoverished parents, the government chose to send the boys home. The government agents
stated, "Indian boys do not take well to trapping after they are sixteen or older." In
addition, when their labour was in demand, as for example during World War Two,
boys were dismissed to become farm labourers (PAC, Howe, 1944).

The school did not face the same difficulties in recruiting and retaining female students. Significantly, not only did more girls than boys attend, but they also remained longer. Fewer girls were discharged to take on family economic responsibilities, and those who did leave often returned (PAC, Lejac School Registers). Available figures show that between the years 1923 and 1936 female enrollment exceeded male enrollment (Department of Indian Affairs, Annual Reports, 1923-1936). Furthermore, more girls than boys achieved an academic standing past grade six (PAC, Lejac School Registers).

THE LIFE COURSE OF FORMER PUPILS

Eventually, the girls and young women left Lejac to return home, most to enter marriages arranged by the priest or his appointed representative, the church chief. Despite the severe limits of their schooling, many found themselves better prepared for adult life than their male peers, whose years of hard work had failed to provide them with the vocational skills they had hoped would make them marketable in the labour force. While they had received no industrial training, the girls had learned a range of practical skills such as canning and pickling garden produce, and knitting. These skills they easily assimilated into the domestic economy, since the Carrier now relied considerably on subsistence agriculture.[1] Small-scale mixed farming was incorporated into the annual subsistence cycle as women found it useful to tend gardens and raise poultry. Garden produce provided women with goods to barter or sell to their Carrier and EuroCanadian neighbours. During the hard times of the Great Depression, for example, Carrier women exchanged food items with white women, receiving in return used clothing to be remade for their children.

Ironically, mission schooling can be credited with preparing Carrier women for social roles once abhorred by the Oblate missionaries. The Oblates placed some former students, mostly orphans, in the regional Catholic hospital. (Those who had remained at Lejac beyond grade eight were particularly well prepared for this role because they had assisted in the school infirmary.) The priests, however, vehemently objected to women entering the labour force. With expanding settlement and economic development, however, women soon found their domestic skills marketable. Overriding the priests' objections, women took jobs as domestic workers in private homes, public hospitals, restaurants, and hotels. Furthermore, having gained experience and self-confidence, many women left the hospitals to join the women working elsewhere (Fiske 1981, 45).

By 1960 many found themselves supporting large families as the influx of EuroCanadian men displaced Carrier men from the labour force while settlement and industrial expansion undermined fur trapping (Fiske 1989, 92). The advent of community self-administration in the 1970s opened new doors for literate women.

Former students of Lejac became office workers and band managers, frequently upgrading their credentials in adult education courses and in para-professional training.

Despite the overwhelming loneliness, hardship, and boredom of their student years, former female students acknowledge these benefits. One former student, who left Lejac at the beginning of the Great Depression, recollects:

I learned useful things, sewing, crocheting, knitting, stuff like that; . . . I learned to look after myself and to be a good mother. I [can] my own salmon and . . . my vegetables too. I learned to do very delicate work with my hands. . . . Then I learned basketry to show my mother I could do it. I revived my traditional skills.

Another remembers:

The girls learned useful things. We did work for the Red Cross. It came in handy when we were mothers. I have ten children. At least I learned to read, write, cook and bake. . . . Without Lejac I would have been nowhere.

Mary John, in telling her life history, poignantly describes the benefits she experienced:

Even then, I knew that there were also good things about school. I could now speak English, and I was making what the teachers called excellent progress in reading, writing, and arithmetic. I had also learned other, more practical things: sewing, cooking, and other domestic skills which the nuns and missionaries hoped would turn girls like me into good farmers' wives. Sister Superior gave me singing lessons each day, and while the lessons were going on, I was as happy as I could be away from my village. (Moran 1988, 48)

Economic advantages were not the only benefits women came to appreciate. Just as other mission schools were influential in forming the coming generations of Indian leadership (Knight 1978, 252ff; Gresko 1986; Miller 1987), so was Lejac instrumental in preparing Carrier women for community leadership. Proficiency in new domestic skills and use of new technology meant that women could diversify and increase their subsistence production. The most capable women were able to organize extended-family productive units that, having collective claims to critical resources, provided the context for control over essential goods and shared labour (Fiske 1989, ch. 6). Control over domestic resources not only afforded women considerable domestic authority and personal autonomy, but it also provided the material base for generating influence in larger kin networks, which are the primary political units of reserve communities (Fiske 1989, chs. 6 and 8). As women drew on other skills essential to community well-being — for example, treatments learned while serving in the Lejac infirmary — they gained prestige and respect and widened their personal social networks within the community.

Although the Indian Act denied women direct participation in their band's affairs before 1951, women utilized their schooling to influence community decision making. In the 1940s, for example, former Lejac students organized local protests against the harsh conditions at Lejac. Carrier women refused to enroll their children and wrote letters to Ottawa demanding changes. During the same period, these same former students organized women's voluntary associations, which were initiated to provide assistance to young mothers and families experiencing personal crises. Soon, however, these leaders were able to draw upon association members to support their petitions to Ottawa for improved community facilities, to organize income-generating activities such as handicraft sales, and to assist their leader in attending a range of conferences and meeting with other women's voluntary associations in Western Canada (Fiske 1989, 291-92). Here also, they drew on their student experiences, maintaining contact with former friends and classmates as they united in their social and political activities.

In the 1950s and 1960s, state intervention into their daily lives increased, and social and economic conditions deteriorated. Industrialization and steady, rapid increases in the white male population displaced Carrier men from the labour market. Incomes from trapping dove sharply. Simultaneously, the state assumed greater control over resource management, all too frequently to the Carrier's disadvantage (Fiske 1989, 97ff). Women broadened their community responsibilities. It was they, rather than men, who had the literacy essential to effective political action. Once again they lobbied and petitioned the government, this time struggling for improved housing, health services, and social assistance.

When the federal government finally removed its ban against women's participation in community electoral politics in 1951, former students were well prepared. Not surprisingly, they were the first women to stand for and win elected office. Several have become prominent community leaders and remain active in interprovincial voluntary associations and regional tribal councils. When asked what Lejac did for her, one Carrier woman replied, "I went on past Lejac, past school. . . . What did Lejac do for me? I became a chief and a professional person."

PARADOXES OF MISSIONIZATION

The irony of residential schooling for women can be appreciated only in the context of Catholic missionary activity and changes in Carrier society, which in themselves created paradoxical constraints and opportunities for women. Long before Lejac Residential School opened, the Carrier social organization had been influenced by Catholic notions of authority and patriarchy. The Oblates had sought to eliminate the Carrier matrilineal clan system, which had previously bound Carrier villages together in ties of marriage and trade, and to exclude women from positions of influence. The theocratic model of authority that they imposed upon the Carrier operated from the late nineteenth century through to the 1930s. It comprised a local hierarchy of chiefs, sub-chiefs, captains, watchmen, soldiers, and councillors whose members the priests drew from established positions of clan and village leadership. The watchmen were the "eyes" of the council, the soldiers its policemen. The former reported misdemeanours to the soldiers, the latter brought the misdemeanants before the chiefs for discipline. Chiefs and sub-chiefs performed as lay magistrates, while the captains administered public whippings ordered by the chiefs. Although the matrilineal clan system did not disappear during this period, it lost significance. Because the potlatch had been outlawed, succession to clan titles and noble positions could not be validated publicly by wealth distributions. Consequently, there was no public forum in which women could claim either traditional or EuroCanadian positions of leadership.

Christian proselytizing eroded women's sources of autonomy and authority. As clan-based trade and exchange disintegrated, women lost opportunities for trading independently amongst themselves. Exclusion from public offices meant that women could not negotiate directly with EuroCanadians regarding matters immediate to their domestic responsibilities — for example, use of resource territories, access to medical care, reformation of the education system. Women were hampered even in their efforts to indirectly influence community affairs. For, not only did priests explicitly forbid women a public voice in church or village affairs, they also ridiculed and berated men who took guidance from women (Fiske 1981, 17, 100).

The missionaries directed a great deal of energy toward the establishment of the patriarchal nuclear family. Men were reminded that "in a family it is the father who is the master" (Morice 1930, 59). Priests demanded father-to-son inheritance of property and supported the government's outlawing of the potlatch (ceremonial property distributions) on the grounds that sons were denied their rightful inheritance, which rendered entire communities destitute. Social stability was to be achieved through the eradication of matriliny, of so-called illicit sexual unions, and of marital dissolution. Watchmen and soldiers were expected to concentrate their attentions on informing against women who allegedly violated their marriage vows or entered into unsanctioned relationships with EuroCanadians. Chiefs responded with harsh punishments, usually public floggings.

"Civilization" carried with it the domestication of women. The Oblates placed great emphasis on women remaining at home, busy with domestic tasks typical of the farm wife, which, in fact, corresponded to many of their traditional duties: sewing, cooking, food processing, and caring for children. At the same time, the priests attempted to restrict women's participation in such tasks as packing, trapping, guiding, and land clearing, which took them away from the community. They also encouraged women to adopt European clothing and hair styles (Morice 1930, 59).

The priests made further attempts to radically alter the behaviour as well as the social importance of women. They attacked the practice of menstrual seclusion and where possible intervened to restrict or stop it. They denounced traditional healers as "witch doctors" and labelled elderly practitioners "ancient hags." Where possible, however, the priests introduced midwife societies, with the expectation that, like the watchmen, midwives would report unsanctioned behaviour of pregnant women to the church hierarchy or the priest (Cronin 1960, 159). In conformity with EuroCanadian gender roles, women's positions within the church organization were confined to informal auxiliary roles.

Carrier women resisted the missionaries' forceful efforts to eradicate traditional practices and to transform the organization of the domestic economy from extended-family productive units to autonomous, male-headed, nuclear-family productive units. They continued to form co-operative productive units comprising female kin, over which senior women exercised authority. Female kin, furthermore, shared the burden of child care, enabling mothers to travel to their fishing sites or to migrate to agricultural jobs at considerable distance from their homes. Ironically, the priests' emphasis on maternal responsibilities served to enhance rather than diminish women's domestic and community leadership. Because men were frequently working away from home, women had ample opportunity to exercise authority beyond their own domestic units. Women soon recognized that, in order to provide for their families and to lower the rate of infant mortality, they needed to act politically. Improved material conditions — for example, a safe water supply, electric power, or adequate housing — could be obtained only with aid from the federal government. Whether organized as a midwife society, church auxiliary, or a state-sponsored community service group, voluntary associations became critical to their political activism. Rather than remaining a subordinate church group, as the Oblates had envisioned, in at least two Carrier communities women's auxiliaries provided a forum for articulating grievances, making demands, and influencing political action (Fiske 1981, 100). Women justify these actions on two grounds. First, some claim that Aboriginal social organization was either matriarchal or egalitarian (Fiske 1989, 128). Second, echoing Catholic ideals of motherhood, women argue that in order to discharge their parental obligations they *must* pursue explicit political strategies; failure to do so is failure to be responsible mothers and grandmothers (Fiske 1989, 292). In short, the interlocking processes of missionization and colonization created paradoxical conditions that unintentionally offered women opportunities to subvert the aims of the priests. Having learned English and having become literate, competent women emerged from Lejac with the knowledge essential for political action. Notwithstanding its patriarchal practice and its harsh routine, Lejac enabled some women to achieve positions of community leadership. As one former student stated, "My sister-in-law runs the reserve. She can do that with her education."

CONCLUSION

The implicit goals of colonial education are to persuade or compel a subordinate population to adapt to the dominant society and in so doing to acquiesce to the political and economic policies of the colonizers. The practices of colonial education are harsh, unremittingly sexist, and unilaterally imposed without consultations with the parents or their community leaders. As is well known, the consequences of colonial education have been unquestionably traumatic for many, perhaps the vast majority, of residential students. Nonetheless, Indian residential schools not only failed to assimilate Aboriginal peoples into EuroCanadian society, but they also unintentionally provided the foundation upon which Aboriginal leaders successfully built structures of resistance. In the final analysis, the missionaries' forceful interventions into Carrier society did not facilitate the anticipated social changes. Carrier women did not accept EuroCanadian models of patriarchal authority, nor did they accommodate themselves to the state's assimilatory policies. Women resisted efforts to undermine their social position and to restrict their personal autonomy. Women (and men) selectively utilized novel skills and knowledge beneficial to themselves. And, in so doing, they effectively subverted the missionaries' intentions by broadening their economic strategies and by developing sophisticated political responses, which to a large measure were spearheaded by a schooled female leadership.

NOTES

A version of this paper has been published in Jane Gaskell and Arlene McLaren, eds., *Women and Education: A Canadian Perspective*, 2nd edition (Edmonton: Detselig Enterprises Ltd., 1991).

1. According to Rolf Knight (1978, 71), Indian farming was already in a decline before the Lejac School opened. Large-scale commercial farming and ranching in central British Columbia were constrained by the harsh climate and a lack of transportation and markets. Subsistence farming was far more significant than cash crops, which failed to offer a secure source of earnings.

REFERENCES

Altbach, Philip G., and Gail Kelly, eds. 1978. *Education and Colonialism*. New York: Longman.

Balikci, A. 1963. "Vunta Kutchin Social Changes: A Study of the Old Crow." Ottawa: Northern Coordination and Research, Department of Indian Affairs, Yukon Territory.

Cronin, Kay. 1960. *The Cross in the Wilderness*. Vancouver: Mitchell Press.

Dunlop, H., OMI 1946. "The Indian Residential School." *Missions* 2, no. 8:16-17.

Fisher, Robin. 1977. *Contact and Conflict: Indian-European Relations in British Columbia, 1774-1890*. Vancouver: University of British Columbia Press.

Fiske, Jo-Anne. 1981. "And Then We Prayed Again: Carrier Women, Colonialism, and Mission Schools." Master's thesis, University of British Columbia.

_____. 1989. "Gender and Politics in a Carrier Indian Community." PhD dissertation, University of British Columbia.

Freire, Paulo. 1970. *Pedagogy of the Oppressed*. Translated by Myra Bergman Ramos. New York: Herder and Herder.

Gresko, Jacqueline. 1986. "Creating Little Dominions within the Dominion: Early Catholic Indian Schools in Saskatchewan and British Columbia." In *Indian Education in Canada, Volume 1: The Legacy,* ed. Jean Barman, Yvonne Hébert, and Don McCaskill. Vancouver: University of British Columbia Press.

Haig-Brown, Celia. 1988. *Resistance and Renewal: Surviving the Indian Residential School*. Vancouver: The Tillacum Library.

Iverson, Katherine. 1978. "Civilization and Assimilation in the Colonized Schooling of Native Americans." In *Education and Colonialism*, ed. Philip G. Altbach and Gail Kelly. New York: Longman.

King, A. Richard. 1967. *The School at Mopass: A Problem of Identity*. New York: Holt, Rinehart, and Winston.

Knight, Rolf. 1978. *Indians at Work: An Informal History of Native Indian Labour in British Columbia, 1858-1930*. Vancouver: New Star Books.

Miller, J.R. 1987. "The Irony of Residential Schooling." *Canadian Journal of Native Education* 14, no. 2:3-13.

Moran, Bridget. 1988. *Stoney Creek Woman — Sai'k'uz Ts'eke: The Story of Mary John*. Vancouver: The Tillacum Library.

Morice, Rev. Father A.G., OMI 1902. *A First Collection of Minor Essays, Mostly Anthropological*. Quesnel, B.C.: Stuart Lake Mission.

_____. 1930. *Fifty Years in Western Canada: The Abridged Memoirs of Father A.G. Morice, O.M.I.* Toronto: Ryerson Press.

Oblate Fathers. Archives of the Oblate Fathers, St. Paul's Province. Microfilm. Provincial Archives of British Columbia.

_____. Records of the Oblate Missions of British Columbia from Oblate Historical Archives, St. Peter's Province Holy Rosary Scholasticate. Microfilm. Ottawa: University of British Columbia Library, AWI R4664.

Patterson, E. Palmer. 1972. *The Canadian Indian: A History Since 1500*. Don Mills, ON: Collier-Macmillan Canada, Ltd.

Public Archives of Canada (PAC). 1938. "Industrial School Files Annual Report." Records relating to Indian Affairs RG 10, vol. 6,553, file 881-1, part 1, 30 September.

Recommended Reading

Christine Miller

As an addendum to this volume, I have compiled a short list of books and articles concerning Canadian Aboriginal women. There are obvious shortcomings in this bibliography, as there are in all such endeavours. It is neither as full nor as up-to-date as I would wish. Nor did I include any of the excellent works of fiction and poetry written by Aboriginal women of Canada. This was done advisedly. Not only did I wish to keep the list within a manageable length, but I also wanted to keep it consistent with the articles in the volume. For these same reasons, I have also decided to exclude works published concerning Aboriginal women in the United States.

While not everyone will agree about the "rightness" or "truth" of the items I have chosen, I have listed only those that I felt did not support the stereotypes with which we are all familiar. This criterion was self-imposed; the results reflect my biases and not necessarily those of the rest of the committee.

Adamson, N., L. Briskin, and M. McPhail. 1988. *Feminist Organizing for Change: The Contemporary Women's Movement in Canada.* Toronto: Oxford University Press.

Ahenakew, Freda, and H.C. Wolfart. 1992. *Our Grandmothers' Lives: As Told in Their Own Words.* Saskatoon: Fifth House Publishers.

Anderson, Karen. 1985. "Commodity Exchange and Subordination: Montagnais-Naskapi and Huron Women, 1600-1650." *SIGNS: Journal of Women in Culture and Society* 11, no. 1 (autumn):48-62.

_____. 1987. "A Gendered World: Women, Men and the Political Economy of the Seventeenth-Century Huron." In *Feminism and Political Economy,* ed. Heather Jon Maroney and Meg Luxton. Toronto: Methuen Publications.

Bastien, Betty, E. Bastien, and J. Wierzba. 1990. Urban Native Family Violence Project. *Native Studies Review* 7, no. 1:136-46.

Blackman, Margaret B. 1981. "The Changing Status of Haida Women: An Ethnohistorical and Life History Approach." In *The World is as Sharp as a Knife: An Anthology in Honour of Wilson Duff,* ed. Donald N. Abbott. Victoria: British Columbia Provincial Museum.

Brady, Elizabeth, ed. 1989. Aboriginal Women in Canada: Special Edition. *Canadian Woman Studies* 10, nos. 2 and 3.

Brand, Johanna. 1978. *The Life and Death of Anna Mae Aquash*. Toronto: James Lorimer and Company.

Brodribb, Somer. 1984. "The Traditional Roles of Native Women in Canada and the Impact of Colonization." *The Canadian Journal of Native Studies* 4, no. 1:85-103.

_____. 1988. "Winonah's in the Spirit Place." *Resources for Feminist Research* (September):49-55.

Brown, Jennifer S.H. 1976. "Company Men and Native Families: Fur Trade Social and Domestic Relations in Canada's Old Northwest." PhD dissertation, University of Calgary.

_____. 1983. "Women as Centre and Symbol in the Emergence of Métis Communities." *The Canadian Journal of Native Studies* 3:39-46.

Brown, Judith K. 1970. "Economic Organization and the Position of Women among the Iroquois." *Ethnohistory* 17, nos. 3 and 4:151-67.

Buckley, Peggy, and Penny Carriere. 1988. "Literacy for Change: Northern Saskatchewan Literacy Programmes." *Canadian Woman Studies* 9, nos. 3 and 4:73-76.

Buffalohead, Priscilla K. 1983. "Farmers, Warriors, Traders: A Fresh Look at Ojibway Women." *Minnesota History* 48, no. 6 (summer):236-44.

Cassin, A. Marguerite, and Alison I. Griffith. 1981. "Class and Ethnicity: Producing the Difference that Counts." *Canadian Ethnic Studies* 13, no. 1:24-42.

Causineau, Deborah. 1987. "Comfort of Belonging: The Justification of Entitlement." *Canadian Woman Studies* 8, no. 4 (winter):81.

Cheda, Sherrill. 1973. "Indian Women: An Historical Example and a Contemporary View." In *Women in Canada*, ed. Marylee Stephenson. Toronto: New Press.

Chiste, Katherine Beaty. 1994. "Aboriginal Women and Self-Government: Challenging Leviathan." *American Indian Culture and Research Journal* 18, no. 3:19-41.

Clatworthy, Stewart J. 1981. *Issues Concerning the Role of Native Women in the Winnipeg Labour Market*. Winnipeg: University of Winnipeg, Institute of Urban Studies.

Cruikshank, Julie. 1975. "Becoming a Woman in Athapaskan Society: Changing Traditions on the Upper Yukon River." *The Western Canadian Journal of Anthropology* 5, no. 2:1-14.

_____. 1979. "Athapaskan Women: Lives and Legends." National Museum of Man Mercury Series. Ottawa: Canadian Ethnology Service, paper no. 57.

_____. 1994. "Claiming Legitimacy: Prophecy Narratives from Northern Aboriginal Women." *American Indian Quarterly* 18, no. 2 (spring):147-64.

Cruikshank, Julie, and Jim Lotz. 1971. "The Changing Role of Canadian Indian Women." A Report Prepared for the Royal Commission on the Status of Women in Canada.

Demas, Doreen. 1993. "Triple Jeopardy: Native Women with Disabilities." *Canadian Women's Studies* 13, no. 4 (summer):53-55.

Driben, Paul. 1990. "A Death in the Family: Strategic Importance of Women in Northern Ojibwa Society." *Native Studies Review* 6, no. 1:83-90.

Dupuis, Jean, and Maurice Vinet. 1985. "Restigouche Family Crisis Interveners." *The Victim's Advocate* 1, no. 3 (June).

Employment and Immigration Canada. 1981. "Native Women and Labour Force Development: A Voice of Many Women" (July).

_____. 1986. "Native Women's Needs Assessment Survey: Final Report." Canada Work Project (January).

Fiske, Jo-Anne. 1988. "Native Women in Reserve Politics: Strategies and Struggles." In *Community Organizing and the Canadian State*, ed. Roxanna Ng, Gillam Walker, and Jake Muller. Toronto: Garamond Press.

French, Alice. 1976. *My Name is Masak*. Winnipeg: Peguis Publishers Ltd.

Garnier, Karie. 1992. *Our Elders Speak*. White Rock, B.C.: Kate Garnier.

Gerber, Linda M. 1990. "Multiple Jeopardy: A Socio-Economic Comparison of Men and Women among the Indian, Métis and Inuit Peoples of Canada." *Canadian Ethnic Studies* 22, no. 3:69-81.

Glasser, Penelope. 1984. "Nokomis: Three Women of Manitoulin." *Canadian Woman Studies* 5, no. 3 (spring):40-43.

Goodwill, Jean. 1971. "A New Horizon for Native Women in Canada." In *Citizen Participation — Canada: A Book of Readings,* ed. James A. Draper. Toronto: New Press.

Graveline, Madeline J. 1986. Northern Native Wife Abuse Prevention Demonstration Project. Thompson Crisis Centre (September).

Green, Joyce. 1987. "The Changing Colour of Feminism." *The Newsmagazine* (November/December):37-39.

Grumet, Robert S. 1980. "Sunksquaws, Shamans, and Tradeswomen: Middle Atlantic Coastal Algonkian Women during the 17th and 18th Centuries." In *Women and Colonization: Anthropological Perspectives,* ed. Mona Etienne and Eleanor Leacock. Toronto: Bergin and Garvey Publishers, Inc.

Holmes, Joan M. 1983. "Childbirth Experience for Native Women." *Breaking the Silence* 1, no. 4 (spring).

_____. 1987. "Bill C-31: Equality or Disparity — The Effects of the New Indian Act on Native Women." Prepared for the Canadian Advisory Council on the Status of Women (released 19 May).

Hudson, Grace. 1980. "Participatory Research by Indian Women in Northern Ontario Remote Communities." *Convergence* 13, nos. 1 and 2:24-33.

Hungry Wolf, Beverly. 1980. *The Ways of My Grandmothers.* New York: Wm. Morrow and Co.

Jackson, Margaret A. 1994. "Aboriginal Women and Self-Government." In *Aboriginal Self-Government in Canada: Current Trends and Issues,* ed. John H. Hylton. Saskatoon: Purich Publishing.

Jacobson, Helga E., and Company. 1982. *A Study of Protection for Battered Women.* Women's Research Centre (January).

Jamieson, Kathleen. 1978. *Indian Women and the Law in Canada: Citizens Minus.* Study sponsored by the Advisory Council on the Status of Women, Indian Rights for Indian Women. Ottawa: Ministry of Supply and Services Canada.

_____. 1979. "Multiple Jeopardy: The Evolution of a Native Women's Movement." *Atlantis* 4, no. 2:157-78.

_____. 1981. "Sisters under the Skin: An Exploration of the Implications of Feminist-Materialist Perspective Research." *Canadian Ethnic Studies* 13, no. 1:130-43.

_____. 1986. "Sex Discrimination and the Indian Act." In *Arduous Journey: Canadian Indians and Decolonization,* ed. J. Rick Ponting. Toronto: McClelland and Stewart.

Keetley, K. 1981. "Native Teen Pregnancy: A Problem in Perspective." A report prepared for the Health and Welfare Canada Health Promotions Branch Grant #1216-9-153, Social Planning and Review Council of British Columbia.

Kirkness, Verna. 1988-89. "Emerging Native Women." *Canadian Journal of Women and Law* 2, no. 2:408-15.

Klein, Laura F. 1980. "Contending with Colonization: Tlingit Men and Women in Change." In *Women and Colonization: Anthropological Perspectives,* ed. Mona Etienne and Eleanor Leacock. Toronto: Bergin and Garvey Publishers, Inc.

LaChapelle, Caroline. 1982. "Beyond Barriers: Native Women and the Women's Movement." In *Still Ain't Satisfied: Canadian Feminism Today,* ed. Maureen Fitzgerald and Connie Guberman. Toronto: Women's Educational Press.

LaPrairie, Carol P. 1984. "Selected Criminal Justice and Socio-Demographic Data on Native Women." *Canadian Journal of Criminology* 26 (April):161-69.

_____. 1987. "Native Women and Crime in Canada: A Theoretical Model." In *Too Few to Count: Canadian Women in Conflict with the Law,* ed. Ellen Adelberg and Claudia Currie. Vancouver: Press Gang Publishers.

Leacock, Eleanor. 1980. "Montagnais Women and the Jesuit Program for Colonization." In *Women and Colonization: Anthropological Perspectives*, ed. Mona Etienne and Eleanor Leacock. Toronto: Bergin and Garvey Publishers, Inc.

Lever, Bernice, and the Richvale Writers Club. 1980. *Singing: Telling It Like It Is Yet Celebrating Survival with Dignity — An Anthology of Women's Writing from Canadian Prisons*. Cobalt: Highway Book Shop.

Matzko, Joyce. 1974. "The Indian Woman and Household Structure in Mill Creek, British Columbia." Master's thesis, University of Victoria.

McElroy, Ann. 1975. "Canadian Arctic Modernization and Change in Female Inuit Role Identification." *American Ethnologist* 2, no. 4:662-86.

McIver, Sharon D. 1995. "Aboriginal Women's Rights as 'Existing Rights.'" *Canadian Women's Studies* 15, nos. 2 and 3:34-37.

Meadows, Mary Lea. 1981. "Adaptation to Urban Life by Native Canadian Women. Master's thesis, University of Calgary.

Mitchell, Marjorie. 1979. "The Indian Act: Social and Cultural Consequences for Native Indian Women on a British Columbia Reserve." *Atlantis* 4, no. 2:179-88.

Monture, Martha. 1987. "Iroquois Women's Rights with Respect to Matrimonial Property on Indian Reserves." *Canadian Native Law Review* 4:1-10.

Monture, Patricia A. 1986. "Ka-Nah-Geh-Heh-Gah-E-Sa-Nonh-Yah-Gah." *Canadian Journal of Women and the Law* 2, no. 1:159-71.

Morgan, Robin, ed. 1984. *Sisterhood is Global: The International Women's Movement Anthology*. Garden City, N.Y.: Anchor Press/Doubleday.

Native Women's Association of Canada, Ottawa. 1988. "Implementation of Bill C-31: Amendments to the Indian Act." *Resources for Feminist Research* 17, no. 3 (September):125-28.

Neilson, Kathryn E. 1971. "The Delinquency of Indian Girls in British Columbia: A Study in Socialization." Master's thesis, University of British Columbia.

Obomsawin, Raymond, and Marie-Louise Obomsawin. 1988. "A Modern Tragedy: Family Violence in Canada's Native Communities." *Vis à Vis: A National Newsletter on Family Violence* 5, no. 4 (winter):1-10.

O'Hara, Maureen. 1985. *Direct Services for Battered Native Women in Canada*. National Native Alcohol and Drug Abuse Program, Health and Welfare Canada (June).

Poelzer, Dolores T., and Irene A. Poelzer. 1986. *In Our Own Words: Northern Saskatchewan Métis Women Speak Out*. Saskatoon: Lindenblatt and Hamonic.

Richard, Mary, chair. 1985. Native Women and Economic Development: Task Force Report. Native Economic Advisory Board, Government of Canada (January).

Richardson, Karen. 1981. "No Indian Women, No Indian Nation." *Ontario Indian* 4:10, 11, 41.

Roberts, Katheryn, ed. *Native Woman Digest*. Edmonton: Lincoln Gumbs Publisher.

Romaniuk, A. 1981. "Increase in Natural Fertility during the Early Stages of Modernization: Canadian Indians Case Study." *Demography* 18, no. 2:157-72.

Rothenberg, Diane. 1980. "The Mothers of the Nation: Seneca Resistance to Quaker Intervention." In *Women and Colonization: Anthropological Perspectives*, ed. Mona Etienne and Eleanor Leacock. Toronto: Bergin and Garvey Publishers, Inc.

Sanders, Douglas. 1975. "Indian Women: A Brief History of Their Roles and Rights." *McGill Law Journal* 21, no. 4:656-72.

Silman, Janet, ed. 1987. *Enough is Enough: Aboriginal Women Speak Out*. Toronto: The Women's Press.

Smandych, Russell, and Gloria Lee. 1995. "Women, Colonization and Resistance: Elements of an Amerindian Autohistorical Approach to the Study of Law and Colonialism." *Native Studies Review* 10, no. 1:21-45.

Spittal, W.G., ed. 1990. *Iroquois Women: An Anthology*. Oshwekan, ON: Iroqrafts, Ltd.

Theriault, Madelaine Katt. 1992. *Moose to Moccasins: The Story of Ka Kita Wa Pa No Kwe*. Toronto:

National Heritage / National History Inc.

Thomas, W.D.S. 1971. "Maternal Mortality in Native British Columbia Indians, a High-Risk Group." In *Population Issues in Canada*, ed. Carl F. Grindstaff, Craig L. Boydell, and Paul C. Whitehead. Toronto: Holt, Rinehart, and Winston of Canada Ltd.

Two-Axe Early, Mary. 1980. "The Least Members of Our Society: The Mohawk Women of Caughnawaga." *Canadian Woman Studies* 2, no. 2:64-66.

Vanderburgh, R.M. 1979. "Women and the Politics of Culture: Class and Gender Conflicts in the Toronto Native Community." *Resources for Feminist Research* 3, no. 3 (November):16-17.

_____. 1982. "Tradition and Transition in the Lives of Ojibwa Women." *Resources for Feminist Research* 2, no. 2 (July):218-20.

Van Kirk, Sylvia. 1980. *"Many Tender Ties" : Women in Fur-Trade Society in Western Canada, 1670-1870*. Winnipeg: Watson and Dwyer Publishing Ltd.

_____. 1987. "The Role of Native Women in the Creation of Fur-Trade Society in Western Canada." In *The Women's West*, ed. Susan Armitage and Elizabeth Jameson. Norman: University of Oklahoma Press.

Whipp, Kathleen. 1985. "Traditional and Current Status of Indian Women: Keys to Analysis and Prevention of Wife Battering on Reserves." School of Social Work, Carleton University (November).

Withers, J. 1984. "Inuit Women Artists." *Feminist Studies* 10, no. 1:85-96.

Young, Doris, and Ustun Reinhart. 1988. "How Powerful We as Native Women Really Are: The Indigenous Women's Collective." *Canadian Dimension* 22, no. 2 (March/April):16-17.

Contributors

JEANNETTE ARMSTRONG is Okanagan and resides on the Penticton Indian Reservation. A fluent speaker of the Okanagan language, she has studied under some of the most knowledgeable Elders of the Okanagan. She has a degree in fine arts from the University of Victoria, and her works have been recognized through such awards as the Mungo Martin Award, the Helen Pitt Memorial Award, and the Vancouver Foundation Graduate Award. She is a recognized and widely published Canadian author and has recently edited a collection of essays, *Looking at the Words of our People: First Nations Analysis of Literature*. Her other creative works include two produced videoscripts and three produced poetry-music collabora-tions. Her collaboration "Indian Woman," on Cargo Record release *Till the Bars Break*, was nominated for a Canadian Juno Award. Works in progress include a music-art-video collaboration of South American and Okanagan indigenous musi-cians and artists and a new novel. She is the director of the EN'OWKIN Interna-tional School of Writing and is an appointed traditional council member of the Penticton Indian Band. A strong advocate of indigenous rights, she was recently appointed to the Council of Listeners in the International Testimonials on Viola-tions to Indigenous Sovereignty.

BETTY BASTIEN is Blackfoot from the Peigan First Nations. She resides on the reservation with her son Peetah. She is currently pursuing a PhD in traditional knowledge and is an instructor in the Native American Studies Department and the Faculty of Social Work at the University of Lethbridge.

JENNIFER BLYTHE is an anthropologist who carried out field work in Moosonee and Moose Factory in 1984 while she was a research associate at McMaster Uni-versity working with Research Program for Technology Assessment in Subarctic Ontario, a multidisciplinary team designed to establish baseline data for the communities on the west side of James Bay in anticipation of future effects of development. She is now an assistant professor in the Faculty of Health Sciences, School of Nursing, at McMaster University.

ROSEMARY BROWN works in Calgary at Arusha, a resource centre that focusses on local and global social justice issues. She is an active member of the Committee Against Racism, a group that has worked in solidarity with the Lubicon Lake Nation since 1984.

SARAH CARTER is associate professor of history at the University of Calgary. She is the author of *Lost Harvests: Prairie Indian Reserve Farmers and Government Policy* (Montreal: McGill-Queen's University Press, 1990).

PATRICIA CHUCHRYK is associate professor and chair of the Department of Sociology at the University of Lethbridge. She teaches and does research in the areas of Latin American studies and women's studies. She has also taught in the off-campus program at Red Crow College on the Blood Indian Reserve.

CHERYL DEERING attended the University of Lethbridge, where she earned a degree in Native American studies and was on the executive of the Native American Students Association. She has co-ordinated workshops for women who have been sexually abused as children and for mothers of sexually abused children. She is particularly interested in women's issues, the Third World, and the effect of colonization and racism globally. She has written and developed an eight-week course entitled "Treatment Readiness: Native Substance Abuse Program" for Aboriginal offenders, and has supported the writing and development of "Male Victims of Sexual Abuse for First Nations." She is now acting as program co-ordinator, developing a treatment program in the Nuu Chan Nulth area.

JULIA EMBERLEY is assistant professor in the women's studies and gender studies graduate programmes at the University of Northern British Columbia. She is the author of a book entitled *Thresholds of Difference: Feminist Critique, Native Women's Writings, Postcolonial Theory* and several articles, some of which have appeared in *Genders, Cultural Critique, New Formations,* and *Feminist Studies.* She is currently completing a book on the cultural history of fur and fashion.

JO-ANNE FISKE is associate professor of women's studies at the University of Northern British Columbia. She has her PhD in anthropology from the University of British Columbia. For the past twenty years, she had been doing research and working with women of the Carrier and Babine Nations in central British Columbia. She has published articles in *Culture, Feminist Studies,* and several other journals.

She has recently completed a monograph on the traditional legal order of the Babine Nation, *Ciz dideen khat — When the Plumes Rise: The Way of the Ned'u'ten.*

BEVERLY HUNGRY WOLF was born in 1950 on the Blood Indian Reserve, where she grew up in a progressive ranching household surrounded by family Elders who practised traditions from the buffalo days. In boarding school (where speaking Blackfoot was severely punished), she learned shame for those same traditions, but since then she has made a lifelong commitment to keeping them alive, encouraged by her husband, Adolf Hungry Wolf, a writer who had studied with those Elders and adopted their ways. Together, the couple have been Keepers of a tribal Medicine Pipe bundle for twenty years. They live with three of their six children on a wilderness homestead in the Canadian Rockies, where they are dedicated to nature and their culture. Beverly Hungry Wolf is author of the acclaimed book entitled *The Ways of My Grandmothers* (New York: Wm. Morrow and Co., 1980) and a book on Blackfoot foods and eating entitled *Buffalo and Berrie,* and she has co-authored several books with her husband. She is currently completing a book entitled *Today's Grandmothers* and is developing courses in the Blackfoot language at the Blackfeet Community College in Browning, Montana.

EMMA LAROCQUE, Plains Cree Métis from northeastern Alberta, is a writer, poet, historian, social and literary critic, and has been a professor in the Department of Native Studies at the University of Manitoba since 1977. For more than two decades she has lectured both nationally and internationally on issues of human rights, focussing on Native history, colonization, literature, education, and identity. She is the author of *Defeathering the Indian* (1975), *Three Conventional Approaches to Native People in Society and in Literature* (1984), and numerous articles on colonization, Canadian historiography, Native literature, racism, and violence against women. Her poetry has appeared in several national and international journals and anthologies.

BRENDA MANYFINGERS, of Cree descent, is married into the Blood Tribe of the Blackfoot Confederacy. She has three children. Brenda has been working in the field of human services for almost 15 years and is a university graduate. She is currently employed with Stoney Nation, managing their Child Welfare Services.

PEGGY MARTIN McGUIRE earned her PhD in anthropology at McMaster University, where she also worked as part of Technology Assessment in Subarctic Ontario. She taught for several years at the Department of Native Studies, University of Saskatchewan, and now works for the Office of the Treaty Commissioner in Saskatchewan.

KATHY M'CLOSKEY is completing her doctoral dissertation, entitled "Myths, Markets and Metaphors: Navajo Weaving as Commodity and Communicative Form," at York University, Department of Social Anthropology. A weaver for twenty years, she has recently undertaken curatorial work as well. In 1995 she curated "Fields and Flowers, Fabric Landscapes of Prince Edward Island" in Charlottetown and is preparing "First Nations / Fine Weavers," which will open at the Burlington Art Centre in Ontario in 1997. Her publications include "Marketing Multiple Myths: The Hidden History of Navajo Weaving" (*The Journal of the Southwest* 36, 3 [autumn 1994]) and "Trading is a White Man's Game," in *Ethnographic Feminisms,* ed. Sally Cole and Lynne Phillips (Ottawa: Carleton University Press, 1995).

CHRISTINE MILLER is of Blackfeet descent. She has taught Native American studies at California State University at Sacramento, University of California, Berkeley, and at the University of Lethbridge, where she held the rank of associate professor. During her tenure there, she spent time at the University of Leeds, England, as part of the Faculty Exchange Program. She has been deeply involved as a volunteer for various community agencies both before and after her retirement in 1992.

MARIE SMALLFACE MARULE was born and raised on the Blood Indian Reserve in southern Alberta and is a member of the Blood Nation of the Blackfoot Confederacy. She was an assistant professor of Native American studies at the University of Lethbridge for several years in the field of politics and economic development, has taught at the Nicola Valley Institute of Technology, and was community and literacy officer in Zambia, Central Africa, under the auspices of CUSO. She has served as executive director for National Indian Brotherhood and as chief administrator of the World Council of Indigenous Peoples. She is currently the president of Red Crow Community College, a First Nations Education institute located on the Blood Reserve, where she is developing a curriculum designed to meet the needs of Aboriginal students. Known for her work as an educator and advocate of human rights for Aboriginal people around the world, she is a recipient of the 1995 National Aboriginal Achievement Awards for education.

VICKY PARASCHAK is associate professor in the Department of Kinesiology at the University of Windsor. She spent five years in the Northwest Territories as a participant observer in community and territorial sport, which included working as a policy officer for the government of the Northwest Territories Sport and Recreation Division. She has also examined sporting practices on the Six Nations Reserve in Ontario, as well as the involvement of Aborigines in sport in Australia.

DIANE P. PAYMENT is a historian with the Department of Canadian Heritage, Prairie and Northwest Territories Region, in Winnipeg. Her areas of expertise are Métis and Francophone history in Western Canada and Métis women's history, particularly as it relates to Batoche, Riel House, and The Forks national historic sites. She has recently co-ordinated an oral history project with Inuit communities in the Auyuittuq National Park Reserve. In 1986 she received the Canadian Historical Association Regional Certificate of Merit for *Les gens libres — otipemisiwak* (Saint-Boniface: Les Editions du Blé, 1983), and in 1994 she received the Canada 125th Anniversary commemorative medal.

LAURA PEERS is an ethnohistorian with a particular interest in Aboriginal cultural history and its representations. She is the author of *The Ojibwa of Western Canada, 1780 to 1870* (Winnipeg: University of Manitoba Press, 1994) and, with Jacqueline Peterson, *Sacred Encounters: Father De Smet and the Indians of the Rocky Mountain West* (Norman: University of Oklahoma Press, 1993).

Index

AADAC (Alberta Alcohol and Drug Abuse
    Commission) 159
Aboriginal women. SEE women, Aboriginal
acculturation
    through colonial education 170
Adam, François
    on medical skills of Aboriginal women 63-64
aesthetics
    discipline of 116-17
age
    employment patterns and 135, 136, 143
agriculture. SEE ALSO subsistence
    on reserves 53, 56
Ahenakew, Edward
    on Aboriginal women as housekeepers 66
Akulukjuk, Malaya 122
Albers, Patricia
    on Sioux women of Devil's Lake 53
alcohol abuse
    at Lubicon Lake 152, 156, 158-59, 160
Allen, Paula Gunn
    on Aboriginal women 4
American Indian Hall of Fame 86
American Indian Movement (AIM) 103, 105
anthropology
    and art/craft dichotomy 116
    as a discipline 108
April Raintree (Culleton) 97-98
Arcand family 31
Armstrong, Jeannette. *Slash* 97, 103, 105-08

art
    craft vs. 113-25
    definition of 113-14
    and labour 117
    weaving as 113
    women's: marginalization of 114; status of
        117-20
Ashcroft, Bill
    on post-colonialism 13
assimilation
    through education 127-28

Batoche
    capture of 27-28
    reconstruction of 30-31
    resettlement at 23-26
Batteaux, Abbé 116
Bear, Lena (Sayese) 71
Beaver, Bev 90, 92
Beaver, Carolyn 91
Beaver Bundle Ceremony 78
Becker, Howard
    on artist vs. craftworker 120
Bélanger family 31
berry picking 58, 154
bias
    in academic studies 12, 13
    gender 39, 42-44
big grass root. SEE turnips, prairie
Billson, Janet M.
    on gender roles 52
Bird, Junius
    on art in textiles 121

bison. SEE ALSO buffalo hunt
  disappearance of 55-56, 69
  Saulteaux dependence upon 41, 42, 43
Blood Reserve 79
Bobbi Lee (Maracle) 98
Bodden, Kenneth
  on Lubicon Lake Cree 153
Bomberry, Phyllis 86, 89, 90, 92-93
Boyer, Elise (Tourond) 33
Boyer, Emma (Ferguson) 33
Boyer, Hélène McMillan 23
Branconnier, Justine 32
Brant, Beth, ed. *A Gathering of Spirit* 97
Brass, Eleanor 62, 71
Brody, Hugh
  on cumulative frontiers 152
Brown, Jennifer
  on company wives 132
buffalo hunt
  role of Métis women 21
Bungi people. SEE Saulteaux people
bush life vs. community life 132, 138

Campbell, Maria 101
  Halfbreed 98
Canadian Arctic Producers (CAP) 122
Canadian Pacific Railway 56
*Canadian Woman Studies / les cahiers de la
    femme* 108
Cardinal-Schubert, Joanne 100
Carlisle Indian School 67
Caron, Jean 23
Caron, Marguerite (Dumas) 23, 26, 27, 31
Carpenter, Edmund
  on visual values 115-16
Carrier nation
  Catholic influence over 171, 178-80
  education and 174-75
Carrière, Damase 28
Carter, Marion 60
Catholic Church
  Carrier nation and 171, 178-80
  Métis women and the 25-26
  patriarchy of 169, 171, 178
  residential schools of 170-73, 175, 176
ceremony
  among Lubicon Lake Cree 162
  and self-concept 129

Champagne, Marie (Letendre) 28, 31
Cheska, Alyce
  on Aboriginal women in sport 85
child care 141, 145, 156, 157, 180
children
  care of 144
  contribution to subsistence 175
  Elders and 157, 158
  Lubicon Lake Cree 157-58
  problems of 129
  in residential schools 171-74, 175-76
  tribal identity and 127, 129
Chippewa, Plains. SEE Saulteaux people
Churchill, Ward
  on Aboriginal sport 84
Clignet, Remi
  on oppressed people 127
Cloutier, Gabriel, abbé 27
Colcleugh, Emma Shaw
  on needlework 63
colonialism
  effect on women 4, 6-7
  in feminist theory 99-100
  of scholarship 12-14, 98
  and tribal identity 128
  "unhappy" books and 101-02
colonization
  of Aboriginal peoples x, 11
  in education 168-70
  effect on tribal identity 127
  effect on women 11-12
colour, women of
  and sport 83, 94
community life
  isolation of residential schools 170
  at Lubicon Lake 157-58
  of Métis women 33
  self-administration of 176-77
  women in 4, 140, 142, 147
conceptual vs. technical 119
  in weaving 123, 125
corn
  grown by Saulteaux 45
craft making 62, 133. SEE ALSO weaving
  art vs. 113-25
  by Cree women 137-38, 140, 142
  history of 117
craftworkers
  status of 117

Craig, Susan B.
  on Aboriginal women in sport 85, 88, 90-91
Cree Development Board 160-61
Cree women
  autonomy of 143
  employment of 131-48
  at Lubicon Lake 151-63
  social ties and 146-47, 160
  work patterns of 134-36
Crowfoot, Chief 70
Culleton, Beatrice
  April Raintree 97-98
  In Search of April Raintree 97
cultural politics 97, 98
culture, Aboriginal
  decline of 55
  education and 127-28
  effect of colonial education on 168-69
  oral tradition and 107-08
  residential schools and 172
  self-determination within 97
culture, EuroCanadian
  effect on Aboriginal culture 48
  women's status and 53
culture, French-Canadian
  at Batoche 24
  and Métis women 20, 22
customs
  Métis 22, 24-25

Daishowa Inc. 163
de Patie, Koreula 123
deaths. SEE ALSO suicide rate
  alcohol-related 158-59
  at Batoche 30
decolonialization
  feminist theory and 98, 104
deconstructivism
  of art history 114
  in writing 102
deer
  Saulteaux dependence upon 41, 42
Deloria, Vine Jr.
  on self-concept 128
Delorme, Catherine 29
Delorme, Joséphine (Fleury) 28
Delorme family 31
Depression, the 132-33
Dept. of Indian Affairs (DIA) 56, 72
  image of Plains women 54-55

Derrida, Jacques
  on the metaphysics of presence 104
Desmarais family 31
diapers, disposable 80
diet 40
  of Lubicon Lake Cree 155-56, 157
  of Saulteaux 41
Dillon, Marion 58, 60, 61, 65
Dion, Joseph F.
  on Onion Lake Reserve 58, 60-61
diseases 57, 80
divorced women
  employment and 139-40, 142, 145
domestic education 172, 173, 176
domestic vs. public life
  in employment 135-36
domestic work 67, 179. SEE ALSO
    housekeeping
  marketability of 176
  Métis women 20, 22
  restructuring on reserves 54
  status of 140
domesticity
  cult of 118
Dorval, Mlle Onésime 25, 32
drawings
  in tapestry production 123, 125
dress
  of Métis 22
drugs. SEE pharmaceuticals
ducks
  hunting 59-60
Dumas, Henriette (Landry) 22, 23
Dumont, Angèle (Landry) 26
Dumont, Gabriel 23, 26, 31
Dumont, Isidore 29
Dumont, Madeleine (Wilkie) 26, 27, 31
dwellings
  on reserves 65

Earth as Mother 77, 81, 127
education. SEE ALSO residential schools
  acculturation through 170
  assimilation through 127-28
  colonial 168-70
  continuing 145
  of Cree women 138, 141
  gender differences 173-76
educational levels
  employment and 135, 139-40, 141, 142, 145
  inequality of 100

el Saadawi, Nawal 102
Elders
  in Métis society 24
  relationship with youth 157, 158
Ellison, Ralph
  on non-white literary tradition 106-07
employment. SEE ALSO domestic work
  attitudes toward 143-44
  choice of 131, 132
  conflicts related to 143
  of Cree women 131-48
  of divorced women 139-40, 142, 145
  domestic life and 144, 175
  at Lubicon Lake 154-57
  marital conflict and 144, 145
  of married women 139, 141-42, 144-45
  of men 137, 140-41
  off-reserve 67
  of single women 139-40, 142, 145
  status of 137, 143-44, 146
environmental concerns 81
epidemics 57

families xi. SEE ALSO children; marriage
  community vs. 146-47
  effect of socio-economic change on 131
  at Lubicon Lake 154-57
  violence in 4
farm labour. SEE ALSO subsistence
  boys' schooling and 173, 174
  of Métis women 31
  women in 61
Father Sun 127
feminist theory
  colonialism in 99-100
  employment and 135-36
  public vs. domestic life 146
  and self-determination 102-05
festivities
  of Métis women 33
Fidler, Peter 46
Fidler, Véronique (Gervais) 27
fine art. SEE art
Fine Day (Cree leader) 60
Fireweed (quarterly) 97
Firth, Sharon 85
Firth, Shirley 85
fish
  in Saulteaux diet 42, 47
Fish Creek, battle at 27
Fisher, Alexandre 29

Fisher, Amélie (Poitras) 28
Fisher, Georges 28
food
  bush vs. store-bought 155-56, 157
  Métis 24
  Saulteaux 41
  selling of 70
forestry 163
Forget, Amedée 61
Fourmond, Father 27
French, Captain 28
fur trade 132. SEE ALSO trapping
  in Cree economy 136
  effect on women's status 54
  Saulteaux and 40, 43-44

game
  decline of 132
  importance to Saulteaux 43-44, 45, 47
  loss of 159
  small: use by Saulteaux 46
Game Ordinance of the Territorial
  government 70
Gariépy, Philippe 27, 29
Gariépy, Rosalie (Parenteau) 27
Gates, Henry Louis Jr.
  on literary tradition 107
Gathering of Spirit, A (Brant, ed.) 97
gender
  in Aboriginal society ix-x
  bias in historical writings 6, 39, 42-44
  division of labour 43, 60
  equality 78, 151, 152, 156-57
  sport and 83, 94
gender differences
  in education 172-76
  in effects of colonization 6, 12
  in status of work 140-41
gender roles 78
  among Cree 136
  among Métis 20-21
  church and 180
  colonialism and 4, 6
  effect of reserves on 52-53
  in subsistence 44
geometric forms
  in art and craft 114, 118-19
Gervais family 31
Gilchrist, F.C. 70
Godon, Catherine 29

Goeres, Mavis 86
Goldfrank, Esther S.
   on reserve life 51
Goldie, Terry
   on sexualization of indigenous culture 106
Gooderham, Instructress 65
gophers
   hunting 59
Goulet family 31
Graham, W.M. 68
Greer, Annie 63
Griffiths, Gareth
   on post-colonialism 13
guerre nationale 24

Halfbreed (Campbell) 98
"Halfbreed" women 21
Hampâté Bâ, Amadou
   on craft workers 120
"happy" books 101-02
Harlow, Barbara. Resistance Literature 99
Hartsock, Nancy
   on women's reproductive work 159-60
health care 80
Henhawk, Doris 91, 93-94
Henry, Blanche (Ross) 28
Henry the Elder 46
Henry the Younger 47
Hickerson, Harold
   on Saulteaux subsistence 41, 43, 44, 48
Hill, Ruth 92
Holzkamm, Tim
   on Ojibway horticulture 46
home vs. public spheres. SEE domestic vs.
   public life
homemakers 141. SEE ALSO housekeeping
Honour the Sun (Slipperjack) 97
Horden Hall 133
housekeeping 61-62, 64-66, 136-37, 141. SEE
   ALSO domestic work
   of Métis women 31-32
   technology and 155
housing
   on reserves 65
Howard, James
   on Saulteaux subsistence 41-42, 43, 44, 47, 48
Hudson's Bay Company 132, 133
Hugonard, Father 67
hunting 57-58
   at Lubicon Lake 151, 154, 156, 159
   in Saulteaux life 39-40, 43

hunting-gathering economy 56, 152, 153

I Am Woman (Maracle) 98
identity
   employment and 144
   tribal 127-29
illnesses. SEE diseases
In Search of April Raintree (Culleton) 97
income
   transfer payments 137, 151
   welfare 134, 154, 156
Indian Act 128
   community decision making by women and
      177-78
   discrimination against women 53
Indian agents 70, 71
Indian status
   loss by women 53
Iniskim 78
interviews
   with Aboriginal women 43
intratextual stories 106, 108
Iroquian society
   women in 53-54
Iroquois national women's lacrosse team 88

James Bay Education Centre 134, 138, 140,
   141, 145
Jamieson, Kathleen
   on the Indian Act 53
   on women in Iroquian society 54
Jamieson, Sandra (Hill) 91
job opportunities. SEE employment
job training
   of Cree women 141
Kant, Immanuel
   on aesthetics 116-17
Keeshig-Tobias, Lenore 100
King, Thomas
   on Aboriginal writings 107
Klein, Alan
   on gender roles before European contact 54

labour. SEE ALSO farm labour; work
   art vs. 117
   gender division of 43, 60, 169-70
   mental vs. manual 115, 117
   social division of 123, 125
LaCapra, Dominick
   on official history 105

Ladéroute, Geneviève 23
Lamphere, Louise
  on women's role in production 157
land claims
  Lubicon Lake Cree 160-61, 163
Lange, Lynda
  on unemployment 143
languages, Aboriginal
  in residential schools 169, 172
Leacock, Eleanor
  on women's role in societal decision making
    161
leadership
  colonial education and 169
  schooling as preparation for 177
  by women 178, 180
Lee, Richard B.
  on hunter-gatherer people 44
Lejac Residential School 171
Lenglet, Auguste 32
Lenglet, Georgine (d'Amours) 32
Leonardo da Vinci
  on painting and science 115
Lépine, Josephte (Lavallée) 26
Lépine, Julia Henry 23
Lépine, Maxime 26, 29
Lespérance, Marguerite 23
Letendre, Angélique (Dumas) 23
Letendre, Marie (Hallet) 23, 27
Letendre, Xavier 23
Letendre, André 29
Letendre dit Batoche, Xavier 23
Lévi-Strauss, Claude
  on writing and history 108
Lickers, Helen 90, 93
literate vs. non-literate
  in anthropology 115-16
literature vs. writings 99
Lubicon Lake
  employment at 154-57
  oil and gas development at 151-63
  socio-economic change at 154-60
Lubicon Lake Nation Women's Circle 163
Lubicon Settlement Commission of Review 163

Magazine to Re-establish the Trickster, The 100
"Man and the Hunter" conference 44
Mandelbaum, David 60
Maracle, Lee 101
  Bobbi Lee 98
  I Am Woman 98

Marion, Narcisse
  daughter of 21
marriage
  among Métis 21, 32-33
  breakdown 157, 158
married women
  employment of 139, 141-42, 144-45
Marxist feminist theory
  employment and 135-36
  public vs. domestic life and 146
mathematics
  and definition of art 114-15
Matheson, Dr. Elizabeth 63
matrilineal system
  of the Carrier 171, 178, 179
McDermott, Andrew
  daughter of 21
McGillis, Julie 29
medical skills
  of Aboriginal women 63-64
Medicine Pipe Ceremony 78
menstrual seclusion 180
Métis women
  after 1885 30-31
  in buffalo hunt 21
  Catholic Church and 25-26
  community life of 33
  customs of 22, 24-25
  heritage of 20-22
  marriage of 21, 32-33
  work of 20, 22, 31-32
métissage 22
Middleton, Maj.-Gen. Frederick 28, 29
midwife societies 180
migration
  of Saulteaux 40
missionaries
  effect on gender equality 78
  in residential schools 170
modernization theory
  employment and 135-36
  public vs. domestic life and 146
  women's employment and 142-43
Moody, Roger
  on indigenous women's movements 104
Moose Factory
  women's employment in 131-48
Moosonee
  women's employment in 131-48
Moosonee Development Area Board 134

moral education
  in residential schools 171-72
mortality rate 3, 57. SEE ALSO deaths; suicide
    rate
Mother Earth. SEE Earth as Mother
mother-child relationship 127
motherhood
  cult of 118
Mother's Auxiliary for Minor Athletics
    (MAMAs) 91
Moulin, Father 25, 27
Myers, Marybelle
  on artist vs. craftworker 120
Myers, Thomas P.
  on moccasins 62

names
  of Métis 24
Napi (Old Man) 78
National Indian Activities Association (NIAA)
    88
natural resources, conservation of 70
nature
  harmony with x, 77-80, 80
needlework. SEE ALSO tapestry weaving;
    textiles
  history of 114-15
  of Plains women 62-63
Nelson, George 46
New Criticism 99, 105
Nicolas, Alexandrine Nicolas (Fleury) 31
Norrish, John 70
North West Mounted Police (NWMP)
  and mobility of women 56
North West resistance 24, 26-30, 57-58
  views of women 27
Nut Lake Reserve 71

Oblates of Mary Immaculate 25, 171-72
Obomsawin, Alanis v, 5, 100
Oglala people 52
oil and gas development
  at Lubicon Lake 151-63
Ojibwa, western. SEE Saulteaux people
Okan (Sun Dance sponsorship) 78
Onion Lake Reserve 58, 60-61
oral tradition 58, 98, 105-09
Ortiz, Alfonso
  on tribal identity 128
Osecap, Marie 59-60, 61, 65
Ouellette, Marguerite (Gingras) 23

Ouellette, Moïse 29
Oxendine, Joseph B.
  on Aboriginal sport 85, 88

painting
  mathematical principles in 115
Pangnirtung weave shop 120-25
Parenteau, Judith 29
Parenteau, Marie-Anne (Caron) 27, 29, 32
Parenteau, Pélagie (Dumont) 28
pass system 68-69, 71
patriarchy
  Batoche as 24
  colonial 104
  effect upon Métis 20-21
  influence on Aboriginal people ix
  in residential schools 171
Paulhus, Alice 33
Peepeekesis, Mrs. 70
Pentecostal bible camps 152, 159, 162
permit system 70, 71
Peters, Captain 26
pharmaceuticals 80
Piapot Reserve 66
Pilon, Barthélémi 32
Pilon, Christine (Dumas) 23, 28, 29, 32
Pilon, Octavie 32
Pino, Pauline 90-91
Plains women
  employment of 67
  images of 54-55, 64-66
  medical skills of 63-64
  move to reserves 51-53
  oral histories of 58-60
  schooling of 67-68
  sports participation 86-90
  work of 58-63
Pocahontas 14, 15
political action. SEE ALSO leadership
  by women 178, 180
Pool, Carolyn G.
  on reservation policy 53
Porter, Cathy 89
potatoes
  grown by Saulteaux 45
potlatch
  outlawing of 179
poverty 3-4, 56-58, 79, 134
power. SEE ALSO leadership
  of women ix, xi, xii, 53-54, 171, 179

Powers, Marla
  on Oglala women 52
Pratt, Charles
  on starvation 56-57
productive work 154-57, 159-60, 170
prostitution 69
Provencher, l'abbé
  on Métis women 21
public life
  domestic vs. 135-36, 139, 157
  exclusion of women from 179
  women in 118
punishment
  of Aboriginal women 69

Qu'Appelle Industrial School 67-68
Quinney, Harriet Sayese 63

racism
  in scholarship 98
  sexism and 103-04
Ranger, Adélaide (Pilon) 32
Rebellion Losses Commission 30
Reed, Mrs. Hayter 67
relief
  Aboriginal people and 57
religion. SEE ALSO Catholic Church
  among Métis 25
  at Lubicon Lake 161-62
  sport and 95
reproductive work
  productive labour vs. 170
  of women 159-60
research. SEE scholarship
reserves
  agriculture on 53, 56
  effect on gender roles 52
  effect on women's status 51-53
  housing on 65
  image of women on 54-55
  life on 79
residential schools x, 161, 167-81
Resistance Literature (Harlow) 99
resistance writing 98, 99-101, 102
Revillon Frères 132
rhubarb, wild 59
rice, wild. SEE wild rice
Riel, Angélique 24

Riel, Henriette 24
Riel, Julie (Lagimodière) 22
Riel, Louis 22, 26, 27, 28
  women and 24, 29
Riel, Marguerite (Monet) 24, 26, 28, 29
Riel, Sara 24
Rosal, Angelita 84-85, 89
Rosaldo, Michelle Zimbalist
  on women's role in production 157
Ross, Donald 29
Round Lake Presbyterian Boarding School 67
Ruskin, John
  on gender roles 118

Said, Edward
  on Palestinian women 103
Sanday, Peggy R.
  on status of women 156
Saulteaux people
  as hunter-gatherer society 40
  subsistence of 39-48
Schmidt, Louis 23
scholars
  Aboriginal women 13
scholarship
  colonialism in 14
  ethnocentric 4
  Native 12
  post-colonial 13
  Western-based 12
schools 157-58, 161
  for Aboriginal children 67-68
  enrollment 175-76
  Moosonee area 134
  residential x, 161, 167-81
Sears, Widow 61
self-concept
  of Aboriginal peoples 128-29
self-determination
  feminism and 102-05
self-sufficiency 79. SEE ALSO subsistence
settlement, European 56
sexism 11, 14
  and racism 103-04
Silman, Janet 86
single women
  employment of 142, 146
Sioux women 53
Sisters of the Infant Jesus 171

Six Nations Reserve
  women and sport on 86-90
skills, traditional
  employment and 137
  loss of, through schooling 169
Slash (Armstrong) 97, 103, 105-08
Slater, Mrs. 62
Slipperjack, Ruby. *Honour the Sun* 97
snaring. SEE trapping
social life. SEE community life
social roles. SEE ALSO gender roles
  changes in 157
  preparation of schooling for 176
Spanish influenza 175
spirituality
  among Lubicon Lake Cree 161-62
Spivak, Gayatri
  on fiction and truth 105
sports
  Aboriginal women and 83-95
  awards for 85-86
  gender and 83, 94
  race relations theories and 83
  religion and 95
  role models in 86
  women's roles in 91
starvation 56-57
state
  dependence upon 79, 157
  and domestic economy 54-55
  residential schools and 170, 172-73
stereotypes. SEE images
Stewart, E.C. 62
St-Germain, Justine (Caron) 29, 32
Storer, Effie
  on medical skills of Aboriginal women 64
story telling
  and print culture 98
sturgeon fishing 46-47
subsistence
  among Lubicon Lake Cree 153
  among Saulteaux 39-48
  education of children and 174-75, 177
  gender differences and 44
  role of children in 175
  role of women in 39, 44-45, 47
sugar making 46, 60
suicide rate
  among Aboriginal women 3
  among youth 129
Sun Dance sponsorship 78

Tanner, John 46
tanning of hides 61, 156
tapestry weaving 114-15
  as art 121, 125
  in Canadian Arctic 120-24
Tekawennake Reporter (newspaper) 84, 87, 91
textiles. SEE ALSO needlework; weaving
  as art 119, 120
  status of 116, 117
Thomas, Winnie 91
throwaway society 81
Tiffin, Helen
  on post-colonialism 13
tipsina roots 45
Tom Longboat Award 85-86, 92
Tourond, Calixte 31
Tourond, Josephte (Gervais) 29-30, 31
Tourond, Josephte (Paul) 26
traditions
  Aboriginal identity and 14
transfer payments 137, 151
trapping
  among the Carrier 176, 178
  in Cree economy 132, 136
  gender roles in 137
  at Lubicon Lake 151, 153, 154, 159
  schooling and 174-75
  of small game 46
Treaty Eight
  and the Lubicon 152
tribal identity 127-29
tuberculosis 133
turnips, prairie 45, 58-59

unemployment
  among men 157
  among the Carrier 178
  identity and 147
"unhappy" books 101-02
Union Nationale Métisse 29
Unocal (gas company) 163

Vagrancy Act 68
Van Kirk, Sylvia
  on Métis women 21
Vandal, Marie (Primeau) 23
VanEvery, Claudine 91
Végréville, Father 29
Venne, Josephte (St-Arnaud) 29
Venne, Salomon 29

victimization
 in writings 101
violence 11, 14, 129
 family 4
visual sense
 primacy of 115-16
voice
 in academic studies 12-13
voluntary work 140

Wadsworth, T.P. 65, 70
water supply
 on reserves 66
weaving. SEE ALSO tapestry weaving; textiles
 as fine art 113
 history of 114-15, 121
 looms 122, 123
welfare income 134, 154, 156
Welsh, Norbert 63
White, Pamela M.
 on women on reserves 54, 55, 64
Wichita women
 reservation policy and 53
wild rice
 in Saulteaux subsistence 45
wildlife. SEE ALSO trapping
 and gas and oil development 153
Williams, Raymond 97
Wissler, Clark
 on the Oglala 52
Wolf, Eric
 on naming and power 113
women, Aboriginal. SEE ALSO Cree women;
  Métis women; Plains women; Sioux
  women
 church and 179-80
 images of 12, 14-15
 Indian Act and 53, 128, 177-78
 power of ix, xi, xii, 53-54, 171, 179
 in primary literature 39
 as scholars 12, 13
 sports participation of 83-95
 strength of 127, 128
 as writers 14, 97-105, 107
women's auxiliaries 180
Woodall, Dixie 91
Woodland Cree Band 163

work 131. SEE ALSO domestic work;
  employment; labour
 of Cree women 147
 of girls in residential schools 172-73
 of Métis women 20, 22, 31-32
 productive vs. reproductive 157
 on reserves 58-63
 of Saulteaux women 39-40
writers
 Aboriginal women 14, 97-105, 107
Writing the Circle 14
writings
 Aboriginal 107
 literature vs. 99
 resistance 99-101

Zeman, Brenda
 on Aboriginal athletes 85